Managing for Knowledge

To my daughter Joanna, with love –
always remember the gift of learning

Managing for Knowledge

HR's strategic role

Christina Evans

BUTTERWORTH
HEINEMANN

AMSTERDAM BOSTON HEIDELBERG LONDON NEW YORK OXFORD
PARIS SAN DIEGO SAN FRANCISCO SINGAPORE SYDNEY TOKYO

Butterworth-Heinemann
An imprint of Elsevier
Linacre House, Jordan Hill, Oxford OX2 8DP
200 Wheeler Road, Burlington MA 01803

First published 2003

British Library Cataloguing in Publication Data
A catalogue record for this book is available from the British Library

Library of Congress Cataloguing in Publication Data
A catalogue record for this book is available from the Library of Congress

ISBN 0 7506 5566 6

For information on all Butterworth-Heinemann publications
visit our website at www.bh.com

Composition by Genesis Typesetting, Rochester, Kent
Printed and bound in Great Britain by Biddles Ltd. *www.biddles.co.uk*

Contents

Figures

Tables

Foreword

With remarkable regularity a 'new idea' surfaces in the management community. Often it results from repackaging a long-lived management issue or truth. Conversely, the current vogue, Knowledge Management, is a genuinely new concept. In summary this involves the processes that ensure all the knowledge, explicit and implicit, that exists in the organisation is organised in a way that enables it to be accessed quickly and easily. This allows for distributed decision making so that new actions, products and services can be built from it at a pace that outstrips similar use by others. Knowledge management simultaneously meets the need to make information freely available while also enabling those with full understanding to move swiftly ahead, thereby rendering the earlier knowledge redundant. In today's fast paced environment, it offers an essential market edge for individuals and for their organisation.

Knowledge management is frequently linked with technology, specifically computer or information technology. IT developments such as database management, bulletin board systems and web technology offer the potential for information to be gathered continuously from a vast array of sources. Also this ensures that it can be accessed in a similar way giving rise to countless permutations of inferences and new possibilities. At the same time, some researchers and gurus, mindful of the capacity of the human mind to make connections between apparently unrelated facts, have urged the study of human aspects of knowledge management rather than concentrating solely on computerisation. The focus here is on collecting the unwritten stories and morés of organisational experience. The shared assumptions, leaps in understanding and intuition that come from standing simple information on its head, may prompt a 'eureka moment'. In turn, this leads to breakthrough thinking.

Nevertheless, most authors and speakers about knowledge management focus on the computer systems that assist the collection of knowledge or, more accurately, information. In this book, rather than relying on technology to manage knowledge as if it were an entity in itself, Christina Evans correctly focuses on human interaction – the need to manage *for* knowledge: that is to organise people, such that they gather and act on the knowledge that is inherently available to them. By directing her attention specifically to HR, she puts this function at the heart of the business since leveraging knowledge effectively is a vital strategic goal of all organisations today. Clearly and directly Christina sets out the role for HR in building a culture where harvesting knowledge as opposed to simply gathering information is the norm. She shows why managing for knowledge is important, how to do it and gives practical examples. She offers guidance to encourage HR specialists to reinvent their role, to become full business partners. Most significantly, she demonstrates the crucial importance for HR to work effectively with knowledge management, the concept and the technical support, in order to create organisations that are successful tomorrow as well as today.

Val Hammond
Chief Executive, Roffey Park Institute

Introduction

The Knowledge Economy – opportunities and challenges for business

It is difficult to pinpoint an exact time when the current interest, possibly obsession, with knowledge management took off. Certainly some of the seminal books from management writers began to emerge in the early 1990s. Yet managing knowledge is not a new concept. Professionals, i.e. individuals whose work depends on them making judgments that are grounded in their knowledge base, have always had to manage their knowledge in order to continue practising.

So why has managing knowledge suddenly moved up the strategic agenda for large corporations? What has changed? A number of fairly significant changes have occurred over the past ten to fifteen years. One significant change has been the shift from manufacturing to service-based businesses, where companies are competing to attract and retain more knowledgeable and more discerning global customers. In this environment speed to market has become all-important.

To compete, some organisations have had radically to rethink how to do business. In the IT sector, for example, most of the major manufacturing companies have transformed themselves into services companies, where they now offer 'total solutions'. In this context knowledge about customers' businesses, i.e. what their business issues are, what their strategic goals are, is crucial. Of course this information is only of value if the organisation then acts on it, in order to deliver what the customer wants, in a cost-effective way, and timely manner, ahead of the competition.

In the race to get a handle on managing knowledge many organisations have come unstuck by investing too much energy in developing formal systems, often IT systems, to facilitate knowledge sharing, at the expense of capitalising on the benefits that come from informal processes.

Organisations have spent millions of pounds on systems to capture, store and improve access to vast quantities of information that is now available, through one source or another, and yet this does not always bring the expected business benefits. I am using the term organisation here as the collective name for its people. As it is people who act on information, not machines, this reinforces the need to focus on mobilising, energising, supporting and enabling individuals at all levels within the organisation to combine their 'Know of' and 'Know how' to deliver existing services more efficiently, as well as to create new services. Perhaps one of the questions that needs to be asked is can we achieve what we want to achieve without an IT solution? If not, should we not at least ensure that any new system can be integrated with what we already have? What seems to have been overlooked is that knowledge doesn't always flow from formal structures and systems, but instead is often the by-product of day-to-day interactions.

Why another book on managing knowledge?

My intention is to stimulate a debate about the role of HR in helping organisations move forward on their knowledge management journey. HR has come under a lot of criticism as it is perceived not to be taking a proactive role in the knowledge management arena. In many organisations it is business teams, or IT teams, that have taken the lead. In practical terms this means that while the systems aspects are addressed, the people and cultural aspects are sadly often overlooked.

A cynical view of the role of HR in managing knowledge could be that HR do not have the skills and knowledge needed to be proactive in the knowledge management arena. After all aren't HR just administrators? What do they know about business and how to make businesses more efficient?

That may have been the old view of HR, but just as the business world has been changing in recent years, so too has the agenda for HR. There are now many good examples of where HR professionals are performing the business partner role, a role which Dave Ulrich suggests is the new mandate for HR. This does not mean that HR have abandoned their administrative role, instead they are finding ways of delivering this part of their work more efficiently, and in doing so are creating the much needed space to operate more strategically.

This was the experience within IBM where the HR function was completely remodelled to channel resources into HR strategy, rather than administrative tasks, in order to support IBM's business transformation in the 1990s[1]. Drawing on techniques from Customer Relationship Management a new HR delivery model was introduced. This reflected the different types of customers that HR have contact with e.g. manager, employee, applicant, together with the different types of interactions e.g. advise, transact, or consult. The delivery model involves a service centre that provides information and advice covering most of the simple questions, an intranet system that enables policy and procedure to be easily accessible at individual's desktop and HR strategy partners, who focus on the strategic issues the business is facing. The global e-HR system has been rolled out to 320,000 employees in 180 countries and is saving the organisation around $320 m (£238 m) a year[2]. It enables HR practices to be quickly updated in line with the changing business. Of course IBM is not the only organisation that is investing in new solutions to enhance the way that it delivers HR services to its different users.

Having been conducting research into the cultural dimensions of knowledge management for some years now I have found a mixed level of interest in the area of knowledge management among HR practitioners. My initial contact with organisations has often been with the IT or KM department. It is only when I have started to ask questions about the processes that support learning, in its broadest sense, or the informal processes for knowledge sharing, that I have then started to connect with the HR community.

My previous research suggests that HR needs to work in partnership with their business colleagues in the knowledge management arena. Indeed some of the case studies that I draw on in this book show the benefits of adopting this approach. In some organisations HR has been part of the catalyst team set up to get knowledge management onto the corporate agenda. In others, the Chief Executive has tasked HR with moving the organisation forward on its knowledge management journey, because of their expertise in the area of learning and change.

Given their knowledge of how to facilitate learning and change there is a real opportunity for HR to move more centre stage in the knowledge management arena.

However, HR will need to re-educate their business partners, and possibly themselves, on what is meant by learning and also how best to encourage and facilitate learning in the modern workplace. Etienne Wenger (1998), a leading researcher and writer in the field of learning, believes that one of the assumptions that many institutions hold about learning is that of learning being an individual process, one that occurs through teaching in locations held away from the workplace. Wenger has developed a theory of learning – a social theory of learning – that is based on the assumptions that (a) learning is as much a part of human nature as eating and sleeping and (b) learning occurs naturally through our active participation in the practices of different social communities. What does this mean for organisations? They need to adopt an integrative training approach, one which focuses on practice and seeks 'points of leverage' to support learning. These 'points of leverage', according to Wenger, can come from learning through everyday practice, as well as by encouraging shared working and learning in communities of practice.

HR can also add value by using their knowledge of best practice occurring outside the organisation to help managers address first-order (i.e. doing the same things, only better) and second-order (i.e. doing different things) change. Part of the value that HR can bring here is in challenging existing assumptions and beliefs about the way business and work gets done. So questioning whether faster is always better and helping the organisation strike a balance between what needs changing and what does not.

However, HR's contribution does not, and should not, stop there. In their strategic partner role HR can add also value in the knowledge management arena by developing a focus on capability building and retention; helping the business develop more efficient business processes, as well as facilitating relationship building, both within and outside the organisation (Evans, 2002).

Building a knowledge-centric culture takes time. As David Parlby, from KPMG, points out, few organisations have reached this stage on their knowledge management journey. While there are some common building blocks, i.e. building, sharing, reusing and retaining knowledge, how organisations move forward depends on their initial starting point and their overall business priorities. The case studies in this book provide examples of where different organisations are focusing/have focused their energies at different stages on their journey. The key message is that knowledge management activities need to add value to the business, it is not just a nice bolt-on to have. Managing knowledge should not be seen as a separate activity, but instead needs to be integrated into day-to-day business processes. The journey is an evolving one too, practitioners need to apply the learning cycle to their knowledge management approach. This requires identifying and using strategic change levers: What are we good at now? Where do we need to improve? How will we do that? Who needs to do what? How will we know that we are moving forward?

This book provides ideas, questions, and tools to enable HR to move their organisation forward on their knowledge management journey. One of the biggest challenges for HR as a function is to position itself as a role model for the knowledge-centric organisation through the way that it is structured, conducts business and builds and enhances its own capabilities. With the right attitude and knowledge HR can achieve this.

Notes

1. Leighton, R. Ensuring employee satisfaction. In *Making e-business deliver.* This is one of a series of business guides, produced jointly by Capstan Publishing and IBM.
2. HR budget at IBM slashed through e-HR. *Personnel Today*, 4 June 2002. See *www.personneltoday.com*

Acknowledgements

There are many people who have helped in shaping the ideas and content in this book. I would particularly like to thank Linda Holbeche, Director of Research at Roffey Park, for suggesting me to Butterworth-Heinemann as someone who could write knowledgably on HR's role in managing knowledge, as well as for her ongoing contribution and support with this project. Equally, I am grateful to Val Hammond, Chief Executive of Roffey Park, for writing the Foreword. This is particularly timely and symbolic given that Val will be stepping down as Chief Executive this year.

I would particularly like to thank Dave Snowden, from the Cynefin Centre for Organisational Complexity, IBM Global Services for his chapter on 'Language and tools for knowledge mapping' and Elizabeth Lank, independent consultant, for helping me shape the chapter on 'Working and Learning in Communities of Practice'.

I am grateful to John Bailey, KPMG; Linda Marks, QinetiQ; Ron Donaldson, English Nature and Alison Lewis, Oxfam GB, for making it possible for me to develop organisational case studies. Also to Jela Webb, Azione, for sharing her experience of how to structure an HR team to ensure maximum impact from a knowledge management perspective. I would also like to thank Linda Emmett, Information Manager at the CIPD, for sharing her thoughts on thinking through the appropriate use of technological solutions for managing knowledge.

Other people whom I would like to thank for giving up their time to share their ideas, or allow me to learn from their experience, include: Ruth Mundy of Jones Lang Lasalle; Elaine Monkhouse, formally of The Oxford Group; Jozefa Fawcett, formally Berkshire NHS Shared Services; Tom Knight of Fujitsu and Richard Archer of The iFramework.

I am also grateful for the enthusiasm, support and challenge from colleagues in my personal network. These include: David Lines, Eden Charles, John Whatmore and John Sparks.

Many thanks too go to Ailsa Marks and the team at Butterworth-Heinemann for being so supportive throughout the whole production process.

Finally, I want to thank my family, particularly my husband David and daughter Joanna, who almost didn't get a holiday last summer because I was so engrossed in writing this book – I'll try to be better organised next time!

Part One

The Strategic Context for HR's Role in Managing for Knowledge

The changing world of business and the imperative for managing knowledge

Knowledge as a key business asset

We are living in the information age where knowledge is now considered the key strategic business asset. '*How do we leverage the knowledge in our business?*' is a fundamental question being raised by senior business leaders, in all business sectors. The Chief Executive of Hewlett-Packard has been quoted as saying '*If HP knew what HP knows, it would be three times as profitable.*'

What knowledge assets are we talking about?

- Structural assets
- Brands
- Customer relationships
- Patents
- Products
- Operational processes

Human assets

- Employee experience
- Employee 'know how'
- Personal relationships

So why has knowledge become such a key business asset? What are the broader economic and technological changes that have contributed to this shift?

Changes in the global business economy

A number of significant changes have occurred in the global business economy, and in society more generally over the past couple of decades (Castells, 1989; Allen, 1992). Allen (1992) points out how a '. . . sense of economic transformation within the western industrial economies has been present for some time, at least since the 1970s.' While there are differing views as to what type of economy we are moving from there seems to be some converging views that information and knowledge are becoming the primary source of economic value.

Castells argues that a series of scientific and technological innovations have converged to constitute a new technological paradigm and that what differentiates the current process of technological change is that its raw material is information, as is is its outcome. He refers to this new paradigm as the 'informational technological paradigm', which is characterised by two fundamental features: (a) the core new technologies are focused on information processing, so its raw material is information, and (b) the main effects of these technological innovations are on processes, rather than products.

The 'informational technological' paradigm is having a fundamental effect on businesses since processes, as Castells points out, enter into the domain of human activity; something that affects social structures and organisational structures. Under the 'informational technological' paradigm information and knowledge become the primary source of economic value and competitive advantage (Castells, 1989; Drucker 1993). As Thomas Stewart points out, the old economy was about 'congealed resources', i.e. a lot of material held together by a bit of knowledge, but the new economy is about 'congealed knowledge', i.e. a lot of intellectual content in a physical slipcase[1].

Knowledge is a source of sustainable advantage given that, unlike other assets, knowledge assets grow with use:

> *Ideas breed new ideas, and shared knowledge stays with the giver while it enriches the receiver.* (Davenport and Prusak, 1998:17)

and

> *Ideas are the instructions that let us combine limited physical resources in arrangements that are ever more valuable.*
> (Paul Romer, cited in Davenport and Prusak, 1998:17)

and

Through knowledge creation, firms [and people] are able to revitalize themselves and set themselves apart from their competitors. (Bird, 1994: 328).

Other leading management writers, such as George Stonehouse *et al.* (2001), argue that there are three factors that influence why one business outperforms another. These are competitive positioning, resource or competitive-based positioning and a knowledge-based approach, i.e. having a focus on knowledge building and organisational learning. Sustainability, according to Stonehouse *et al.*, comes from the level of importance that is placed on information and knowledge within the organisation. They suggest that competitive advantage only arises when an organisation is able to generate new knowledge, something that is heavily dependent on an organisation's learning environment.

The combined effects of globalisation, influenced by new technologies, and better communication and transport facilities means that consumers now have more choice over the goods and services available to them. They are constantly being inundated with new product offerings from global companies. For organisations this means that they cannot afford to be complacent about how they conduct business. They cannot assume that the products and processes that made them successful in the past will continue to do so in the future.

Davenport and Prusak argue that companies now require quality, value, service, innovation and speed to market, in order to remain successful in business; the business imperative then is one of knowing how to do new things well and do them quickly.

But businesses have also got to keep an eye on their cost base and seek new ways of managing this. One of the ways in which many organisations have done this is through reviewing their core competence, and outsourcing business activities that do not map directly onto their core competence. Over recent years we have seen an increase in the number of organisations that have outsourced their manufacturing, and in some case part of their service function, to countries where labour costs are lower than in their native country. The area around Bangalore in India, for example, is now a world centre for software production; an example of where the globalisation of knowledge is unaffected by traditional boundaries. Of course by shifting production to different continents, organisations can take advantage of different time zones, which means that they can offer a twenty-four hour service to customers in a cost-effective way.

Changes in technology

Despite the way in which changes in technology are affecting all of our lives, it is easy to forget the speed at which change is taking place. As Table 1.1 indicates, technological changes, which in the past spanned generations, now take place within much shorter timeframes.

Table 1.1: Time to market – how the world of technology is speeding up

Technology	Time to reach 10 million customers (years)
Pager	41
Telephone	38
Cable TV	25
Fax machine	22
VCR	9
Cellular telephone	9
Personal computer	7
CD-ROM drive	6
Netscape Internet browser	0.5 (i.e. six months)

Over the past couple of decades we have seen significant and rapid changes in Information and Communications Technologies. Two important technologies evolved during the 1980s and 1990s. One was a change in telecommunications technologies providing a hundred-fold increase in the amount of data that can be transmitted over computer networks. Another was the growth in the number of networked computers enabling more open communications systems and new ways of working.

These technological changes have enabled new organisational forms to develop, for example networked organisations, virtual organisations and e-businesses – all of which are based on a different set of assumptions about the way business should be organised and managed. In these new business environments, hierarchical structures have been found to be less effective as they get in the way of providing a differentiated and responsive service to customers. In addition, they are based on a different set of assumptions about the way business should be organised and managed.

These combined technological changes have also led to a number of observable changes in the way that work is structured and organised. First, information that in the past would have been restricted to individuals in certain job roles, can now be made more accessible both vertically and horizontally, within and across organisations; such a change can affect how and where business decisions are made. Second, these new technologies have enabled work to be location-independent thus transcending traditional geographical boundaries. With the relevant technologies, work, as pointed out above, can be distributed around the world in order to minimize production costs. Finally, these new technologies have opened up the possibilities for individuals to work from home thus bringing about a return to a way of living and working that existed in the pre-industrial era, in which work, family and community life were closely intertwined (Baruch and Nicholson, 1997).

Castells argues that in the knowledge economy individuals who are unable to acquire the relevant skills, or who do not invest in continuous learning, may find themselves excluded from the labour force. Continuous learning throughout all strata of the workforce is critical to survival in today's ever-changing business world (Coolahan, 1998).

Knowledge-based businesses apart, more and more jobs now involve the use of Information and Communications Technologies (ICT). ICT skills are seen as being essential in the modern workplace (Labour Market & Skills Trends, 2000). However, as more and more organisations opt to have their IT systems developed and serviced by third party suppliers, this will have implications for the skills mix within organisations. What will be required is IT literate employees who understand the business, but IT literacy will come to mean knowing how to use computers more so than knowing how to manage them (Evans, 2000).

What are the implications of these continuous changes in technology for HR? First, HR professionals will need to become more IT literate themselves, sufficient enough to be able to enter into meaningful discussions with their IT counterparts. Second, they will need to consider the implications for the organisations' future resources, skills and capabilities. Third, they will need to help prepare employees for new roles and opportunities that are likely to emerge from emerging technologies.

The changing nature of work and the workplace

The combined effects of globalisation and economic uncertainty have put businesses under increasing pressure to manage their operating costs. This has led many businesses to review their core processes and capabilities to identify ways in which they can speed up product development and service delivery, and of course manage their costs. Going back to basics has been one of the strategies adopted. To achieve this, organisations have chosen to outsource non-core business activities.

Today's workplace is distinctly different to how it was twenty years ago. Many organisations have introduced flexible production models, including flexible employment options. The number of individuals employed on flexible work contacts increased by one and a quarter million between 1986 and 1993[2]. Part-time working is still the most common form of flexible work option with around 26% of the workforce working part-time (Labour Market Statistics, December 2002).

However, there are structural differences within this overall figure. One is that the largest proportion of part-time working occurs within the Distribution, Business & Miscellaneous Services, as well as Public Services sectors. A second is that the majority of those who work part-time are women, particularly women aged 25 to 39, with dependent children[3]. But, part-time employment among men, particularly younger men (aged below 25) and older men (aged 50 and over), has been increasing too. The rise in the number of younger men working part-time may be associated with changes in the availability of grants for higher education, leading young people to seek alternative sources of funding for their university education. The rise in number of older men working part-time could be the result of the changing organisational practice of encouraging early retirement, from age 50 onwards. Or it could be that the increasing pressures in the workplace, as a result of continuous change, are leading some individuals to rethink what they want from a career. Work–life balance became a hot topic in the late 1990s, particularly for individuals (Filipczak, 1994; Glynn, 2000). There are signs that organisations, as well as the Government are beginning to take this issue more seriously.

The establishment of the 'Employers for Work–Life Balance' forum is one indication that employers are beginning to pay attention to individuals' concerns about work–life balance. The forum, founded and chaired by Lloyds TSB Group plc, provides a forum where employers can share policies and practices relating to work–life balance (so itself knowledge-building). There are currently twenty-two member organisations. Work–life balance has also become part of the political agenda. In March 2000, the Minister for Employment and Equal Opportunities launched its Work–Life Balance Challenge Fund. This scheme is intended to provide support to private, public and voluntary sector employers who are committed to initiating work–life balance policies and practices.

The introduction of flexible working practices has organisational benefits too. These include: the ability to provide a more responsive service to customers; the ability to attract employees from diverse backgrounds, who otherwise might be excluded from traditional employment models; attracting and retaining skilled professionals; and retaining employees looking to have a balance between their work and home lives.

However, when considering structural change, such as the introduction of flexible working practices, organisations also need to consider and plan for the impact that this might have on their ability to manage their knowledge (Evans, 2002). While having more mobile and flexible workers may make it easier to deliver a more responsive service to customers, unless properly managed, this could have an adverse affect on an organisation's knowledge capabilities. In addition, organisations will need to plan for the fact they may have less time to capitalize on their employees' 'know how'.

The combined effects of structural change i.e. the shift from manufacturing to service-based businesses (which are more information and knowledge dependent) and technology is having an effect on the skills needed within the workplace. To-day's businesses are more knowledge intensive. Statistics provided by the OECD indicate that the percentage of GNP that comes from knowledge-based business is now around 50% (OECD, 1999). This is leading to an increased demand for cognitive skills (i.e. problem-solving, communication, and interpreting information), which have become more important and in demand than manual skills (DfEE National Skills Task Force, 2000). Where these skills are in short supply, organisations are finding that they are struggling to recruit and retain employees (Gubman, 1998).

Equally the percentage of the workforce employed in managerial, professional and technical roles, working in 'information occupation' is increasing (Allen, 1992; DfEE Labour Market & Skills Trends, 2000). Employees who fall into the category of professional and technical workers are among those listed in the statistics on 'hard-to-fill vacancies' (DfEE Labour Market & Skills Trends, 2000).

These combined changes have important implications for employees. There is a danger that it could lead to polarisations in the workforce, with knowledge workers becoming an elitist group within organisations and within society more generally (Castells, 1989). Ian Angell, Professor of Information Systems at the London School of Economics, suggests that in the Information Age it is not simply a question of replacing 'old jobs' with 'new ones', it is about building 'intellectual muscle', in the form of intelligent knowledge workers, as this will be the source of growth.

The pace of change in the modern business world means that the life-span of certain knowledge is getting shorter and shorter. Individuals in all employment sectors, not just those working in knowledge-intensive businesses, need constantly to update their skills and knowledge in order to maintain their employability. In the modern workplace continuous learning is becoming the norm. But there is an issue here with regard to who should pay for this learning – should it be businesses, individuals themselves, or should the Government be expected to contribute some funding too?

Raman Roy, the Chief Executive of Spectramind, a call centre based in India, sums up the changes that have occurred in the nature of work in the late 20th century:

Geography is history. Distance is irrelevant. Where you are located is unimportant. I can log on anywhere in the world.

With work today being like the Martini advert – anytime, anyplace, anywhere – this has created new challenges for organisations. Many large organisations are adopting the mobile office principle whereby staff may spend some of their time working in a central office, some working at a client site, some working at a satellite office, or some of their time working at home. These changes have implications for the organisation's knowledge management and human resource systems.

In order to be able to work anyplace, anytime, anywhere individuals need to be provided with the right technological infrastructure (laptop, mobile phone) and they also need to have access to up-to-date centralised information systems that can be accessed from any location. One of the difficulties, however, of having a global and mobile workforce is that it can be difficult to ensure certain types of knowledge sharing. Creating a sense of community can be difficult in organisations in which the majority of employees are mobile, leaving them feeling isolated and lacking a sense of belonging.

The changing landscape of careers

The structural changes in the workplace discussed above, has had an effect on individuals and their 'careers'. Here I am deliberately using the term 'career' in the plural, given the renewed interest in the notion that the term career can be applied to other life-areas, not just an individual's paid work (Barley, 1989).

From the 1950s, when the notion of a managerial career really began, up until the 1980s, individuals had experienced relative stability and predictability in career terms. The dominant view of a career, and to some extent still is, that of:

A succession of related jobs, arranged in a hierarchy of prestige, through which persons move in an ordered predictable sequence. (Wilensky, 1960)

The structure and order associated with this career definition provided individuals, and indeed organisations, with a sense of security.

However, during the 1990s, many organisations re-structured, or de-layered, largely as a way of managing their cost base. As a result, traditional career models, based on Wilensky's definition, were eroded as organisations began to flatten their structures. In addition to the cost-saving element, organisations saw flatter structures as a way of speeding up the decision-making process and hence providing a more responsive customer-focused service.

As flatter organisational structures do not lend themselves to conventional career opportunities (Holbeche, 1999), employers and employees have found themselves searching for alternative career models. One new career model that has emerged is that of the 'boundaryless' career. This is characterised by movement across levels/functions either within a single organisation, or across multiple organisations. The 'boundaryless career' is based on an assumption that work will encompass a variety of tasks and

. . . the person, not the organisation, is managing their career. It consists of all the person's varied experiences in education, training, work in several organisations, changes in the organisational field . . . it is not what happens to the person in any one organisation. (Mirvis and Hall, 1994: 369).

The 'boundaryless' career then opens up the career space, such that an individual's career can encompass both paid and non-paid work and where the boundaries between these two domains are more fluid.

Other writers define a career as 'repositories of knowledge':

I see careers as accumulations of information and knowledge embodied in skills, expertise and relationship networks, acquired through an evolving sequence of work experiences over time (Bird, 1996:326), where

The contents of a career are located in what is learned from experiences – in the information, knowledge and perspectives that are acquired, or changed, over time as a result of a series of work experiences. (Bird, 1994: 327)

Another career definition that is gaining interest, particularly given concerns about work–life balance, is that of a career being seen as part of a whole life-system:

. . . where two careers and two sets of personal and family concerns are integrated into one lifestyle. (Schein, 1996)

We can see this way of thinking about careers creeping into the behaviours of some individuals in terms of the changes they are making in their own lives in order to gain a more satisfactory work–life balance. Despite the increasing availability of part-time and flexible working, employers cannot, or will not, provide the type of flexibility that employees are looking for. This then leads to employees, particularly highly skilled professionals, seeking alternative work options, such as self-employment (Evans, 2001).

It has been argued that the current recruitment and retention difficulties in the NHS, for example, will not be resolved until the NHS adopts a more flexible stance on its flexible work arrangements. It is not surprising therefore that retaining talent, which if we unpack this is really about retaining organisational 'know how', has become one of the top strategic issues for organisations.

Building a shared understanding of knowledge and knowledge management

Definitions of knowledge

One of the difficulties that organisations experience, when trying to introduce knowledge management, is helping individuals build an understanding of what is meant by the terms knowledge and knowledge management.

The term knowledge is in itself a difficult concept. It is a subject that has intrigued and occupied the minds of many of the great philosophers. Unlike many other assets, knowledge isn't something that you can touch, or feel, hence the reason why it is often described as the invisible, or intangible asset. Some knowledge exists outside the individual, in text format, but a large percentage of knowledge resides within people. One of its other elusive characteristics is that the value of knowledge is highly contextual, i.e. you only know what you need to know, at the time when you need to know it; something that many organisations have discovered far too late.

While many knowledge management practitioners argue that we shouldn't get too hung-up on definitions, it is important to ensure that there is some common understanding about what knowledge the organisation is trying to manage. Tom Boydell[4], a leading writer on learning organisations, has developed a framework for thinking about knowledge. This consists of four types of knowledge and three knowledge levels. The four types of knowledge include:

(a) knowing about things,
(b) knowing how to do things,
(c) knowing how to become yourself,
(d) knowing how to achieve things with others;

and three knowledge levels:

1. knowing how to implement,
2. knowing how to improve,
3. knowing how to integrate.

Davenport and Prusak, leading writers in the field of knowledge management, refer to knowledge as:

> . . . *a fluid mix of framed experience, values, contextual information, and expert insight that provides a framework for evaluating and incorporating new experiences and information. It originates and is applied in the minds of knowers. In organisations, it often becomes embedded not only in documents or repositories but also in organisational routines, processes, practices and norms.*
> (Davenport and Prusak, 1998:5).

Davenport and Prusak point out that knowledge is different from information, since information only becomes knowledge when transformed by one or more of the following processes:

- Comparison – how does information about this situation compare to that of others?
- Consequences – what implications does this information have for decisions and actions?
- Connections – how does this bit of knowledge relate to other pieces of knowledge?
- Conversation – what do others think about this information? It is this particular activity that emphasises the importance of social interaction for the knowledge creation process.

In my own practitioner work, I tend to concentrate on four different types of knowledge:

Know of, or know about

This is often referred to as 'operational level' knowledge, i.e. knowledge that is used as part of individuals' day-to-day work. In a retail environment, operational level knowledge might include awareness of the current week's special offers, new promotions, store layout changes etc. In a legal environment, operational level knowledge might include changes in legislation relating to employment law.

This type of knowledge lends itself to being codified and hence more readily accessible through intranet systems, or transmitted via mass communication techniques (e.g. through e-mail, memos).

Know how

This again is often referred to as operational level knowledge. However, the type of knowledge here is tacit knowledge, i.e. our accumulated experience of how things work and also how things get done. It is the type of knowledge that gets called upon when problem-solving and decision-making and sets the context within which knowledge gets applied. It is for this reason that tacit knowledge is more difficult to codify.

Accessing 'know how' isn't something that can always easily be extracted through the use of interviewing techniques. This was an important discovery made by the Xerox corporation when researching how to design information systems to support the way people really work (Seely Brown, 1998). The initial stage of the Xerox research involved interviewing certain groups of employees about how they went about their day-to-day jobs. When clerks working in the organisation's accountants department were interviewed about their jobs, what they described in the interviews pretty much matched the information in their job description.

However, when these same clerks were observed at work by anthropologists a very different picture of their jobs emerged. The anthropologists observed how although the clerks referred to formal procedures as they went about their day-to-day work, they also had to adapt many of their day-to-day work activities in order to get the job done. What was concluded from this study was that employees use formal procedures as a way of understanding what needs to be done, rather than to identify the actual steps that need to be taken to get from A to B. Instead the clerks draw on 'workarounds', i.e. informal steps, which are un-documented, and which managers are often unaware of. Given these findings it is clear why induction and initial on-the-job training for new members of the team become so important. Without this an organisation is likely to find that new employees follow documented procedures that do not deliver the intended results. The result: dissatisfied customers and disheartened employees.

Know why

In the complex and ever-changing business world that we operate in today employees need to be more strategically aware. They need to know where their organisation is going and why. They also need to know about the organisation's value system and how this links to the organisation's strategic direction. This is important for two reasons. One is to ensure that the decisions that individuals make as part of their day-to-day jobs are consistent with the organisation's overall strategic direction. The second reason is so that individuals can understand how they can best contribute to the organisation's strategic goals.

If individuals are clearer about where and how they can contribute to the organisation's future then this will help them feel more connected. Robert B. Reich, Professor of Economic and Social Research at Brandeis University, argues that in the modern workplace employers need to work at creating 'social glue'. Reich suggests that 'Collaboration and mutual advantage are the essence of the organisation. They can create flexibility, resiliency, speed and creativity – the fundamental qualities of the 21st century.' To help build 'social glue', individuals, according to Reich, need to be given opportunities to work on projects which make a real difference and where the organisational goal is aligned with the individual's own personal goals and values.

In today's ever-changing business world individuals also need to be aware of the economic, social and political changes taking place around them, so that they can have intelligent discussions about the likely implications for the business, as well as their own careers. Building this external perspective can help individuals spot emerging trends, as well as see existing landscapes through a new pair of lenses.

Some of the ways in which organisations are helping individuals build their 'know why' are discussed in later chapters in this book.

Know who

As much of an organisation's knowledge resides within individuals' heads, knowledge of who is who, both within and outside the organisation, and what knowledge can be unlocked through networking is critical. The ability to build and maintain social networks, as we shall see later, has become one of the critical knowledge-building competencies.

In any organisation it is important to have this taxonomy of knowledge in mind when developing policies and practices for managing knowledge. Without this organisations may focus their energies and other resources on developing one particular type of knowledge, leaving themselves vulnerable in other areas.

Other KM practitioners have adopted other methods for categorising the types of knowledge that organisations need to focus on managing (Knight, 2001). The 'knowledge types' method pioneered by Knight and his colleagues in ICL, for example, include knowledge types such as:

- Product and service knowledge – the business 'content' relating to the customer experience.
- Process knowledge – how to get things done.
- Customer and supplier knowledge – knowledge about relationships.
- Project knowledge – focused on organisational memory and learning.
- Technical, or expert knowledge – supporting people with know how.

Defining knowledge management

Just as there are difficulties coming up with a single definition of knowledge, so it is with identifying a single definition of the term knowledge management. Some practitioners feel it is important not to get too hung up on definitions, or indeed get embroiled in a lengthy debate about the differences between data, information and knowledge. However, if individuals are to engage in a dialogue about knowledge management then they at least need to have a working definition of what knowledge management is, within the context of their own organisation. Some definitions that I have gathered while researching in this area include:

> . . . *the process through which we translate the lessons learnt, residing in our individual brains, into information that everyone can use.* (internal consultancy team)

> . . . *not just doing the existing business better, but about new business approaches to thrive in a market that is radically changing.* (DERA)

> . . . *it is about action and change, not just about installing intranets and managing documents.* (Cap Gemini).

> . . . *creating, managing, applying and sharing explicit knowledge (that exists typically in documents, databases and as part of*

processes) and tacit knowledge (embedded in people and their experience) in order to 'make a difference' in overcoming poverty and suffering. (Oxfam)

The Document Company – Xerox prefer to use the term Managing for Knowledge, as opposed to Knowledge Management. By this they mean

. . . creating a thriving work and learning environment that fosters the continuous creation, aggregation, use and re-use of both personal and organizational knowledge in the pursuit of new business value.

What is different about The Document Company – Xerox and the Oxfam definitions is that they link the 'What' and the 'Why' associated with managing knowledge, which at least helps people to put changes into a wider context.

Does knowledge management only apply to knowledge professionals?

Before we can answer that question we need to consider what is meant by the term knowledge worker. In her book, *Managing Knowledge Workers*, Frances Horibe defines knowledge workers as people who use their heads (i.e. through their ideas, analyses, judgements, or syntheses) more than their hands to produce value. She refers to traditional roles, such as R&D, management, and salespeople as being archetypal knowledge workers. Using this definition, IT professionals, HR professionals, as well as people in different creative fields, would all come under the category of knowledge workers.

Another definition is that of a knowledge worker being a worker who knows more than his/her boss about how to do their job, or can do his/her job better than the boss could (Knight and Howes, 2002). Knight and Howes point out, the notion of 'team working' is based around assembling people with different skills and using specialists with relevant knowledge to tackle specific projects, managed by someone who does not have the in-depth knowledge of team members. This also works both ways, in that team members will not have the same type of knowledge as their managers.

But what about individuals who work on the customer service desk in a retail environment, or work on the helpdesk in a service company, can these be considered knowledge workers? Certainly they have to make judgements about how to deal with a particular customer problem/complaint and they no doubt have ideas about how to enhance customer service, based upon their experience of dealing with customer problems and complaints day-in and day-out.

There is a danger that if we define the category of knowledge worker too narrowly then we could exclude a large number of individuals who have a lot to offer from a knowledge management perspective.

How do HR professionals see knowledge management?

Research by Vanessa Giannos (2002) identified a number of different perspectives on knowledge management among HR practitioners. These include:

Ensuring the learning acquired is shared with others within the organisation (to save re-inventing the wheel). (Consultancy)

Ensuring that the information that employees need in order to make effective and informed decisions is quickly and easily available. (dot.com company)

Ensuring the right people with the right knowledge and skills are in the right position and making the most impact. (Firm of solicitors)

Having structures, systems and processes in place that encourage and facilitate the creation of knowledge and its transfer across organisational boundaries. (Telecommunications company)

Ensuring that the knowledge held within the organisation is fully available . . . by providing the right environment, culture, structure and processes to motivate and encourage knowledge-sharing at all levels. (Educational institution)

So what then are the common themes in all of these different definitions?

- Learning
- Sharing
- Having people in the right place at the right time
- Effective decision-making
- Creativity
- Making people's jobs easier
- Generating new business and business value

For these things to happen requires a culture where individuals are motivated enough to want to share their knowledge with others, such that they themselves grow, as well as enabling the business to grow and survive too.

Are organisations taking knowledge management seriously?

Several organisations conduct regular surveys on the state of play of knowledge management within organisations. KPMG's Knowledge Management Survey[5] indicates that:

- 80 per cent of organisations have some knowledge management projects in place.
- 40 per cent of organisations have a formal KM programme in place.
- 25 per cent of organisations have appointed a Chief Knowledge Officer.
- Funding for KM activities comes from central corporate budget, followed by MIS function, then marketing.

However, findings from an annual survey of management trends by Roffey Park Institute – The *Management Agenda* – indicates that Knowledge Management isn't a key business process within all organisations yet. The *Management Agenda* monitors and reports on trends affecting organisations and individuals within the changing workplace. The research is based on a questionnaires sent out to small, medium and large organisations drawn from all business sectors within the UK.

The key findings from the Knowledge Management section of the 2002 *Management Agenda* highlighted that:

- Knowledge management is a key business process in only 49 per cent of participating organisations.
- In only 45 per cent of participating organisations is knowledge management linked to key results areas.
- Only 23 per cent of participating organisations had an Executive Director with overall responsibility for knowledge management.
- Only 15 per cent of organisations reported having a Chief Knowledge Officer.
- Only 41 per cent of participating organisations have knowledge management competencies included in their competency framework.
- There is a lack of shared understanding of what knowledge management is about. Individuals commented that knowledge management hadn't been defined within their organisation and that this led to confusion about what the organisation was trying achieve.

This confusion is echoed by one of the HR Directors that I interviewed as background to writing this book. She pointed out how, in her opinion, there is still a lot of confusion about responsibilities and accountability for knowledge management.

Confusion has arisen about who is accountable for knowledge management, because it is not the exclusive remit of IT, or HR. There are important implications for other business functions, such as marketing. Knowledge management needs to be viewed strategically by the business because of the potential impact on the bottom line. Value can be unlocked by recognising that an organisation's knowledge pool is greater than the sum of its constituent parts.

What this particular HR Director was clear about though was that knowledge management is not a nice to have, but a business imperative, which means that HR really need to be taking knowledge management seriously:

Efficient knowledge management is about having business processes which link to organisational design and development. This is where HR needs to have a broader business focus and develop its relationship with IT and other functions.

Where is your organisation on its knowledge management journey?

Speaking at a seminar on Knowledge Management David Parlby, from KPMG, referred to five stages in an organisation's knowledge management journey[6]. These are represented in Table 1.2.

Where would you place your organisation in this five-stage model? Are you knowledge chaotic, knowledge-centric, or somewhere in the middle? If you are at the knowledge-centric stage then you are probably one of the few organisations that have reached this point. The KMPG survey revealed that only about 10% of organisations have reached stages four and five. Even the big consultancies, whose knowledge-value is recognised in their market capitalisation, are still struggling with the cultural aspect of knowledge management. This is despite having made significant investment in their knowledge management systems and often adopting what some consider to be a big stick approach, i.e. linking to work processes and ensuring staff conform by linking to performance and reward systems.

Getting to the knowledge-centric stage requires adopting a balanced implementation approach, combining a **Mechanistic Knowledge Management** approach (i.e characterised by a strong emphasis on IT solutions and organisational practices that tend to be top-down and highly prescriptive) and an **Organic Knowledge Management** approach (i.e. emphasis on open and evolving structures and processes, where there is a strong emphasis on the people processes).

Table 1.2: Stages in an organisation's knowledge management journey

Stage	Name	Characteristics
1	Knowledge-chaotic	• unaware of concept • no information processes • no information sharing
2	Knowledge-aware	• awareness of KM need • some KM processes • technology in place • sharing information an issue
3	Knowledge-enabled	• benefits of KM clear • standards adopted • issues relating to culture and technology
4	Knowledge-managed	• integrated frameworks • benefits case realised • issues in previous stages overcome
5	Knowledge-centric	• KM part of mission • Knowledge-value recognised in market capitalisation • KM integrated into culture

The Organic Knowledge Management approach is felt to be more fruitful for the development of tacit knowledge. It requires an approach whereby knowledge is created through volunteering, encouraging self-organised communities, building an open environment where the motivation for knowledge sharing comes from the desire to leave some form of legacy. In this way knowledge sharing becomes a self-reinforcing activity.

Where is your organisation on its knowledge management journey?

If you feel that your organisation is at the knowledge-chaotic stage then perhaps a first step for HR would be to conduct its own internal audit. Questions that you might include are:

For the organisation as a whole
- Where does knowledge management fit within the organisation's strategic plans?
- What do people in different parts of the organisation understand by the term knowledge management?

- Where do they think responsibilities for managing knowledge should rest?
- What do people see as the blocks and enablers to managing knowledge within your organisation?
- What do they think could be done to minimize the blocks and strengthen the enablers?
- What practices already exist that could be considered as helping to build the organisation's knowledge capabilities?
- What do people know about the practices that exist within other organisations?

For teams
- What are the things that get in the way of them performing at their best, e.g. certain types of information, tools, processes, certain organisational practices or rituals?
- How much is known about the skills, expertise and interests of team members? Where is this information held? How is it kept up-to-date?
- What practices are in place to enhance knowledge transfer within and across teams?
- How receptive are teams to learning from the experiences of others outside the team? How is this facilitated?
- What practices are in place to capitalise on individuals' knowledge as they join, grow and move on from the team?
- What is the psychological contract between team members for developing and sharing knowledge?

For individuals
- Where does managing knowledge fit with individuals' concept of a career?
- How are individuals investing in themselves in order to keep their own knowledge up-to-date and in demand?
- What support/resources do individuals find most useful in developing their knowledge?
- How do individuals help others develop their knowledge?

These same questions could also be used and/or adapted when carrying out periodic evaluations of how well the organisation is managing its knowledge.

The need for a strategic approach to managing knowledge

The knowledge management journey in many organisations often begins in a piecemeal way with a local initiative, kicked off by a group of like-minded forward-thinking individuals. This was the experience within ICL, for example, where a group of colleagues got together to address the question of 'How can we add true organisational learning to the existing emphasis on training and developing people?'

Case study: The knowledge management journey within ICL

ICL, now Fujitsu, is an international company which focuses on helping its customers '. . . *seize the opportunities of the information age'*. In the early 1990s the organisation began transforming itself away from a computer manufacturing company into a service-led organisation. It was this change which made it a strategic imperative for the organisation to gain leverage from its world-wide intellectual capital.

However, in an organisation that at that time consisted of 22,000 employees, operating in 70 different countries, many of whom were mobile workers, or working on flexible contracts, getting a knowledge management initiative off the ground was not an easy task.

The first knowledge management project was initiated by an informal network of individuals, in the early 1990s. This group came together to address the question of

How can we add true organisational learning to the existing emphasis on training and developing people?

A couple of years later a formal project, Mobilising Knowledge Programme, was established with the support and backing of the then Chief Executive, Keith Todd, as a way of accelerating ICL's business transformation. The project was headed up by a full-time programme director, responsible for co-ordinating a cross-company knowledge management initiative. It was recognised that at the initial stage of the organisation's knowledge management journey a separate project team was needed in order to champion the knowledge management approach. However, it was always the intention that managing knowledge was ultimately to become a line management responsibility.

The Mobilising Knowledge project team, consisting of individuals with different skills drawn from different parts of the business, ran a series of focus group discussions with front-line employees to establish what information they needed to do their jobs effectively. This activity yielded some common themes regarding the information needs of individuals. This included information about:

- ICL as a business
- ICL services and customers
- ICL customers and partners
- Processes and policies in use across different parts of the company
- Who the company experts were and how to get in touch with them
- Time-saving tools, such as up-to-date telephone directories and site maps.

The first deliverable for the project team was the introduction of Café VIK (Valuing ICL Knowledge), which was a web site on the organisation's intranet. The use of the term Café was of symbolic importance. Being a global organisation the project team wanted to create a virtual environment that had some of the character-istics and attractions of a physical Café.

An important feature of the launch of Café VIK was a series of briefing sessions throughout the organisation. These were no ordinary briefing meetings. Instead the project team used Café style props to set the scene, so they bought inexpensive café style tables and chairs and some PCs. After the formal part of the presentation individuals could then gain hands-on experience of exploring Café VIK and what he had to offer.

Speaking at a Roffey Park seminar, Elizabeth Lank, Programme Director – Mobilising Knowledge, commented that this approach worked really well. Even though ICL is a technology-based company Elizabeth Lank pointed out that the project team came across individuals who were technophobic, thus having support on-hand to help individuals explore what Café VIK had on offer was a good tactic.

Another important element of the Mobilising Knowledge Programme was the introduction of the 'New World' office accommodation programme, where offices where systematically remodelled with far fewer, mostly 'hot' desks (about 30 per cent fewer desks in some cases). Private offices were removed too. The first private office to go was that of the Chief Executive. This was a fairly dramatic symbol that change was coming.

With the move to mostly 'hot-desking', many more meeting rooms, quiet rooms for solitary working, and comfortable meeting spaces, near coffee machines, were introduced. Coffee and tea were also made free at this point. The message that the organisation wanted to get across was that you don't come to work to answer e-mails – you can do that when working at home – instead you come to work to do what you can uniquely do at work: meet with and talk to colleagues, discuss work and exchange information.

ICL's second generation of its intranet was launched at the start of 1999 and was completely built around the idea of communities: providing the same tools for functional business units as for virtual communities of practice. It proved a great success, with the 50 or so communities that were part of the original set-up quickly becoming more than 500 communities within a year, and the majority of ICL's then 19,000 staff participating in multiple groups. Communities ranged in size from as few as 15 participants to 4000, with most settling around an optimum number of 100–200. By the time of ICL's full merger with Fujitsu in spring 2002, 500 items of new content were being added to the site every week. There is now a steady stream of volunteered content, much of it high quality.

While local initiatives are important, there is a view that these initiatives then need to be set within a strategic framework (Knight, 2002). A process that involves establishing:

Knowledge management drivers and the link with organisational strategy

What are the pressures that the organisation is facing? Why is managing knowledge important to us as a business?

Knowledge management strategy

Where do we need to be? What are the key levers for change? These might be a focus on people, processes, leadership, or technology. Some of the common strategic levers for knowledge management include: customer knowledge; knowledge in products and service; knowledge in people; knowledge in processes; organisational memory; knowledge in relationships and knowledge assets (Skyrme, 2001).

Implementation

How do we move forward? Here consideration needs to be given to implementation from a top-down, lateral and bottom-up approach.

Measuring the results

How are we doing? Here consideration could be given to adopting a balanced scorecard approach, focusing on the four elements of financial, customer, process and future.

As other writers point out it is important that wherever an organisations starts on its knowledge management journey, or wherever the initial focus is placed, it is important to adopt a holistic approach (Probst, Raub and Romhard, 2000). Probst *et al.* see the core building blocks of knowledge management as:

Knowledge identification – How do we ensure that there is sufficient transparency of external and internal knowledge? How do we help employees to locate the information that they need?

Knowledge acquisition – What forms of expertise should we buy in from outside? Are we making full use of the expertise embedded in the external relationships that we have?

Knowledge development – How can we build new expertise and capabilities?

Knowledge sharing and distribution – How do we get the knowledge to the right places?

Knowledge utilisation – How do we ensure that the knowledge that we have is applied productively for the benefits of the organisation?

Knowledge retention – How do we ensure that we retain the knowledge that we have? How knowledge enabled is the organisation?

Evaluation – How well are we doing on our knowledge management journey? What have been our key successes and failures? Where should we focus our energy going forward?

Summary

This chapter has discussed the key economic, technological and social changes that collectively have led to information and knowledge becoming a key source of competitive advantage. With the increasing emphasis on service, as opposed to manufacturing, innovation and speed to market have become key differentiators in today's global business world.

The ability to learn to do new things (i.e. products, services, processes) and then deliver more quickly than competitors is crucial. To do this organisations and individuals need to become better at information management, as well as managing different types of knowledge: 'know how', 'know who' and 'know why'.

In many organisations there is still confusion about what managing knowledge is really about. This has caused confusion regarding responsibilities for managing an organisation's knowledge. For organisations to move forward on their knowledge management journey there needs to be greater acknowledgement that:

Knowledge resides in people, not in systems, although systems contain valuable data and information that can help the knowledge process, and

Knowledge creation is fundamentally a social process, it is created through the interactions between individuals as they go about their daily lives.

Pause for reflection

- Which of the external forces outlined in this chapter represent the most significant threats and/or opportunities for your organisation?
- How does your organisation monitor trends in the external world so that it is prepared for the implications and opportunities, from a knowledge management perspective, of these structural changes? Who takes responsibility for this activity?
- What different interpretations of knowledge management exist within your organisation? What is the HR view of knowledge management?
- What good practices already exist within your organisation for ensuring 'know of', 'know how', 'know who' and 'know why'?

Notes

1. Stewart reference was cited in F. Horibe, *Managing Knowledge Workers*.
2. See Watson, G., in Neathey and J. Hurstfield (1995), *Flexibility in Practice: Women's Employment and Pay in Retail and Finance*. Equal Opportunities Commission.
3. Dex, S. and McCulloch, A. (1995), *Flexible Employment in Britain: A Statistical Analysis*. Research Discussion Series No. 15. Equal Opportunities Commission.
4. Boydell, T., Levels and Types of Knowledge. Presentation at Roffey Park Institute. Autumn 1999
5. See Skyrme, D. J. (2001), *Capitalizing on Knowledge, from e-business to k-business*. Butterworth-Heinemann.
6. Parlby, D., Turning Knowledge Into Value. Knowledge Management Conference. Strategic Planning Society. October 1999.

2

The changing role of HR – from operational to strategic HR

The role of HR has changed significantly over the past couple of decades and is continuing to change as the HR profession strives to gain acceptance as a strategic business partner. In many organisations HR is performing a very different role to that of twenty to thirty years ago. Its role has evolved from that of payroll clerk and welfare supporter, through corporate policeman and industrial relations expert, to that of a business partner role.

A key area of change has been in the label given to those working in the field of Personnel. The Personnel label, other than in public sector organisations, has been largely superseded with that of Human Resources. This change coincided with the decline in the importance associated with industrial relations, both in economic and political terms, and the decline in the membership and influence of trade unions (Guest, 1998). In the 1970s and early 1980s when industrial unrest dominated UK industry many personnel practitioners gained their credibility through negotiating with the Trade Unions about pay and working conditions, on behalf of the organisation.

The distinctions between the traditional personnel role and that of HRM (Holbeche, 1999) are summarised in Table 2.1.

The HRM agenda according to David Guest (1998) is concerned with: ensuring commitment from employees; creating a focus on values, mission and purpose; developing an environment-based on high trust and building an organisation consisting of flexible roles, flatter structures and where there is autonomy and self-control within the work that individuals do (Guest, 1998).

Table 2.1: Contrasting traditional personnel and HRM

Characteristics of the traditional personnel role	*Characteristics of the emerging role of HRM*
Reactive	Proactive
Employee advocate	Business partner
Task force	Task and enablement focus
Focus on operational issues	Focus on strategic issues
Qualitative issues	Quantitative issues
Stability	Constant change
Tactical solutions	Strategic solutions
Functional integrity	Multi-functional
People as an expense	People as assets

The HR function, according to Dave Ulrich (1998), is crucial to organisations achieving excellence. Excellence, according to Ulrich comes through a focus on learning, quality, teamwork, re-engineering, knowing how things get done within an organisation and also how people get treated; all of which are HR issues and hence achieving organisational excellence requires the work of HR.

Ulrich suggests that given the business challenges that organisations face today – globalisation, profitability through growth, technological change, intellectual capital and continuous change – success depends on organisations building core capabilities such as speed, responsiveness, agility, learning capacity and employee competence. Developing these capabilities, in Ulrich's view, is the mandate for HR. This he suggests requires a focus on four key areas.

Partner in strategy execution

Ulrich doesn't argue that HR alone should develop the business strategy, this he argues is the joint responsibility of an organisation's executive, which hopefully HR should be part of. HR's role in strategy making should be that of guiding the discussion about how the organisation should be organised in order to carry out its strategy. In essence this means HR taking on the role of architect, advising on what organisational systems and processes already support the organisation's strategic goals and which ones need some attention, and how best to set about changing these.

The Executive Director of group resources at Xerox Europe argues that if HR wants to have an equal seat at the table they have to have things that they can contribute. Part of that contribution means adding directly to the productivity of the business.

Ulrich argues that HR also needs to take stock of its own workloads, setting clear priorities, which are aligned with the real operational needs of the business. To become accepted as a business partner, HR may need to acquire new skills and capabilities and may need to acquire new tools for their toolbox.

Linda Holbeche, Director of Research at Roffey Park Institute, argues that a strategic agenda for HR is likely to include a number of key areas: recruitment and retention of talent; improving the quality of management; enabling high performance and creating and building organisational climates and culture which supports what the organisation wants to do (Holbeche, 1999).

Administrative expert

HR has traditionally performed an administrative role within organisations. However, Ulrich argues that in their new administrative role HR need to shed their traditional image of policeman and instead seek to improve the administrative procedures both within their own function, as well as within the business as a whole. They need to seek out the inefficient processes that get in the way of the organisation excelling and suggest ways in which these processes can be improved. In essence what HR needs to do is identify the bottlenecks in the organisation's core processes and then work with their business colleagues to find ways of removing these.

Employee champion

Ulrich argues that with the changing psychological contract of employment HR should be made accountable for ensuring that employees are fully motivated and engaged. He argues that it is HR's role to ensure that line managers understand the critical link between employee motivation and organisational performance and how this link can be sustained.

HR also have to play the role of employee champion. This requires delivering development programmes that ensure personal growth, helping employees meet the demands placed on them in the workplace, as well as taking on an advocacy role, i.e. acting as the voice of employees in discussions with management, ensuring that this is heard and understood.

Change agent

The final area of expertise that HR needs to address to be a strategic partner is helping the organisation build its capability to embrace and manage change. Here then HR need to demonstrate their knowledge of how successful change can be brought about. This requires HR to ask their business colleagues some basic questions:

What? – What are we trying to achieve? What will it look like when we have changed?
Why? – Why do we need to change? What will happen if we don't change?
Who? – Who is going to be responsible overall for the change programme? Who else needs to be involved?
When? – When will we get started? When will the necessary resources be made available?
How? – How should we get started? How will we know if the changes are working?

What does this changing role of HR mean in terms of the key competencies that HR professionals need to demonstrate?

Based upon extensive research among 2000 HR professionals, in three separate studies, Dave Ulrich (1998) has identified five key high-level competencies needed for HR professionals working at the strategic level. These are: understanding of the business, knowledge of HR practices, ability to manage culture, ability to manage change and personal credibility.

Test yourself against the five core competences needed to perform at a strategic HR level.

For each of the competencies defined below, rate yourself on a scale of 1–5 where 5 = highly developed and 1 = needs attention.

Core HR competencies	Personal rating	How others might rate you
Business awareness and understanding		
☐ Understands the financial indicators of business success (e.g. balance sheet, profit and loss, return on assets)		
☐ Understands customer success measures (e.g. satisfaction surveys, segmentation criteria)		
☐ Understands and applies competitor analysis techniques (e.g. industry trends)		
☐ Able to translate own work into the same financial and customer-focused language used in the business		

Core HR competencies	Personal rating	How others might rate you
☐ Able to describe HR's impact in terms that business leaders will understand		
Delivery of HR practices		
☐ Able to identify the value of different HR practices		
☐ Able to diagnose business problems and translate these into effective HR solutions		
☐ Able to benchmark own organisation's HRM systems against those of other high-performing organisations		
☐ Able to develop strategies for attracting and retaining key people		
☐ Enables the business to put in place the right structures to meet operational needs		
☐ Knowledgeable about HR systems and practices, internally and externally		
Management of culture		
☐ Able clearly to articulate the desired culture needed to support the business strategy		
☐ Provides credible explanations as to why employee commitment is a critical success criteria for culture change		
☐ Able to build employee commitment to the desired cultural shift		
☐ Understands the learning interventions needed to kick-start culture change process		
☐ Identifies the behaviours needed to support cultural change		
Change management		
☐ Understands the business case for strategic change		
☐ Identifies and articulates the key measures and success criteria		
☐ Understands and applies different theories of change to bring about successful change		
☐ Persuades people at all levels of the need to change		
☐ Develops the necessary support infrastructure for change		
☐ Has the confidence to challenge issues that are getting in the way of change		

Core HR competencies	Personal rating	How others might rate you
Builds personal credibility		
☐ Has an established track record of success		
☐ Commands the respect and trust of colleagues		
☐ Regularly sought out for opinions and insights about HR matters		
☐ Demonstrates willingness to take personal risks		
☐ Lives the organisation's values		

Developed from the work of Becker, Huselid and Ulrich (2001) on The HR Balanced Scorecard.

My own research with HR directors and managers has identified that there are other competencies that HR professionals need to develop. In particular it seems that HR professionals need to demonstrate leadership. To do this HR needs to:

Make things happen – they need to deliver the operational services efficiently, as well as deliver new and enhanced services linked to the business strategy. To do this HR needs to develop its influencing and political skills.

Become a trusted advisor – they need to win the respect of their Chief Executive and other senior managers. They need to be seen as professionals whom senior managers can be confident that they can confide in and share some of their fears and concerns. But this needs to be balanced with maintaining a certain distance at times from the top team, as well as being able to hold your own ground, particularly on issues where HR feels that senior managers are not upholding the organisational values.

Be attuned to changes in the organisational climate – HR needs to keep its ears and eyes open so that they are attuned to how individuals and groups within the organisation are feeling and what the key tensions are out in the organisation.

HR also needs to be able to demonstrate to their business colleagues that they are approachable. In order to symbolize to their business colleagues that HR is open and approachable one of the things HR could consider is reviewing where it is physically located. In many organisations HR shuts itself away in offices that are not easily accessible. If managers and employees are to see HR as being approachable they need to be physically more accessible. Perhaps they should consider physically locating themselves in a more central location. One suggestion would be for HR to set up part of the Help Desk function in the firm's reception area, in this way being more accessible to employees. This may encourage employees to drop in and strike up conversations about good practice – thus having a similar effect to the 'corridor conversations' that we all know can often be very knowledge rich. Another option, given the trend to mobile working, would be for HR to spend some of their time working at a mobile workstation in different business areas. In this way they could pick up some of the real operational issues and niggles that individuals struggle with day-to-day, and that get in the way of high performance.

Contribute to the overall development of the organisation as a business – here HR needs actively to contribute to building the business agenda and sharing responsibility for organisational performance. It can use its skills to help advance strategic thinking within the business. This means gaining itself a reputation as 'thought leaders', providing a conceptual framework to translate business strategy into key HR deliverables. One HR manager described HR's mission as being 'to gain a reputation of being thinkers who deliver'. This means HR needs to deliver on two or three key deliverables that will really make a difference to the business.

In addition HR also needs to demonstrate some of the softer skills associated with the profile of leadership in the future (Jean-Marie Hilltrop, 1998). These include being:

- Self-reliant: initiative, vision, creativity, risk-taker, self-motivation
- Expert: enthusiastic, professional, intellectual curiosity; life-long learner
- Networked: communication skills, negotiation skills, problem-solving skills, project management, open-minded
- Resilient: stress tolerance, flexibility, team-worker, adaptable, determination

However, as Ulrich points out, it is not enough for HR to be competent at what they do, they also need to demonstrate attitude (Ulrich, 2000). 'HR with attitude' involves:

- turning knowledge into action;
- making informed choices about how to invest in HR practices to assure business results;

- associating with peers in the HR profession and line management with the confidence that you have something of value to offer;
- demonstrate confidence, decisiveness, risk-taking and action-orientation.

Does everyone in HR need to demonstrate all of the competencies and attributes outlined above? Does everyone need to be working in the strategic partner role? After IBM had transformed the way that its HR services were delivered, as part of their overall business transformation in the 1990s, several different skill levels of work emerged (Leighton). These include:

- The strategic level – this encompasses policy and process owners, who are responsible for specific policy and processes and HR strategy partners, who are responsible for focusing on the strategic issues of the business units.
- The complex interaction level – dealt with by HR professionals who specialise in a particular HR process.
- The simple interaction level – which could be non-HR professionals, who are able to answer simple questions on current policy and process.

How can HR develop their competencies?

Spend time working in the business – HR managers need to be business managers too. One of the best ways for HR to build an understanding of the business is to take time out of their function to work in/alongside the business. This could be anything from organising a short 'back to the floor' work arrangement, to negotiating a more solid chunk of time to work full-time on a specific business project. Steve Cronin, the Executive Director of group resources at Xerox Europe, argues that HR should not be seen as a career for life, instead HR professionals need to develop their career in more diverse ways. There seems to be growing consensus that some of the best HR professionals are those who are able to straddle the boundary between business and their own profession. From a career perspective, those with experience outside HR are increasingly in demand because of their wider leadership skills and enhanced knowledge.

Invest in formal learning – this could either be short professional development courses, or something that involves a more extended period of study, such as gaining a further qualification. If the latter option is chosen then some of the options that HR professionals could consider is whether to choose a more focused HR qualification, or to study for a more generalist qualification, such as an MBA, which has greater portability.

Alternatively the organisation could consider running its own internal HR development programme. A suggested content, drawn from a programme developed by the HR team within a major international bank is show in Table 2.2.

Invest time in informal learning and knowledge building – Chapter 5 sets out the critical importance of learning with and from other professionals. HR professionals need to invest in building links with others within their profession, as well as with professionals in other functional specialisms. Investing time in

Table 2.2: Example of an in-company HR development programme

Day	Morning	Afternoon
1		● Changing role of HR – key drivers for change ● What does a world-class HR look like? ● A vision of HR within this organisation ● Challenges HR needs to be prepared for ● Barriers to success ● Critical success factors for HR
2	● The product development cycle ● Policy on HR Product Management ● HR Product Plans ● Behaviours needed to support HR Product Management	● Simulation exercises ● Learning review
3	● The vision for Service Delivery ● The importance of standardisation ● Streamlining HR processes ● Peoplesoft implementation ● Employee self-service – the visions and aims	● Internal consultancy cycle and skills – Part 1 ● Self-assessment of own competencies
4	● Internal consultancy cycle and skills – Part 2 ● Managing change	● Talent management – Introduction, overview, workshop and simulation activities
5	● Leveraging the HR network ● Contributing to virtual teams ● Personal action planning	

networking enables you to keep in touch with significant changes in the external world, open up the mind to new ideas, raise awareness of what you don't know, as well as provide opportunities for sharpening up existing thinking.

Secondment to other organisations – recognising that sometimes it isn't always easy or possible to develop new skills and/or try out new roles within one's existing organisation. Another development option would be to organize a secondment to another organisation.

Take up a non-executive position – seeking out a non-executive position can help to gain greater exposure to senior business leaders from diverse business sectors. These roles are undoubtedly very challenging and stretching, but create opportunities for honing political and influencing skills.

Get a good coach – every successful sports personality has a good coach, they are unable to sustain their performance without one. Increasingly business leaders are recognising the importance of having a coach to help them enhance their performance. Having a coach is not a sign of failure, but instead a symbol of taking charge of one's own career. Like their business counterparts, HR professionals should ensure that they have the support and challenge provided by a good coach.

Sue Cox, formally Head of HR at Shroders, the international asset management company, and now working as an independent coach with HR professionals, shared her thoughts on how to select the right coach at an HR networking event that I attended. Some of the areas that Cox thinks are important to consider include:

- Check out the coach's background and roles played. If the coach hasn't worked directly in HR make sure that they understand the function.
- Find out their motivation for being a coach.
- Establish how well networked they are – the more contacts the coach has then the more potential resources that you can draw on.
- Establish whether or not they have a supervisor – or whether they have a coach themselves.
- Get the coach to share with you the range of tools that they use.

Summary

The role of HR has changed significantly in recent years, and no doubt will continue to change as HR continues to develop the role of strategic business partner. The new mandate for HR in high-performance organisations is to help build the organisation's core capabilities, such as speed, responsiveness, learning capacity and employee competence. At a practical level this means that HR itself needs to demonstrate leadership. This requires: delivering new and enhanced services, in addition to providing the operational basics; becoming a trusted adviser to their business colleagues; being in tune with the tensions that are getting in the way of performance, as well as contributing to the business agenda. For HR practitioners this means having to invest in developing their own competencies, as well as building in-depth knowledge about the business that they are trying to enhance. Indeed there are some practitioners who believe that HR should not be seen as a career for life, but instead HR professionals need to consider developing their careers in more diverse ways.

Pause for reflection

- How is the HR function perceived within your own organisation? How close are you at becoming accepted as business partner?
- Who do you see as being the most successful HR players, and why?
- Where do you see HR adding value within your own organisation?

3

Towards a blueprint for building a knowledge-centric culture

Chapter 1 described five stages that organisations experience on their knowledge management journey. Stage 1 being knowledge-chaotic and Stage 5 being knowledge-centric, i.e. where knowledge management practices are integrated into the organisational culture. But what are the characteristics of a knowledge-centric culture? As an outsider how would I know whether an organisation is knowledge-centric? What signs would I look for? This chapter is an attempt to try to answer these questions. It is based on findings from my own research, combined with ideas and thoughts from other writers, about the cultural dimension of managing knowledge.

Characteristics of knowledge-creating organisations

In his book, *Living on Thin Air*, Charles Leadbeater sets out a number of core principles which he believes are critical ingredients for knowledge-creating organisations. He defines these core principles as:

- *Cellular* – having organisational structures that are adaptive. If structures are too rigidly defined then organisations will not be adaptive enough; on the other hand, if too loosely defined, organisations will not be distinctive enough.
- *Self-managing* – individuals and teams need to be self-managing in order to unlock innovation and creativity. An

important pre-requisite for self-management is the free flow of information up, down and across an organisation. Leadbeater cites the practices within CMG, a UK-based computer services company, where there is open access to personnel files, including how much individuals are paid. This open information approach enables individuals to challenge executives on the salaries paid to both themselves and others. The rule is that executives are 'obliged to respond' to these challenges.

- *Entrepreneurial* – to thrive in a knowledge economy all individuals will need to become more entrepreneurial, i.e. develop the ability to spot and act on opportunities for growth and/or change.
- *Equitable membership and reward* – in order to counter-balance the effects of self-management, organisations will need to provide reward systems that help to create a sense of membership.
- *Deep knowledge reservoirs* – organisations need to view knowledge as a core capability and thus focus on developing specialist expertise, rather than rely on a collection of generalists.
- *The holistic company* – the holistic company is one that recognises that it can benefit from knowledge assets that reside outside of its own structure.
- *Collaborative leadership* – in cellular organisations Leadbeater sees the role of the centre as being less concerned with monitoring and checking and more concerned with direction setting, communicating values, raising ambitions and encouraging others to adopt an 'outside-in approach' to conducting business.

These core principles are based on Leadbeater's observations of practices in knowledge-creating organisations, particularly technology companies in Silicon Valley. They are challenging operating principles for organisations and individuals to come to terms with.

It seems that what is required in knowledge-creating organisations is the development of a new moral code, one which, according to Sumantra Ghoshal and Christopher Bartlett (1998), requires a fundamental shift in management philosophy and the role of senior managers. Their view of what this shift entails involves:

- Building new organisational structures that enhance initiative and personal responsibility.
- Tapping into the unused potential of individuals.
- Building an environment that supports individual knowledge and skills development.

- Strategic senior management that engages lower level managers in a dialogue in how to sustain competitive advantage.

Barriers to effective knowledge sharing

Some of the more common factors that can inhibit knowledge transfer within organisations, together with some possible ways of addressing these tensions are shown in Table 3.1.

Research by Cranfield School of Management identified that the barriers to knowledge sharing fall into three key areas: structure, people and management.

Structure
- Inflexible company structure
- Fragmented organisation
- Functional silo mentality
- Failure to invest in the right systems

People
- Inertia to change
- Lack of time
- Lack of motivation to share
- Turnover of staff
- Insufficient attention to inducting new people

Management
- Fear of giving up power
- Difficulties of passing on power
- Unwillingness to challenge company style

One of the other areas that needs to be considered when trying to encourage employees to participate in knowledge management projects is addressing the '*What is in it for me?*' question. Which if we unpack this requires thinking about the following questions:

- How will knowledge management affect me in my current job?
- Will it make my life at work any easier?
- Will it affect how I am rewarded?
- Will it affect my future employment prospects?
- What will I need to do differently?

There are no simple 'off the peg' solutions. Many organisations are having to find solutions which work best for them, through

Table 3.1: Cultural tensions affecting knowledge transfer within organisations (after Davenport and Prusak, 1998)

Knowledge transfer tensions	Possible solutions
Lack of trust	• Build relationships of trust and common ground through balancing virtual and face-to-face contact. • Ensure that the communication's approaches supports knowledge transfer.
Different language and frames of reference	• Ensure common ground through team working, job rotation and other forms of collaborative working. • Develop a shared language or utilise 'boundary spanners'.
Perspective held of productive work	• Establish places/events for informal and formal knowledge exchanges. • Encourage experimentation and play. • Help managers reframe their perspective of where and how work gets done.
Rewards go to knowledge holders	• Reward those who share and reuse knowledge.
Absorptive capacity in receivers of knowledge	• Educate others on the benefits of flexibility. • Plan time for knowledge processing, application and use.
Belief that knowledge relates to certain groups/positions	• Create an environment where quality of ideas are more important that status of source.
Intolerance of mistakes and lack of support when help is needed	• Tolerate errors from creative work and help individuals learn from these.

experimentation. Some common themes include: allowing users to drive systems and practices, rather than imposing these from the top; encouraging a sense of playfulness and fun as a way of engaging individuals in knowledge management activities, as well as providing systems which help individuals feel part of a wider community.

Designing a blueprint for a knowledge-centric organisation

Most of us don't have the luxury of designing an organisation from scratch, in the same way that we might design a green-field production site. But imagine for a moment that you had been given this task. How would you set about building an organisation that was perfect from a knowledge creation and sharing perspective? What would be the key components?

From my own research, combined with thoughts from other authors who have written about the cultural dimension of managing knowledge, it seems that there are a number of key elements as indicated in Figure 3.1.

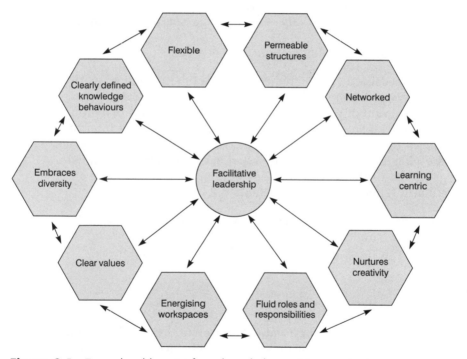

Figure 3.1   Towards a blueprint for a knowledge-centric organisation

Clearly defined cultural values

Ahmed, Kok and Loh (2002) have defined a number of cultural norms that they believe are essential for knowledge building and sharing. These include:

- Challenge and belief in action
- Freedom and risk-taking
- Dynamism and future orientated
- External orientation
- Trust and openness
- Debate and listening
- Cross-functional interaction and freedom
- Committed and involved leadership

My own research (Evans, 2000) identified the value base in knowledge-enabled organisations as:

- Openness
- Trust and integrity
- Tolerance of failure
- Respect for individual contributions
- Generosity and reciprocity – knowledge sharing, not knowledge hoarding
- Co-operation and collaboration

Trust has become a vital ingredient in the modern business world, particularly given the shift towards virtual organisations, organisations that do not physically exist but instead consist of a group of companies/people all working in an area of common interest.

One of the areas that organisations need to pay attention to is addressing the cultural paradoxes that occur in managing knowledge. Some of these paradoxes, as defined by Probst, Raub and Romhardt (2000), are shown in Table 3.2.

How many of these paradoxes exist within your organisation?
What other paradoxes are you aware of?
What do you think HR's role should be in addressing these?

Embraces diversity

Perhaps one of the cultural values that should be added to the above lists is that of valuing difference, in whatever shape or form, e.g. background, perspectives, experience.

An organisation that does not encourage and support diversity is one that is destined for extinction according to Eden Charles, a leading Diversity and Change consultant[1]. Diversity, he argues, is crucial for success in a business world that consists of diverse markets and diverse consumers. It is not nice to have, but it is a critical component of business success.

But what does your organisation understand by diversity? In many organisations the terms Equal Opportunities and Diversity

Table 3.2: Paradoxes associated with managing organisational knowledge

We train our employees	. . . but	we do not let them use their knowledge
We learn mostly in projects	. . . but	we do not pass on our expertise
We have an expert for every question	. . . but	few people know how to locate him/her
We document everything thoroughly	. . . but	we cannot easily access our knowledge store
We recruit only the brightest	. . . but	after three years we lose them to our competitors
We know everything about our competitors	. . . but	not much about ourselves
We ask everyone to share their knowledge	. . . but	we keep our own secrets
We co-operate in order to learn from others	. . . but	we do not know what our learning goals are

are often used interchangeably and yet they are distinctly different. Equal Opportunities practices focus on addressing unfairness in the recruitment, selection and retention practices. They also tend to focus on targeting particular social groups for specialist attention.

An organisation that considers itself diverse, however, operates from a different standpoint and set of assumptions. Organisations that embrace diversity, so individual differences, in whatever shape or form, are valued for just that, their differences. Doing different things and doing things differently are acknowledged ways of producing new perspectives. Difference, according to Gryskiewicz (1999) a leading writer in the field of creativity, provides the all-important sense of turbulence, from which creativity flows. Diverse, but complementary skills, are also felt necessary to produce the friction that generates creative sparks.

Organisations that truly embrace diversity, according to Eden Charles, adopt the following principles:

- Include a broad-range of people; no one is excluded
- Individual differences are recognised

- All employees are helped to maximize their potential and contribution to the organisation
- Individuals are encouraged to free themselves up
- Concentrate on the issue of movement of people
- Believe that diversity is the concern of all employees, not just HR practitioners

As HR practitioners this suggests a need to focus on practices that:

- Enable differences to be recruited and retained
- Encourages and draws out different ways of thinking
- Appraises and rewards people for their ability to make a valued difference
- Encourages different networks to thrive
- Facilitates the practice of helping teams get to know each other's differences and challenges the assumption that this is not productive use of time
- Fosters networking, to maximise exposure to differences
- Acknowledges that individuals learn differently and provides a range of learning opportunities for them to draw on
- Help teams to address collective needs as a prerequisite for working together, rather than just concentrating on getting things right with one or two members (Herriot and Pemberton, 1995)
- Enable individuals to develop a diverse set of interests, thus maximising opportunities for diversity of knowledge and experience

From the organisation's perspective a more diverse workforce provides a deeper pool of talented people that more closely reflects the pluralistic, multi-cultural client base of the 21st century business world (John Bank, 1999).

Nurtures creativity

For knowledge to become the source of sustainable advantage organisations need to develop a culture where creativity is encouraged and supported. Creativity is vital for developing new knowledge assets e.g. new products, services, or processes, which sets the organisation apart from its competitors.

The term creativity, as with the term knowledge, is one that individuals and organisations have difficulty understanding. Theresa Amibile from Harvard Business School, one of the leading experts on creativity, defines it as 'The production of novel and appropriate ideas by individuals or small groups[2].' She defines innovation as 'The successful implementation of creative ideas within an organisation.'

Amabile argues that the individual components of creativity are:

Expertise: knowledge about particular domain points; technical skills and talent in the domain.

Creativity skills: flexible cognitive approach; energetic persistent approach to work and an orientation to risk-taking.

Task motivation: motivated by a deep interest in the area and challenges presented by their work.

However, environmental factors play an influencing role in shaping creativity, for example the availability of resources, management practices, as well as the organisation's motivation to innovate.

In his book *Releasing Creativity*, John Whatmore argues that creativity within organisations arises through the interaction between the task, the team and the organisation, with leadership being a vital enabler for connecting these three overlapping areas. His research identified some of the organisational disabling influencers for creativity as:

- Too much focus on the task and/or the client and not enough on the process/people aspects
- Too much control and bureaucracy
- Hierarchical structures
- Paternalistic culture
- Boxed thinking
- Unrealistic time constraints
- Not users or nourishers of ideas
- Lack of recognition that people have a variety of objectives
- Low support for personal development
- Physical spaces divisive

and in terms of the role of leaders, where leaders:

- have less interest in the personal development of people in their team
- have too high a workload to have enough time for team members
- are not a 'people person'
- are not skilled in 'process' skills

- only having partial responsibility for group activities e.g. selection of team members
- do not give people the space to be creative themselves

Given the right conditions creativity will flourish. An important part of that is getting the right leadership in place. How can leaders make a difference? According to John Whatmore there are a number of factors to consider:

> *There are so many practical considerations: the task to fit each person in a way that will not wreck another person's opportunities*

and

> *Motivating inquisitiveness and encouraging self-exploration, and finding ways in which they can understand for themselves*

and

> *By giving responsibility and guidance for them to learn for themselves, to learn by discovery, and then letting them have a go . . . giving them 'the dignity of risk'.*

How does this type of enabling leadership develop and who should be responsible for developing an organisation's leadership? These are key questions that HR professionals, working in a strategic role, need to consider and ones that will be returned to in Chapter 5.

Permeable and agile structures

Charles Leadbeater argues that in knowledge businesses it is vital to have organisational structures that are adaptive and networked given that in the complex and ever-changing business world that we now live in no single company can develop the solutions needed to stay successful.

Many new consumer products today are developed through collaborative ventures between different strategic partners. A collaborative network according to Leadbeater '. . . should provide companies with distributed intelligence, sensing new opportunities, combining different skills and sharing ideas to create and exploit new knowledge' (Leadbeater, 1999: 131).

It is not just in the private sector where partnership working is important, public sector companies too are being encouraged to work in partnership with a range of different stakeholders. However, in partnership arrangements the rules of the game are different. Managers can no longer rely on the authority that goes with their position to get things done. Instead they have to win the trust and respect of each of the partnering organisations, something that takes time to develop.

Working with more fluid and permeable structures requires a different mindset and management style. Traditional organisational forms and structures bring with them a sense of security for individuals – people know their place and what is expected of them. Managers too have a better sense of how to manage and indeed often feel more comfortable managing within traditional structures.

As Charles Handy (1996) points out there are important implications of working in virtual organisations. First, greater attention needs to be given to selecting the right people. This suggests a need to think about a different approach to recruitment, one that enables both parties to get a better feel for whether there is likely to be a 'good fit'. Second, the size of an organisational unit will have implications for the level of trust. The bigger the unit the less chance there will be to really get to know colleagues and hence establish relationships of trust. Third, as vision and values will really count, time will need to be allocated to talking about these things. Fourth, as trust is fuelled by talk then communication, by a multitude of means, is crucial. In virtual organisations communication needs to be well managed, to avoid the situation of 'out of sight, out of mind'. But if organisations want to survive then they will need to find ways of dealing with these crucial areas, rather than continuing to stick with what has worked in the past.

Flexible

Flexibility and agility have become two of the most coveted business competences in the last couple of decades. However, achieving flexibility is not a straightforward process. First organisations have to develop a shared understanding of what is meant by the term flexibility, then they have to review their practices to find out which ones get in the way of achieving flexibility.

The flexible firm needs to make creative use of each of the four flexibility categories:

Temporal flexibility – this relates to the time-span within which work is carried out. The options that come under this form of flexibility include: part-time working, short-term contracts, annualised hours, job-share, or V-time (where an individual reduces their hours to just below full-time on a temporary basis) and zero-hours or bank (where individuals work for an organisation but do not have any guaranteed contracted hours), and associated schemes (which include individuals who offer specialist services to organisations on a short-term, project-by-project basis).

Locational flexibility – this relates to the physical location where work is carried out. This form of flexibility encompasses: teleworking, working at home, or a combination of working at home and at the office. Teleworking can enable individuals to benefit from temporal as well as locational flexibility, i.e. offering greater flexibility over the overall number of hours worked and also the time window within which work takes place. Research by Gartner[3], a leading technology research and advisory consultancy, identified that around 44 per cent of organisations plan to invest nearly half of their IT budget on systems to increase business agility, including putting the infrastructure in place to support mobile working.

Numerical flexibility – this relates to how organisations manage their overall resources in relation to the work that needs to be done. As part of an organisation's overall resource strategy they may choose to sub-contract some of their services or indeed outsource complete functional areas. Contracting out work to self-employed professionals would come under this category.

Functional flexibility – this relates to the way in which different services and/or skills are combined in order to provide a more responsive service to customers. Many customer service organisations, such as retail, financial service and hospitality, have sought to enhance their overall level of flexibility through the introduction of multi-skilling. Certainly, for individuals, this can be attractive since it enables them to develop a broader skills base, thus adding to their employability. In addition, where individuals get an opportunity to develop new skills by working in different functional areas, this provides them with an opportunity to develop their knowledge about the linkages between different functional areas. Armed with this knowledge employees can then engage in a dialogue about how to enhance these linkages and hence overall performance.

There is another form of flexibility that needs to underpin each of the above categories of flexibility – mindset flexibility. Mindset flexibility means being open to new ways of thinking about how work can be achieved and indeed how and where business should be conducted. This requires a time investment in order to gather intelligence ('know of') about the practices in place in other organisations. Another example of mindset flexibility is where individuals are able to adjust to leading on one project, and being a team member on another.

However, although the range of flexible employment options offered by employers has been on the increase since the mid-1980s, some individuals feel that organisations are still not flexible enough. This is one of the reasons that some professionals opt for self-employment (Evans, 2001).

The removal of layers of management does not necessarily make organisations more flexible and agile. Clearly removing unnecessary bureaucracy is important if organisations want to speed up the decision-making process. Customers do not want to have to wait weeks for decisions to be made/ratified by senior management or institutional committees. Sadly the introduction of flatter organisational structures has earned some organisations the reputation of being anorexic, i.e. suffering from corporate amnesia, from stripping out key knowledge assets without any regard to the longer term implications for the business. As a result these organisations now have less flexibility as they have less resource to draw on in order to take advantage of new business opportunities.

Fluid roles and responsibilities

Fluid role and responsibilities go hand-in-hand with looser organisational structures. Instead of having tightly defined job descriptions individuals will need to become more adept at working with fluid role descriptions. Like entrepreneurs, employees will need to become comfortable with wearing many hats, as well as developing the ability to wear multiple hats simultaneously.

Some of the new roles required to build and maintain a knowledge-centric organisation are discussed in the next chapter.

Learning centric

The pace of change in businesses today makes it difficult to keep abreast of existing knowledge let alone identify what new knowledge will be needed in the future. One thing is certain as Arie de Geus, formally of Royal Dutch Shell, points out '*Learning faster than your competitor may be the only sustainable competitive advantage.*' Peter Senge, points out '*The need for understanding how organisations learn and accelerate that learning is greater today than ever before. The old days when a Henry Ford, Alfred Sloan or Tom Watson learned for the organisation are gone. In an increasingly dynamic, independent and unpredictable world, it is simply no longer possible for anyone to figure it all out at the top. The old model "the top thinks" and "the local acts" must now give way to the integrative thinking and acting at all levels.'* (Peter Senge, 1998: 586)

But what mindset shift would be needed for organisations to become learning-centric? What would it take for learning conversations to become as natural events in the workplace, as the conversations that individuals have about their favourite football team, or the TV programme that they watched the previous evening?

If only we could encourage individuals to be enthusiastic about dissecting practices/events in the workplace to tease out good practice and lessons learnt. Sadly individuals often get switched off learning, because of their earlier experiences of formal learning, i.e. at school or college.

One of the biggest challenges that learning institutions face is that of how to motivate individuals to engage with the process of learning, this can also be a challenge for organisations too. There are relatively few organisations that would class themselves as 'learning organisations'.

Becoming a learning-centric organisation requires instilling behaviours whereby all individuals are prepared to question and challenge the routines that get in the way of effective and efficient practices. It also requires a shift in organisational thinking too, whereby time spent reviewing how things get done (i.e. process), is perceived as being as important as what gets done (i.e. outputs/deliverables). In today's ever-changing business world organisations need to embrace second-order change (i.e. doing different things, not just doing existing things better); a process that is often best facilitated through collaborative working.

Equally, organisations need to be clear about the extent to which they are prepared to invest in building generic human capital (i.e. skills and knowledge which enhance employees' productivity irrespective of where he or she is employed) and specific human capital (i.e. skills and knowledge which only apply to current employer). Chapter 6 discusses some of the issues relating to this strategic decision.

Clearly there are important leadership issue here since leaders (this includes HR) are the ones in a position to act as role models to others in the organisation, or at least give their stamp of approval for changes proposed by team members. By working in partnership with the line, HR can help the business review their business processes to tease out inefficiencies and make plans to address these.

One of the other lessons that learning organisations need to address is the importance of recognising when they don't have all of the capabilities in-house to do what the business wants to do.

Recognising and accepting this at least gives the organisation the opportunity to borrow, or learn, from the experience of others outside the organisation. This was the strategy adopted by Shell Oil as part of its transformation from traditional products to an operations focus (Gubman, 1998). This transformation involved the organisation concentrating on developing its organisational capabilities for finding, producing, transporting and marketing gasoline. As the organisation realised that it didn't have the experience/capability to do the things that they wanted to do on their own, they decided to form a partnership arrangement with other organisations, such as Amoco. The key lesson that the organisation learnt from this experience is that of knowing when it is best to do things on your own, and when it is best to work in partnership with others.

Networked

Networking has been identified as a core competence in knowledge-based businesses (Bird, 1994; Davenport and Prusak, 1998). It is the means by which businesses acquire business critical knowledge. But as we have seen in the example above about Shell Oil, it is also the means by which businesses acquire and build effective strategic partnering arrangements, which either help fill a gap in existing knowledge, or complement existing knowledge.

Through networking organisations are able to build knowledge supply chains that extend outside of their own organisation, similar to physical distribution supply chains. Most service providers today have some form of partnering arrangements with other organisations to help them deliver their business.

The networks that businesses belong to will need to remain fluid, changing as and when the business changes.

Individuals within organisations need to be networked too. As well as helping to build human capital, networking is important for building social capital (i.e. 'the oil that lubricates the process of learning through interaction' (Kilpatrick and Falk, 1998)).

Facilitative leadership

Facilitative leadership is the heart of a knowledge-centric organisation. Without supportive leaders then creativity will not emerge and individuals will not be willing readily to share their knowledge. John Bank defines the characteristics of facilitative leadership as:

- Having vision and values to support diversity.
- Demonstrating ethical commitment to fairness.
- Having a broad knowledge and awareness regarding primary and secondary dimensions of diversity and multi-cultural issues.
- Being open to change based on diverse inputs and feedback about own personal filters and blind spots.
- Mentoring and empowering diverse employees.
- Acting as a catalyst for individual and organisational change.

Peter Senge suggests that in the global marketplace companies need to foster a new leadership model, one that is based on principles, particularly mutual trust[4]. Empowerment, according to Senge, does not work without trust. Trustworthiness comes from behaviours such as equity, justice, compassion, integrity and honesty. Trustworthiness will not evolve, according to Senge, in the old command and control management structures.

Other writers point out that in a knowledge-centric culture, one of the key roles for HR is to develop leaders who can nurture 'pockets of good practice' in which individuals are encouraged and enabled to identify and apply usable ideas for local and organisational wide benefit (Bailey and Clarke, 1999).

Physical architecture to support collaborative working and learning

The physical work environment has certainly changed over the past twenty years. In the 1980s open-plan offices started to replace traditional office environments, particularly where organisations were located in out-of-town business parks. One of the design features of these open-plan buildings was to scatter coffee machines around each floor, making coffee more accessible; the aim being to demonstrate looking after the employees. However, one of the practices that emerged was that people took coffee back to their desks and continued working, rather than breaking for a coffee and a chat with colleagues.

In the 1990s there has been a trend towards more mobile working, with certain categories of employees only working in a central office environment on two or three days a week; the rest of the time being spent working on client sites, or working from home. Organisations realised that these large open-plan offices were being under-utilised and the accountants were quick to work out the cost of this under-utilisation. The result – the introduction of hot-desking, where individuals no longer have their own personal workspace, but instead book a shared workspace as and when they plan to be in the office.

Richard Scase points out 'If, in the past, the workplace was the place where work was done, in the information economy it is the place where ideas are exchanged and problems solved. This means that the architecture and the design of the workplace needs to encourage employee sociability' (Scase, 2002:87)

Scase suggests that the physical architecture of the future workplace will consist of: large reception area; 'public space' for meetings with colleagues and customers; hot-desking area; project rooms and confidentiality suites for private meetings.

There are signs that organisations are already re-designing their office environments with some of these considerations in mind. Despite the trend towards more mobile working many organisations are beginning to see the importance of investing in the right physical environment to encourage knowledge building and sharing. There seems to be a growing acceptance of the critical importance, from a knowledge management perspective, of bringing teams together, particularly those who are geographically dispersed or working in virtual teams. The view is that it is in these shared spaces – physical, mental and virtual – knowledge flows. Some examples of changing practice, in line with Scase's thinking about the future workplace, include:

Jones Lang Lasalle, a global provider of real estate and investment management services, has set up break-out spaces on two of its floors in its Head Office. These areas form part of the central areas, located close to the lifts and main thoroughfares, thus making them easily accessible. Each of these break-out areas contain coffee machines, PCs and plasma screens for presentations. These breakout areas can be used for formal meetings, presentations, as well as informal meeting spaces.

The European headquarters of Electronic Arts, the world's largest interactive entertainment software company, was designed to provide a campus atmosphere. A key feature of the building is a fully glazed open street overlooking a lakeside setting.

This area is used to hold impromptu meetings over a coffee, or to test latest releases of games at one of the games platforms. This new head office environment was designed with people firmly in mind. It has a self-service cafeteria, a fully equipped gym, a general store, a library, a sports bar and a floodlit outdoor sports court.

IBM UK – as more and more people within the organisation now work more flexibly this has created an opportunity for the organisation to consider rationalising its office space, or at least transform its usage. Personal desks at IBM's UK head office are gradually being transformed into mobile workstations, which individuals connect to as and when they require. As traditional office space becomes free, this has created an opportunity for the organisation to build in more coffee lounges and informal meeting areas, creating more spaces for individuals to hold informal meetings.

GlaxoSmithKline's new head office has a river running alongside the building's central avenue, which is filled with shops and cafes for staff to meet socially.

However, one of the dilemmas that many organisations face is that of reducing costly overheads, such as the cost of central office space. As organisations grow in size they often look for ways of using existing office space more efficiently rather than having to engage in expensive building work. Several of the organisations that I made contact with as part of the background research for this book have experienced a dilemma regarding the space allocated to central restaurant facilities. Each of them had deliberated over whether to remove their restaurant facilities, thus freeing up space to allocate to offices. While financially this decision seemed to make sense, on reflection many felt that this would have drawbacks from a knowledge management perspective. Organisations that have removed central restaurant areas, replacing them with coffee machines and food dispensers, have found that this is not conducive to encouraging informal networking. With nowhere to sit to drink their coffee individuals have no choice but to take this back to their desks – from a knowledge management perspective this is a lost opportunity.

Clearly defined knowledge behaviours

A summit of Chief Knowledge Officers, organised by TPFL[5], identified the core competencies for working in a knowledge culture as:

- Curiosity and learning ability
- Demonstrates initiative
- Have a collaborative and team playing attitude
- The capacity to make intellectual connections
- Humility
- The ability to focus on outcomes
- Ability and willingness to share and receive knowledge
- ICT literate – able to use the information and communication tools available
- An appreciation of information management techniques – the ability to be able to locate and use information is felt to be a core competency for everyone in organisations, not just those working in specialist roles.

My own previous research identified several behavioural characteristics associated with knowledge workers (Evans, 2000), these
include:

- Having a holistic view of self and the broader world within
  which they operate
- A strong sense of purpose, i.e. an understanding of why what
  they are doing is important
- A passion for what they do and create
- Demonstrate a strong sense of self, i.e. awareness of the impact
  of own actions on others
- Show respect for other people's views, ideas and opinions
- Demonstrate a willingness to work collaboratively, i.e. to be
  open with others and trust others to be the same
- Have a sense of generosity, i.e. willingness to make time to
  exchange ideas with others
- Demonstrate a tolerance for uncertainty and risk-taking
- Networked – able to build connections, inside and outside the
  organisation, as well as participate in communities of
  interest.

Enablers of these critical behaviours include:

- Communication – need to develop a common language base so
  that everyone can engage in knowledge-building dialogues.
- Equitable rewards – common performance criteria that everyone has access to; framework for career development, together
  with appropriate support; an opportunity to gain equity in the
  organisation through some form of share scheme.
- Networking forums – both face-to-face and on-line.
- Trust – indicators to consider to ensure that sharing is taking
  place include: response times for information requests by
  colleagues being satisfied; awareness of different roles individuals play so they can help to connect others as quickly as
  possible.

Summary

This chapter has introduced and discussed the key components of
a knowledge-centric culture. These include: clearly defined
values and knowledge behaviours; permeable structures; energising and sociable workspaces that enable creativity to flow and
support collaborative working; fluid roles and responsibilities; an
organisation that values and embraces diversity. Linking all of
these components is facilitative leadership: leadership that really

encourages, enables and supports knowledge creation and sharing, at all levels, and who see this as being their primary role. The rest of this book fleshes out many of the characteristics of knowledge-centric cultures.

Pause for reflection

- How does your organisation stack up against each of the elements in the model introduced in this chapter?
- Are there elements where you think that your organisation could be used as a role model for other organisations? If so, in what way? Are there pockets of good practice within your own organisation?
- Which elements do you feel that your organisation needs to pay more attention to?

Notes

1. E. Charles. Diversity: A draft Laurel Trends Paper. 2002. Further details about this practitioner's work can be obtained from *Info@EdenCharlesAssociates.co.uk*
2. T. Amabile. The Work Environment for Creativity. Oxford Forum for Assessment & Development, 2001.
3. An Agile Age. A study by Gartner and reported in *Computing*, 18 July 2002.
4. Masters of the Universe. Global HR, 01 October 2001. *www.personneltoday.com*
5. S. Ward. Mobilising Knowledge: Skills for working in knowledge environments. *www.TFPL.com*

Part Two

Building a
Knowledge-centric Culture

4

Structures, roles and responsibilities in a knowledge-centric culture

Changing organisational structures

The shift from manufacturing to service-based businesses that are heavily dependent on knowledge as a key differentiator, has resulted in organisations rethinking the structure(s) needed to deliver a more responsive and efficient service to their global customers, as well as maximising opportunities for organisational learning.

Traditionally, decisions about organisational structure related to choices such as:

- Should we organise around products, markets, or function?
- Should we organise globally, nationally, or regionally?
- Should we structure for efficiency and flexibility?
- Should we be centralised or de-centralised?

Up until the early 1980s, most large organisations were designed around the principles of Taylor's scientific model of management. A defining feature of organisational design was ensuring control through the managerial hierarchy. There was a clear demarcation between the role of managers and other employees, with responsibilities and accountabilities clearly mapped out. The role of managers, under the Taylorist model, was to ensure that others in the organisation were doing the right things, at the right time.

However large bureaucratic structures, based on command and control management, have proved to be less effective in today's ever-changing business world. Organisations have found that command and control structures: hinder decision-making, get in the way of creativity, are inflexible and difficult to change. In addition, in structures where jobs are specialised, relationships are formalised, and units are compartmentalised, knowledge does not readily flow. In the modern knowledge-enabled organisation success comes from speed, flexibility, integration and innovation. This contrasts with the success criteria applied previously: size, role clarity, specialisation and control.

So is there an alternative way of structuring organisations to enable knowledge to flourish and flow?

From their own research Sumantra Ghoshal and Christopher Barlett (1998) have identified that some organisations (e.g. Skandia, McKinsey, ABB) are replacing their traditional structures with what can best be described as an 'integrated network structure'. This model enables organisations to develop distributed specialised capabilities and expertise, linked by horizontal flows of information, knowledge and other resources. The 'integrated network structure' is just one example of the boundaryless organisation.

In addition to distributed and specialised units, multi-functional and multi-disciplinary team working also form part of the normal way of doing business in 'integrated network structures'. These structures are inherently more flexible; teams and groups can be more easily formed, re-formed, as well as disbanded. However, organisations need to be wary of becoming attached to any single way of working. They need to be willing to adopt different structures depending on what the business is trying to achieve. What is crucial is that managers and individuals need to embrace the 'mindset flexibility' discussed in Section 1.

Trust is a fundamental ingredient in making 'integrated network structures' work. This provides the glue that binds people together. Individuals need to be confident that colleagues, and others who are part of the networked organisation, will respond quickly to requests for information, support and help; speed being one of the three main success factors in networked organisations. The ideal state is a situation where whenever a problem arises in one part of the organisation others automatically step in to help, without waiting to be asked, or commanded to help. Relationships in networked organisations need to be founded on the principle of inter-dependency, as opposed to dependence, or independence.

Pause for thought: Is your organisation 'boundaryless'?

Table 4.1 contains a number of statements that characterize the boundaryless organisation. Take a few moments to think about and rate your own organisation as it is now. You may like to complete from an HR perspective and then at some point get your business colleagues to complete too, and then compare your responses. No doubt you will get different perspectives in some areas, at least it will provide some information on which to have a meaningful discussion. It will also provide an opportunity to gather success stories which can be used to help encourage and support future change.

Although survival in today's business world requires flexible and adaptable structures, some writers and business leaders point out that this can create a number of tensions for organisations. Homa Bahrami (1996), for example, points out how in the traditional workplace the key area of focus is maintaining control, whereas in knowledge-intensive organisations flexibility and autonomy are critical. Autonomous organisations are characterised by innovation, local recipes, rapid response, future products and have a long-term vision. Bahrami argues that this requires a workplace characterised by the following attributes:

- Multiple centres – the traditional organisational model where the centre is all-powerful does not fit in a business world where organisations need to be constantly changing in response to ever-changing markets. Instead organisations need to structure themselves as a 'federation' or 'constellation' of inter-dependent business units that are more adaptable and able to support each other with their knowhow. The organisation then is both centralised and decentralised. The centre has a crucial role to play in ensuring cohesion between the various inter-dependent business units. It also has a role to play in ensuring a balance between stability and change and in providing the right steer at the formative stages of high-risk ventures. Each independent unit uses its own discretion about how to deal with business imperatives for their own area as they arise, but set within a clearly defined overall strategic framework.
- Diverse structures – in dynamic and ever-changing environments, organisations need to draw on a range of different structures: project teams, micro-organisations, as well as utilising core employees in different roles. They also need to draw on a blend of different management styles and cultural perspectives. The cultural diversity of an organisation's top management sends out an important symbolic message to others.

Table 4.1: The 'boundaryless' organisation – a self-assessment activity

Behaviours in boundaryless organisations	*Response (Always, Sometimes, Never)*
Decisions are made on the spot by those closest to the work and/or customer	
Routine work is carried out through efficient end-to-end processes	
Problems are tackled by multi-level teams, without formal rank getting in the way	
Expert resources can be quickly assembled and moved around the organisation when needed	
Managers are comfortable with front-line responsibilities, as well as working at the strategy level	
Teams spontaneously form to explore new ideas	
Strategic resources are often on loan to customers and suppliers and vice versa	
Customers, suppliers and other key partners are involved in strategic change initiatives as a matter of course	
New product/process ideas are evaluated for their wider application/usage	
Leaders rotate between operational and geographic boundaries	

- Multiple alliances – organisational structures that incorporate a number of strategic alliances, or collaborative partnerships, provide a means for pooling complementary capabilities, dealing with the need for rapid product development cycles, as well as providing an alternative way of building strategic flexibility.
- Cosmopolitan mindset – operating in a global business world requires everyone in the organisation to adopt a cosmopolitan mindset that incorporates different culture assumptions and values. Equally organisations need to be prepared to take advantage of having a pluralistic culture, one that can bring different perspectives and solutions.
- Emphasis on flexibility – the need to ensure flexibility in its people is as important as building structural flexibility. Organisations need to consider recruiting people who are experts in a given area but who are able and willing to apply their expertise to other areas. Employees, as much as the organisation, need to adopt a flexible mindset so that they can quickly adjust to new assignments and/or new business opportunities without the need for extensive re-training.

Another design consideration is that of whether to create Centres of Excellence, i.e. specialist work teams who can offer in-depth specialist knowledge accessible to the organisation's diverse business, thus helping to prevent wasteful duplication. The concept of Centres of Excellence emerged in the last decade as large corporations began to reconsider the benefits of centralised versus de-centralised structures. They were initially seen as a solution to the problem of 'wasteful duplication', i.e. where one division spends tens of thousands of pounds on consulting fees to get a new business operation off the ground, only then to discover that another division had already implemented something similar.

As well as helping to address a specific business need, i.e. harnessing and capitalising on existing knowledge, there are other benefits too. First, Centres of Excellence can provide a way of reducing expenditure on external consultancy. If existing organisational knowledge is used more effectively, then organisations can make more effective use of their consultancy budget, targeting it at areas where in-house expertise is missing. However, for this to happen, managers need to be persuaded to consult with these centres, prior to initiating major projects, rather than going off and doing their own thing.

In addition, these centres need to ensure that they can provide a responsive service to the business, if not they will just become another bottleneck in the delivery process. Second, the establishment of Centres of Excellence can open up career opportunities for existing 'knowledge experts', providing a way of dealing with the issue of retention. They could also be used as valuable learning ground for future experts, providing that the organisation is willing to accept the overhead of releasing individuals from their existing responsibilities. Third, as the reputation of these Centres of Excellence grows it may be possible to sell this expertise to external businesses. This is a strategy that has been adopted by organisations such as BP and BG Technology.

However, the need for Centres of Excellence, as well as their core deliverables, is something that requires continually re-visiting to ensure maximum value to the organisation.

In addition to establishing Centres of Excellence, organisations also need to consider how best to structure/design for building new knowledge linked to ensuring the organisation's future success. This may mean setting up a physical department, similar to R&D, or it could be utilising virtual teams who have a brief to work on projects that are more future orientated.

A study of knowledge work within Fortune 500 companies by Susan Mohrman and colleagues[1] concluded that with the right organisational design organisations are in a better position to deliver their business better, learn faster and change more easily. As Paul Myers (1995) points out, this finding suggests that line managers need to consider the organisational structures needed to facilitate knowledge building and sharing, rather than focus purely on technological solutions.

Organisational size and impact on knowledge building and sharing

Another area that needs to be considered when designing knowledge-enabled organisations is that of organisational size. Davenport and Prusak (1998) point out that one of the difficulties that organisations face is how the size and geographic location of its workforce makes it difficult to locate existing knowledge. From their own research they identified that it is easier to locate critical knowledge in organisations that consist of up to three hundred people. However, once organisations go beyond this size manag-ing knowledge becomes more difficult, particularly where employees are located in different geographical locations. Here then organisations frequently establish new roles, change respon-sibilities associated with existing roles, as well as look for technological solutions to facilitate what Davenport and Prusak refer to as the problem of global knowledge transfer.

Changing roles and responsibilities in knowledge businesses

With traditional structures within knowledge-based businesses being broken down and replaced with more fluid structures this inevitably has an effect on individuals' roles and responsibilities. As Bahrami (1996) points out 'An individual's effectiveness in getting things done is based on results and credibility, perceived reputation, and network of relationships, rather than formal authority, job descriptions, and position in the hierarchy. In this context, titles, seniority, spans of control, formal power and hierarchical position are not necessarily significant determinants of individual success and organisational power'. In knowledge-based businesses individuals, as well as managers, need to adjust to new structures and ways of working.

With knowledge becoming the key business asset this has created a need for new specialist roles, as well as a revision of the responsibilities associated with existing roles. These new roles include:

Chief Knowledge Officer

The role of the Chief Knowledge Officer (CKO) is to lead on developments relating to the infrastructure, processes and cultural dimensions of an organisation's knowledge management approach. Their remit is often that of developing the concept of knowledge management within the organisation, in partnership with senior managers from IT, HR and business development areas. TFPL[2], a specialist recruitment agency for knowledge workers, defines the responsibilities of CKOs as:

- Identifying and prioritising changes that need to be made to leverage the organisation's information and knowledge.
- Implementing processes, infrastructure and organisational procedures to enable the building and effective utilisation of a corporate knowledge base. This includes ensuring that: information needs are understood and acknowledged; information resources and intellectual assets are identified and managed on an integrated basis; processes exist to facilitate the acquisition and sharing of information and knowledge; appropriate structures for the development of staff are available; the utilisation of information and communication; ensuring the right technology to support the organisation's KM objectives.
- Encouraging all staff to participate in the building, utilisation and protection of the organisation's knowledge base.

• Identifying and integrating other support services relevant to the support of the organisation's knowledge management system.

According to a FT survey[3], individuals who take on the role of CKO need to be able to wear many hats: entrepreneur (willingness to champion risky new initiatives), consultant (able to match new ideas to business needs), technologist (fully IT literate) and environmentalist (able to design settings and processes to maximize knowledge building). It is not surprising then, given the demands of the role, that the more successful CKOs are often hybrid people, who have had a broad-based career, and have a broad-range set of skills and interests.

Information Officers/Information Services Officers

The amount of information that people might possibly need to access in their jobs has grown enormously in recent years. Many people now suffer from information overload, i.e. not being able quickly to locate and access the information needed to do their jobs.

As mentioned earlier competitive advantage in today's business world is not just about having the right products, it is about speed to market and also being able to respond quickly to the needs of customers. Thus speed of access to the right information has become critical. With customers becoming more and more demanding businesses need to make sure that they have the right infrastructure in place to capture, search and disseminate information.

Having now realised what a skilled job information sifting is, many organisations have created new roles, to ensure that it is able to access and manage its information sources. While the label that organisations give to these new positions varies, the role is essentially the same. In essence the people in these roles act as intelligent search engines for others in the organisation. They are skilled in different search technologies, as well as which search engines to access for different types of information. They also have an educational function in that they help to educate other employees on how to get the best out of tools such as the intranet and the Internet.

Accenture, the global and mobile consultancy firm, have established a Knowledge Centre Network as part of its overall knowledge management approach. This team is responsible for gathering and sifting critical business intelligence, making it easily accessible to colleagues. Around twenty people work in the

Knowledge Centre Network within the UK. As well as gathering key business intelligence by scanning information produced by business information providers, such as Gartner, the team also carry out bespoke searches for client-facing teams within the rest of the organisation. As some of these requests come from colleagues working in other parts of the world the Knowledge Centre Network offers a 24 hour service, 7 days a week.

The NHS is drawing on the skills of its librarians to help build an environment in which clinicians and other healthcare professionals can gain access to the critical information that they need to do their jobs. At a national level one area of development has been creating a National Electronic Library for Health. But there are also local initiatives taking place within the NHS too.

Case study: The Berkshire NHS Shared Services Unit[4]

Within the county of Berkshire there are six Primary Care Trusts, a Mental Health and Learning Disabilities Trust, an Ambulance Trust and two general hospitals. In May 2000 a KMC Network was formed as a way of encouraging knowledge sharing across the wide range of health professionals working within the Berkshire region. The funding for this partnership venture has been provided through a number of sources: Department of Health, South-East NHS Regional office and Windsor, Ascot and Maidenhead PCT (the overall project sponsors). The KMC network is being championed by the workforce development team within the Shared Services Unit.

The KMC Network project has a number of key deliverables:

- Creating KM centres (KMCs) within Berkshire. These centres enable healthcare professionals to have access to a wide range of national and other information sources related to health and learning. 'Human portals' i.e. the KM co-ordinators who work in the KMCs provide advice and guidance on how to access the information that is needed. KM co-ordinators also encourage local practitioners to share their knowledge with colleagues.
- Creating an infrastructure that aligns KMCs with other knowledge-building activities.
- Marketing e-learning facilities for health and social care staff within Berkshire. Each KM centre will become a licensed Learndirect site, enabling healthcare and other professionals to have access to a wide range of courses.
- Provide a 'signposting' service to connect the diverse healthcare resources across Berkshire, this way capitalising on the explicit and tacit knowledge available within the county.

Clearly organisational size, combined with the nature of the work that needs to be done, will have a bearing on the number of people that need to be employed in these new information management and knowledge management roles. The big question though is whether these new roles will become a permanent feature of organisational structures, or whether they are simply transitional, i.e. only needed until organisations become more experienced at managing knowledge. For example, until organisations have at least reached Stage 4 of the Knowledge Management Journey discussed in Chapter 1.

However, given the time that it can take to get from the knowledge-chaotic to the knowledge-centric stage, it is likely that some of these roles will become a permanent feature. HR then will need to keep a watching eye on this. They will need to ensure that others in the organisation do not use the presence of these new roles as an excuse to avoid developing their own information management skills. If this becomes the case, what could happen is a shift in power from the information management illiterate to the information management literate, a situation that could prove counterproductive to building a flexible and responsive organisation.

Building KM responsibilities into existing roles

Earlier research of mine identified that in knowledge-enabled organisations line managers, individuals and specialist teams all have an important role to play in developing the organisation's knowledge base (Evans, 2002).

The role of managers

Provide information for people to develop their 'know why'.

Somewhat of a cliché now but change is a constant in today's business world. It is for this reason that individuals need to have regular opportunities to hear about where the organisation is going, what that means in terms of future challenges, how they can best contribute, as well as talk about some of their current concerns and difficulties. While much of this information could be communicated electronically some business leaders feel that it is often better communicated face-to-face.

Allan Ditching, the Chief Information Officer of Progressive Corporation, a major Ohio-based automobile insurance company, holds bi-weekly Donuts-with-Ditch sessions; a practice which he initiated when he worked at AT&T (Myers, 1995). These informal sessions, run with groups of no more than 10 people at a time, provide a forum to hear people's concerns, gather information, as well as get at some of the real issues that are getting in the way of people's jobs. Ditchling believes that Donuts-with-Ditch type sessions provide a valuable forum for communication and interaction between senior managers and employees. These types of communications forums can provide opportunities for those at the centre to build 'patterns of information' about operational difficulties that might otherwise not come to light until too late.

There is an opportunity here for HR professionals to lead by example. Stephen Cronin, Executive Director, Group Resources, at Xerox Europe, for example believes that '*It is in the nature of hierarchy that the higher you rise, the more remote you become . . . the more senior you are, the less you know, the more dependent you are.*' (Overell, 1999). It is for this reason that Cronin initiated the practice of senior managers holding regular round-table discussions with staff at all levels within Xerox Europe. At these discussion forums, or 'surgeries' as they are sometimes referred to, senior managers provide information about where the business is going and invite employees to share their ideas on how they see the future. Employees are also encouraged to share their anxieties about the future at work. Each senior manager is set a target number of round-table discussions to be held; these form part of their performance objectives.

Support the free movement of people

Frances Horibe (1999) argues that managers can help build knowledge in an organisation by supporting the free movement of people. As much of an organisation's knowledge resides in individuals' heads then this seems like a sensible strategy. However, Horibe recognises that managers may need incentives to encourage them to do this, as a natural inclination for managers is to hold on to good people rather than facilitate their movement to other teams. She suggests that to encourage the free movement of staff, the organisation (i.e. the senior decision-makers) needs to consider being over-resourced, thus creating the slack to allow movement within the organisation, as well as offering specific rewards for managers who willingly support the free movement of people.

Trial new team structures and ways of working

In order to free individuals to work in more creative ways many organisations have introduced new team structures, or created flexible units that are isolated from the rigid operating core (Volberda *et al.*, 2001). Citibank, for example, adopted this approach when it was developing its world-wide consumer operations and its 24-hour telephone banking service. One of Citibank's branches in Greece, where much of the development work took place, became known as the organisation's 'banking laboratory'.

A similar approach was adopted by the Prudential when they were developing the Egg account. Here a separate team, where the managers and team members worked on a more equal basis, was established. The DigiLab team, set up by the BBC to build knowledge about the capabilities of digital video camcorders (Evans, 2000) is another example of where specialist teams can help meet a particular knowledge need at a given point in time.

When assembling project teams another consideration to help build and spread knowledge is actively to include 'novices' in the team. This is a strategy adopted by one of IBM's top systems software managers at Hursley Park (Kavanagh, 2002). This particular management approach can have a number of benefits. First, as novices often ask naive questions, this can help stimulate other team members to question their own ideas, thoughts and working assumptions. Second, these 'novices' get an opportunity to learn directly from more experienced team members, thus helping to address the issue of knowledge transfer and retention.

Locate the knowledge experts and extend and reward their remit

Within every team there are certain individuals whom others, either within the team, or outside, consult with to tap into their knowledge. These individuals are often called upon to assist in trouble-shooting projects. But equally they may be good connectors of knowledge, both within and outside the organisation, because of their vast network. The value that these 'knowledge experts' bring to an organisation is often under-estimated. However, the amount of time that these individuals spend either helping others resolve their problems, or sharing their knowledge in other ways, is often not budgeted for, or adequately acknowledged/rewarded. A consideration for line managers then is to re-visit the role descriptions/job descriptions of 'knowledge experts' and their performance objectives, so that these reflect this often 'taken for granted' role. Chapter 11 introduces a tool, Social Network Analysis, which can be used to identify the different knowledge roles that people play in knowledge businesses.

Build and facilitate knowledge connections

With the role of managers shifting from 'subject expert' to more of a facilitative role, a key task for managers is to build and extend their own network connections, both within and outside the organisation, as well as to facilitate knowledge exchanges among others within the organisation.

Managers have an important role in helping individuals understand the importance of networking in today's business world. The more network contacts an individual has then the greater his/her sphere of influence. In addition it creates more learning opportunities, as well as opening up more opportunities from a career development perspective.

Encourage and support informal learning

As 70 per cent of what we learn comes from informal learning approaches, managers have an important role to play in supporting and encouraging informal learning environments. These can range from: supporting Communities of Practice; creating spaces within the office environment where team members can come together for informal discussions; introducing a knowledge exchange slot at team meetings, or adopting the apprenticeship model of learning for individuals at different stages of their career. Chapter 6 goes into more detail about the need to re-visit learning in the knowledge economy.

With technology being a key tool that many individuals use as part of their day-to-day work, many of the practices used in the past to build and share knowledge can become lost or replaced with a technological solution. The Chair of a NHS Conference on Knowledge Management for Clinicians reminded his audience that there is still value to be had in some of the traditional knowledge-sharing practices used within the profession. Here he was referring to the traditional 'ward round' practice where trainee doctors follow a qualified clinician around on his/her ward rounds, thus bridging the learning between theory and practice. In the past, if a question was asked on the ward rounds that no one could answer, one of the trainee doctors would be instructed to write the question down, go away and find out the answer and return with this at the next ward round.

Re-visit assumptions about what counts as productive work

Closely linked to the point made above about the need to create spaces for informal learning is the need to re-visit assumptions about what counts as productive work. Several other writers have been quoted as saying that talk is real work in the knowledge business as it is through conversations and dialogue that we extend our 'know of', 'know why' and 'know how'.

In today's knowledge economy managers need to re-frame their perception of what counts as productive work. They need to become more tolerant of what Apgar (1998) refers to as the 'Doughnut club', i.e. the place where virtual teams meet to talk about problems they are experiencing with customers and get feedback on what they are doing and also 'engineering as many accidental meetings as possible'.

Make sure staff build in time for thinking and best practice scouring

One individual who shared his experiences with me of working in a creative field spoke of how his MD supported him by encouraging him to take time out to think. The MD constantly reminded him to take time out, to get out of the office environment and to find new thinking spaces.

Help staff value what they know

The English Nature and QinetiQ case studies (see Section 3) highlight one of the common dilemmas for knowledge workers – they do not always value what they know. If people do not value what they know, then they may not blow their own trumpet, which can be restrictive from a career perspective. Feedback, from managers, and colleagues, either through 360-degree feedback processes, or though information from KM systems, can be useful in helping people get a better sense of their own value-add.

I have uncovered several stories as part of this phase of the research that reinforces the need for managers to re-visit what counts as productive work.

The journalist's story – this is the story of a journalist who was challenged by his manager for looking at a book at his desk – the book happened to be a dictionary.

The utilities engineer story – in this particular organisation the senior management team took a decision to cancel the service engineers' weekly team meetings. For the most part of the week these engineers worked independently out in the field, attending the team meetings meant that they had to make a special journey back to base. Clearly while attending the team meetings the engineers were not able to respond to calls from customers, this was considered not to be in the best interest of customers. However, in cancelling the weekly team meetings what the management team had overlooked was the amount of informal learning that took place, before, during and after the team meetings. The meetings provided an important opportunity for knowledge transfer with the less experienced engineers picking the brains of the more experienced engineers.

The salesman story – this is the story of a salesman who had worked for thirty years in the sales department of a large American company (Probst *et al.*, 2000). His daily routine involved having chats with his immediate colleagues, as well as walking around the office chatting with other people in the department. However, a review of the sales figures by a new manager director identified that this particular salesman did not actually sell very much and thus he was dismissed. Once he had left, a number of difficulties began to emerge in the department. These included: difficulties with communication and co-ordination across different sub-sections, a dip in morale and new employees found that they had no one to indoctrinate them into the company's unwritten rules. In short, the organisation had misread the role that this particular salesman had played in transferring knowledge through his daily walkabouts.

Case study: Influencing knowledge creation and sharing – the critical role of managers

The role of line managers has changed significantly in recent years, as have the skills needed to perform effectively in a line management role. In the past, much of a line manager's authority came from his/her own knowledge base. Indeed in many organisations individuals were promoted on their ability to do their current job, rather than following an assessment of their ability to perform in a managerial role. It is not surprising then that there are many square pegs in round holes in leadership positions, particularly in scientific, technology and creative-based organisations. Organisations that now fall into the category of knowledge businesses.

Having worked with managers in knowledge-based organisations I am aware of how quickly their knowledge can become out-of-date, particularly when they are no longer doing hands-on work. One of the big issues, and indeed risks, for leaders in knowledge businesses is that they may not have in-depth knowledge about the work carried out by their function/area. As time elapses managers become more and more dependent upon their team to provide in-depth up-to-date knowledge to input into the management decision-making process. This shift can leave some managers feeling vulnerable, because of the dependency on their teams for certain types of knowledge. What is needed often is a different kind of leadership approach.

So if in knowledge businesses managers are no longer the 'knowledge experts', what should their role be? What type of leadership is required? Where should they focus their energy?

Jela Webb, formally Senior Manager Knowledge Management and Development, the New Learning Organisation, the centralised learning and development department within a major financial services company, and now the Director of Azione, a knowledge management consultancy, shared some thoughts with me about how she used to structure and manage her team to ensure maximum impact from a knowledge perspective.

First, she ensured that the team was structured appropriately in order to provide an efficient service to the business, as well as to maximise the resources within the team, from a knowledge management perspective. The team was structured into three areas: a team of information and knowledge professionals, a team of excellence and an R&D team.

The R&D team supported the relationship managers who worked closely with the business units to identify their learning and development requirements, which they then took forward into a development solution. The solution may have been a short instructor-led course, a workbook, or e-learning product, or a combination – an 'integrated learning solution'. Each relationship manager had responsibility for a specific business area, e.g. retail banking, corporate banking, insurance, etc.

The team of excellence were just that. They had detailed knowledge of tools and techniques to help develop the right learning and development solution for the business, such as Balanced Scorecard, Business Process Re-engineering, intranet design, as well as being fully cognisant of the best way in which to use technologies to maximise the learning experience.

The R&D team had a remit of maintaining an external focus, gathering information about HR best practice in other organisations, as well as keeping up-to-date with what the gurus were saying about HR and the changing workplace. The team were encouraged to develop relationships with other organisations, even if these were competitors, as a way of enhancing their knowledge base. Interestingly, good relationships with competitor organisations evolved. In the true spirit of knowledge sharing individuals were happy to discuss relevant issues while being mindful of the need not to breach confidentiality, or disclose price-sensitive information.

Members of the team of excellence and the R&D team also worked on project teams developing new learning solutions for the businesses. In this way the project teams benefited directly from their specialist knowledge and expertise. What Webb insisted on though was that people from the team of excellence and the R&D team did not get assigned overall Project Management responsibility. She felt that this would not be effective use of their expertise. She also felt that this would draw these experts into areas that would take them away from the task of knowledge-building and utilisation. However, she had to fight hard to maintain this position with her business colleagues.

Despite having an HR background, Webb found herself managing teams where she didn't have the detailed knowledge of all of the work carried out in her area. This meant that she had to adopt a different leadership style, one that was more facilitative, with an emphasis on coaching and mentoring. She commented how managers need to learn not to be afraid to admit when they do not know something and to trust the judgment of individuals within the team. This helps individuals to build self-confidence, as well as develop their skills through acting in an advisory capacity to their own line manager. Webb found that her team felt valued and respected for their opinions.

Another area that Webb focused on to facilitate knowledge-building and sharing within her area was communication. Many of Webb's team worked flexible hours, herself included. Some also worked from home for part of the week. Given people's different working patterns she felt it important that the whole team got together for a team meeting once a week. The team meetings were used as a time for individuals to update others on where they were at on their respective projects. This was important. Even though several members of the team might be working on the same business project they could each be working on a separate part of the overall project. The team meetings were also used as an opportunity for skills development. The more junior members of the team, for example, were able to use the team meetings to develop their presentation skills. Team meetings were also used as an opportunity for team members to talk about some of the problems that they had encountered over the week and how they had resolved these.

The team also held regular lunch-and-learn sessions. A variety of topics were covered at these sessions, not all of which were directly related to the team's work. There was a multiple objective then of broadening, as well as deepening, people's knowledge base. Business colleagues were sometimes invited along to the lunch-and-learn sessions, not as speakers, but as listeners and observers, so that they could develop their knowledge base too.

This case study illustrates that the line manager role is critical in organisations trying to build a knowledge-centric culture. They can provide a good role model from a knowledge management perspective, as well as establishing boundaries and targets for their team for knowledge management activities.

The role of individuals

While managers have an important role to play in setting the context and in creating the environment within which individuals can develop and share their knowledge, individuals have an important role to play too in building the organisation's knowledge base.

Share insights and reflections with others

When running development programmes one of the things that developers often encourage delegates to do is to share their insights and reflections, so why then do we not do this as a matter of course as part of daily business life?

The HR team within one of the major consultancies that I have worked with have adopted a practice of e-mailing their 'What struck me' thoughts to colleagues at the end of each week, as a way of sharing knowledge.

Let others know what you are interested in knowing more about

It is very easy in today's high-tech world to suffer from information overload and a sense of being overwhelmed by the vast amount of information that possibly needs to be located and absorbed. However, there is a lot to be gained from sharing what we know, and what we are interested in knowing more about, with others. In this way you can each act as another pair of eyes, or ears, helping to connect each other with valuable information sources. This approach is particularly important for those working in more autonomous/independent roles, as the opportunity for informal knowledge exchanges may not occur through the course of daily work. My own doctoral research which investigated how self-employed HR professionals manage their learning and knowledge identified that these individuals come to rely on contacts in their knowledge networks for circulating information that matches with their areas of interest and business (Evans, 2001). Equally all professionals can benefit from sharing the learning task, as the following case study illustrates.

Case study: Sharing the learning task
(*Source:* Evans, 2002)

Jim McMorran is a GP based in Coventry. He qualified as a doctor in the mid-1990s from Oxford Medical School. During his time as a medical student Jim and six fellow students (one of whom was his brother) established a routine of writing up and sharing their clinical notes with each other. As Jim and his fellow students also had a strong interest in Information Technology they looked for ways in which they could apply their IT expertise and at the same time make the task of building their clinical knowledge easier.

Together Jim and his fellow students designed and developed a relationship database system. The content of this initial database was based on their lecture notes, as well as information located from references suggested during lectures. But what evolved was the beginnings of a shared knowledge resource.

As the database grew it became a sought-after reference point for other medical students. Initially, access to other medical students was provided locally through the Cairns Library in the Oxford Clinical School. Wider access was later made possible through a rudimentary version of the database, published by Butterworth-Heinemann in the mid-1990s. It was this version that was awarded the prestigious John Perry Prize, by the Primary Care Specialist Group of the British Computer Society.

Now qualified doctors, this initial rudimentary database has been further developed into a product known as GPnotebook (see www.gpnotebook.co.uk), which other professionals working within the primary healthcare profession can access via the internet. GPnotebook provides a source of concise practical clinical information, with an easy to use rapid indexing system, in the style of a pocket book. The content of GPnotebook is aimed at UK primary healthcare physicians. However, as it is also recognised as being a useful resource for other healthcare professionals, it is now included as a resource on the National Electronic Library of Health.

The database has been designed to allow rapid access to information specific to a user's query without the user having to trawl through a vast list of references. For practitioners, GPnotebook acts as an aide-memoire to different clinical conditions, i.e. the symptoms, underlying causes and sources of treatment. In addition to providing a clinical reference, GPnotebook acts as a useful tool for clinical governance and continuing professional development.

Maintaining the GPnotebook system enables Jim and his former fellow students (who now work either as GPs, specialist registrars, or in clinical research) to work in a collaborative way to keep their professional knowledge up-to-date. Each member of the team takes responsibility for reading and summarising a set number of medical journals each month. These summaries are then added into the GPnotebook system and cross-referenced with existing information.

What this group of clinicians have demonstrated is how partnership/collaborative working has enhanced their own professional development, as well as making their jobs much easier as they now have easier and faster access to the most up-to-date clinical information when treating patients.

While the benefits of this collaborative approach to knowledge-building are clear, it does have its downside. Each member of the group invests a considerable amount of their own time on this activity. Collectively they spend around 40 hours a week, either in the evenings or at weekends, reading journals, summarising and updating the database; a time commitment which has had to be negotiated with their families.

Trust has been paramount to the continuing success of this knowledge-building activity. Reading and summarising professional articles is a skill in its own right, a skill that each of the group members has had to develop. However as Jim and his colleagues have known each other for several years now they have learnt to respect each other's professional judgement. Now that the system is becoming more widely utilised the information published in GPnotebook is peer-reviewed and cross-referenced (thus making it evidence-based). These changes were felt important to ensure the credibility of the information source.

Reflecting on their experience of developing GPnotebook Jim and his fellow clinicians feel that keeping the GPnotebook system up-to-date has become a backdrop to their lives. The personal learning has been enormous *'We have all learnt a lot about medicine, but more than that we have learnt to work as a team. We have had fascinating insights into the world of online commerce and the business of publishing. But without doubt the most satisfying part of the work is that we can now share the fruits of our labour with thousands of people around the world.'*

Suspend judgement on ideas until tried and tested

One of the things that can put individuals off sharing their ideas with others is the put-downs that they can get from others, particularly from people who have been with the organisation longer than they have. What needs to be addressed is the 'not invented here' mantra. The Chaparral Steel Company has gone one further than this. They have introduced an operational slogan of 'not re-invented here', acknowledging that creativity is a process of synthesis – the building on of ideas (Leonard-Barton).

An important message for both individuals and organisations is to accept that knowledge reuse is just as important as knowledge creation. We cannot all be great inventors or pioneers, however, we are all capable of learning from the practice of others. Eric Abrahamson (2001), a leading change management guru, argues that organisations that are experiencing continuous change need to adopt the behaviour of rewarding 'shameless borrowing'.

The Spanish have a phrase which is relevant to the knowledge era and that is 'Well stolen is half done'. Equally we need to follow a rule of thumb of 'Pinch with pride, but give credit where credit is due', otherwise you may find that you become excluded from knowledge circles.

Blow your own trumpet once in a while

This is something that in this country we are not always that good at. While conducting this research there have been several people who have told me that they feel uncomfortable using the term 'best practice', as it implies that they are experts in a particular practice. However, it is important that individuals shout about what they know, or have learnt, and what they are interested in learning more about.

Many organisations now have systems available where individuals can post their successes (e.g. skills databases, internal newsletters, personal web pages). If your organisation has a 'Yellow Pages' database make sure that your details are kept up-to-date. Get in the habit of reviewing your achievements and development goals after each project and/or assignment and updating your details. If there is an opportunity to have a home page on your organisation's intranet then take it. Often this can create the space to say more about yourself than the information held within a 'Yellow Pages' system.

Develop your knowledge-building capabilities

Participating in a knowledge-community requires some key competencies to be developed. These include research/investigative skills, questioning skills, listening skills, experimental or 'what if?' type thinking, observation and critical reflection, as well as networking.

Communications Theory suggests that a network's potential benefits grow exponentially as the number of nodes (i.e. contacts) build and expand.

But as Wayne Baker points out we need to be trustworthy in our knowledge-building interactions 'Repeated interaction encourages cooperation. If you sponge information and never give, your sources will dry up. But give and you shall receive. This does not mean that you should become an inveterate gossip. Be a tactful, judicious supplier of information and a trustworthy, responsible user of information' (Baker, 1996:213).

The ability to build social connections is also important for successful career management within the knowledge economy. The more people we connect with the more opportunities we are likely to uncover. In addition it can help to expand our sphere of influence.

Building and keeping knowledge up-to-date, as we saw earlier in the GPnotebook case study, is something that all individuals need to plan into their daily life routines.

Help colleagues to develop their 'know how'

Several organisations are beginning to specify the knowledge-creating behaviours that they want to see present in day-to-day practice. The KPMG case study in Chapter 6 shows how the organisation is building a coaching culture, based on an assumption that all employees are expected to apply and share their knowledge. Knowledge-building behaviours, linked to the firm's values, form part of the firm's assessment practices.

In DERA, the level of contribution that an individual makes, i.e. by sharing their 'know how' with others, is reflected in the organisation's performance management system (Evans, 2000).

Summary

Organisational structures have changed over the past couple of decades, largely in response to external pressures. Whereas in the past, organisational success has been influenced by factors such as size, role clarity, specialisation and control, success today hinges on speed, flexibility, integration and innovation.

However, many business leaders believe that in order to compete in the global economy organisations need to combine the best characteristics of both big and small companies. They need to be able to capitalize on the economies of scale, the resources and the talent available within the large corporation *but* at the same time benefit from the flexibility and autonomy often present within small organisations.

However, whatever the size and scale of an organisation, one thing is crucial, organisations need to consider their needs for knowledge creation, re-use and transfer in their discussions and decisions about organisational design. This can mean, as we have seen in this chapter, creating new roles, as well as changing the responsibilities associated with existing roles. This includes the changing role of HR. What is also important is to ensure that everyone in the organisation plays their part in developing, sharing and utilising knowledge, and does not leave it to a select few. The next chapter looks at the specific role of HR in building a knowledge-centric culture.

Pause for reflection

- What structures get in the way of your organisation accessing and making the most of its knowledge?
- What new knowledge roles have emerged in your organisation? How do you see these developing over the next 3–5 years?
- How might you weave some of the material in this chapter into learning and development resources for managers?
- How can HR help line managers, as well as others within the organisation, to think about some of the emerging knowledge roles in the future?

Notes

1. See Mohrman, S., Cohen, C. and Mohrman, A. M. Jr. (1995), *Designing Team-Based Organizations: New Forms for Knowledge Work*. Jossey-Bass.
2. More details about TFPL can be found on their website *www.tfpl.com*.
3. Mastering Information Management Survey: The role of the chief knowledge officer. *Financial Times*, 8 March 1999.
4. See Fawcett, J., Knowing me – knowing you? *Knowledge Management*, April 2002.

5

HR's role in building a knowledge-centric culture

HR has a pivotal role to play in helping to build a knowledge-centric culture and yet their involvement to date has been limited and patchy. It is fair to say that HR practitioners, particularly those working in operational/administrative roles, have had little or no involvement in knowledge management. The main interest in knowledge management has come from those working in a developmental role. Yet as other writers point out, the irony is that HR is well placed to take an active role in knowledge management since they are the guardians of a variety of data about the organisation's employees, which could be used to ensure a more strategic knowledge management approach is adopted.

With the role of HR changing from operational to strategic, as discussed in Chapter 2, HR professionals should be in a better position to adopt a more strategic standpoint with regard to knowledge management.

So what should HR's role be? Where can HR add value?

An interview with Linda Holbeche, Director of Research, Roffey Park Institute

If designing an organisation from scratch what key things need to be considered to maximise opportunities from a knowledge perspective?

Focus on getting the structure right: Where possible aim for small units and project-based working, in this way enabling more ideas to flow and be put to good use for the business as a whole.

Develop facilitative leadership: I have an interesting story about this from a client of mine who are providers of investment management services. In one of the teams the leader was new to the role. He had been promoted from within. One of the corporate goals for the organisation is the cross-selling of projects, as a way of maximising overall efficiency and returns. However, there is a tension with this particular goal and the company reward system, which is not team-based.

When he took up his new role this particular leader instructed his team to forget about cross-selling of projects and instead focus on improving their own team's performance. The team set about creating their own simple knowledge management database in which they captured critical information about each of their clients. Each team member was encouraged to develop their antennae so that they became attuned to information about current and prospective clients that they could use in a strategic way. The informal contract between team members meant that they were each attuned to picking up critical information about each other's clients. Very quickly the team built up a database containing information which others in the company 'would die for'.

Because of their approach the team quickly gained a reputation for being one of the most highly effective and successful. Needless to say other managers wanted to identify what made this particular team so successful. However, the mistake that the organisation made was having identified the source of this particular team's success it tried to take control of the database that the team had developed and turn it into something that could be used by others in the organisation. The result was less than satisfactory, both for this particular team and the organisation as a whole.

Build a good IT Infrastructure and ensure that everyone is trained to use it.

Build relationship with suppliers: Even in situations where services have been contracted it is important to build a good working relationship with third-party suppliers. A good third-party supplier needs to understand your organisation's business. So it is important to spend time developing the relationship and working on joint developments and learning projects.

How can HR really make an impact from a knowledge management perspective?

They need to work with the key decision makers to identify what the priorities are and focus on those. They need to help the organisation work out what its core capabilities are and also those of individuals within the organisation. Once they have helped identify the gaps between what is needed and what is required they can then develop a plan to address the gaps, either by recruiting in the missing capabilities (either short-term, or as a permanent appointment), or focus on development plans.

HR need to be championing and enabling a culture that is knowledge enabled. HR should not see themselves as the guardians of corporate culture, but instead be enablers of the corporate culture and be supportive of the necessary changes. They need to be talking to their colleagues out in the business.

They can act as catalysts for culture change, helping to spur on those aspects of the culture change that are important for future business success. They should encourage new ideas and ways of working and also ensure that high calibre people are recruited into the business.

Another key area where HR can make a big impact is helping the organisation implement the right structure, one that supports high performance. HR should help build an infrastructure that is adaptable and skilled. This requires addressing some higher-order goals, such as:

- Organisational design and structures. This requires a range of strands to be followed in parallel. Structures need to have permeable boundaries to allow the free movement of people. However, attention needs to be given to balancing the strengths and weaknesses of small autonomous units. While small units can enable autonomy and freedom, they can lead to duplication and wastage. Large structures on the other hand can stifle innovation, be cost-intensive and lack a customer focus. We should perhaps then think of organisational structures as 'loosely coupled icebergs'. Where the organisational structure consists of small units, with flexible boundaries, then it needs to pay attention to developing people who are capable of working in this way.

- Careers and career structures. The organisation needs to attract people who are predisposed to being flexible and adaptable. Once inside the organisation, these people need to be inducted well. Where individuals are placed in key roles where they are developing new capabilities, or working in uncharted territories, the organisation needs to make sure that their capabilities are really being utilised. If not then these high-performing individuals will become disillusioned. Of course having recruited the best, the organisation needs to work at retaining the best.
- Performance management. Individuals need to know what is expected of them and what rewards to expect when they deliver. HR needs to develop a reward system where people are rewarded for knowledge-building and sharing.
- Developing a learning focus to enable the organisation to build its capabilities.
- Succession planning. This requires constant attention, not just a one-off initiative. HR will need to keep on challenging line managers about their succession planning approach. Consideration needs to be given too to protecting the organisation's Intellectual Capital.

Strategies and policies for each of these areas need to be followed through with a partnership approach to implementation with line managers, the IT function and other key functional teams.

HR needs to work out what they are good at themselves (their own USP) and focus on that. One of the things that HR needs to avoid is getting itself locked into an operational trap, where they find themselves with a finger in every pie, but are not really having a strategic impact. They shouldn't expect to do everything themselves. They need to know what areas to tinker with that will have maximum impact for the business. As a team they need to have a list of key areas to focus on. This may mean at times working on a number of what might seem disparate projects, but which in fact are joined-up.

The HR function needs to see itself as an integrating function. This may mean getting involved in areas that they haven't been involved in before, e.g. ergonomics and office and space planning. They could consider taking on the role of Workspace Adviser, helping to draw together the IT and physical office requirements that enable knowledge to flow.

They may also need to help the business get back to basics and keep in touch with real operational difficulties. Take M&S and Asda, for example, they have both initiated a 'Back to the floor' programme. After the trading difficulties, M&S managers spent time on the sales floor listening to what customers and staff want.

In ASDA, all store managers spend one day a week on the sales floor working alongside their colleagues.

What can HR do to help their organisation retain knowledge?

In merger situations, or indeed any major change programme, HR needs to be involved in the organisation's People Plan at a very early stage. Without this the organisation is likely to lose its most able people.

When we were doing the mergers research at Roffey Park we found some interesting data about employee retention during merger situations:

- 39 per cent fail to retain their best talent.
- 67 per cent fail to deploy talent effectively.
- After making people redundant, many organisations then find that they have to start recruiting again as they don't have the resources they need to perform in the new business.
- There are two phases of exit in a merger situation. Those who go immediately, without waiting to see what new opportunities there might be. Those who play the waiting game, waiting to see if what is on offer meets their expectations.

HR's role at this early stage in the change process should be to:

- Help identify what the organisation of the future will look like.
- Identify what capabilities the organisation will need. What it is good at already and what it needs to become better at.
- Identify the capabilities of the merging organisation, so that synergies can be determined.
- Establish which bits of the organisation are most at risk and hence need to be protected.
- Talk to managers about the way jobs are likely to pan out.
- Keep their ear to the ground, to identify issues of discontentment identifying what is real and what is fiction.

To achieve this HR will need to work in partnership with their counterparts in the newly merged organisation, even though their own position may be unclear at this stage. As the new structure emerges, HR needs to focus on:

- Introducing new structures and processes, such as collaborative working and cross-boundary team working.
- Ensuring that the right people get positioned in the right jobs. Here it is important not to overlook junior people.
- Making sure that people are inducted into their new roles, so that they understand what is required of them.

- Targeting people whom they think need to be retained and ensure that the right rewards and incentives are in place to retain them. This may mean having to provide retention bonuses, or placing individuals in roles that provide developmental stretch.
- Facilitating the process of new teams working together.
- Developing people management policies and practices that are fair for all parties in the newly merged organisation. This includes ensuring that career structures and systems meet the needs of the changing organisation.
- Putting processes in place for learning from the change process, thus helping to build the organisation's capabilities for managing change in the future.
- Focus on identifying the key people that need to be retained and put systems in place to help them manage their careers.

What about HR's own capabilities, what should they be focusing on?

HR need to be well networked themselves, both within the organisation and outside. They need to be influential at all levels and build up their own personal credibility. It is important for HR to understand the business that they are working in. How can they be effective if they don't understand the business? To be effective they need to spend time with their business colleagues building an understanding of what their issues are.

David Dell, the Research Director of the Conference Board Inc., a research network in America, argues that HR needs to learn to redirect themselves and their organisation towards a culture where collaborative and cross-functional team working is the norm and where the organisation is able to attract and retain the best talent on the market (Roberts-Witt, 2001).

If, as Tom Knight (2001) argues, the goal of any knowledge management approach is to change the way people behave, then clearly HR has a crucial role to play. While HR cannot in itself change an organisation's culture it has the 'know how' to influence and support the transformation of an organisation's culture.

Where should HR start?

Work with business leaders to help clarify the start and endpoint

Work with business colleagues to build a clear picture of what a knowledge-centric culture would look like within the organisation and assess the gap between where the organisation is now and where it wants to be. Chapter 10 contains some tools that could be used for this activity. In addition, generate a discussion around the 'blueprint for a knowledge-centric organisation' discussed in Chapter 3. Do you agree with this blueprint? Do colleagues? What elements might be missing?

There may be a need to gather some basic data, by asking the following basic questions:

- What knowledge do we have now and where is it located?
- Do we know what we are good at and what we are not so good at?
- Is the information that people need to do their jobs being systematically disseminated?
- Does the organisation systematically gather information/intelligence from outside? What happens to this? How is it used?
- How does new knowledge get created and shared? What groups/areas/individuals are better at this than others?

Identify and agree on a few strategic goals

In the General Motors (GM) Corporation, for example, HR have been set a number of strategic goals that relate to managing knowledge (Roberts-Witt, 2001). One is to identify and eliminate unnecessary bureaucracy within the corporation. This involves reviewing different organisational practices to identify inefficiencies and barriers to rapid implementation and then redesigning these processes so that they are smoother and quicker. Another is to recruit, develop and retain flexible and mobile workers. A third strategic goal is to identify employees who only intend to stay with GM for a limited period of time so that the implications for the organisation's knowledge base can be managed, as well as deciding how best to manage and reward individuals during the short time that they plan to be with the organisation.

Agree priorities for change

Having defined the end-state, the next step is agreeing the priority areas for change/action. It is far better to focus on a few key areas, rather than spread resources too thinly. Agreeing a few key priority areas for change will also make it easier to monitor and report on how well changes are being embedded. Often easier said than done, but each of the senior management team will need to agree on the priority areas for change.

Many change initiatives often fall by the wayside after the initial flurry of activity, due to a number of now well-documented factors (Kotter, 1995). These include:

Error 1: Not establishing a great enough sense of urgency, often referred to as not having a burning platform.
Error 2: Not creating a powerful guiding coalition.
Error 3: Lacking a clear vision.
Error 4: Under-communicating the vision.
Error 5: Not removing obstacles to the new endpoint.
Error 6: Not systematically planning for and creating short-term wins.
Error 7: Declaring victory too soon.
Error 8: Not anchoring change in the new culture.

With these factors in mind it seems essential that when embarking on their knowledge management journey the organisation sets up some form of steering group, consisting of key players from different parts of the organisation (e.g. HR, IT, Marketing, Business Strategy, Internal Communications, Customer Services). This is one way of demonstrating how seriously the organisation is taking the subject of knowledge management. One of the roles of this forum will be to ensure that a plan is put in place to ensure that the organisation does not make the same errors listed above. Leadership of this forum is crucial. It needs to be someone who is a respected player, has the ear of senior colleagues, and is very approachable.

Engaging managers across the organisation in the KM dialogue

Drawing on a well-accepted knowledge management technique, i.e. learning from the experience of others, the following case study which sets out the experience of how a car rental company set about developing a service culture, might shed some light on this question.

Case Study: Building a customer-focused culture in Enterprise Rent-A-Car (*Source:* HBR, July 2002)

Through customer feedback Enterprise Rent-A-Car, an American-based car rental company, identified that its customer service was not as good as it could be, or as good as senior mangers wanted it to be. However, one of the difficulties that the organisation faced was that of getting its field managers, who worked largely autonomously, to accept that there was a problem that needed fixing.

The first step for the organisation was to get their managers to recognise and own the problem. Senior managers worked with field managers, and others in the organisation, to develop a more robust customer satisfaction survey tool. While adopting this approach meant that the survey tool took longer to develop, it had the advantage that the approach helped get management buy-in.

As part of the change process, senior managers agreed to other changes suggested by the field managers themselves such as separating out customer satisfaction results by individual branch and switching from postal to telephone surveys.

A couple of years on from initiating the change process, the organisation identified that there was still room for improving performance, so it turned up the heat, introducing more changes. One particular change was revising the criteria for promotion. The new criteria meant that field managers were not allowed to move up without having achieved customer service satisfaction scores at, or above, the company average. Having adopted this stand-point the organisation then had to stand its ground, which meant having to take the tough decision not to promote managers who had achieved good growth and profits, but who hadn't met the criteria for customer satisfaction scores.

This case study is a classic example of real leadership in action, i.e. making tough decisions and being prepared to stick with them in order to move the culture so that it is in line with the strategic goals. That said, in a discussion that I had recently with a KM practitioner about how to motivate certain individuals, e.g. sales people to share their knowledge, the response was 'Most organisations are not willing to use a "stick approach". If a salesperson is bringing in revenue, then organisations will not penalise them for not sharing their knowledge'. The big question then is should they? If knowledge-sharing is crucial to the future success of the business, should this be reinforced through rewards and sanctions? If business leaders aren't prepared to get tough on this, shouldn't HR? At what point should this topic enter into the dialogue?

Help demystify knowledge management

As we saw in the earlier chapters in this book there are many different definitions of knowledge and indeed of knowledge management. This can be very confusing for individuals. If individuals cannot get a clear picture in their minds about what a knowledge-enabled culture looks and feels like then they will not be able to contribute. HR then has a critical role to play in helping senior managers articulate what a knowledge-centric culture means to them, why it is so important to the business and what this means in terms of the changes that need to be introduced.

This is also an important stage for HR to start to drip in some of the behavioural changes that will need to be developed in order for the organisation to move forward. This includes the leadership behaviours that will be required. It is here that HR will need to demonstrate their political awareness and influencing skills – given that their senior colleagues may not be so willing to change their own behaviour.

Develop a knowledge awareness programme

Individuals cannot engage in a dialogue about knowledge management unless they have an understanding of what it is, its importance to the business and what that means for them. The previous chapter set out some of the different roles and responsibilities relating to knowledge management. Where HR could add value is in producing a knowledge awareness programme, or even producing a toolkit that can be used as a learning tool. The Department of Health, for example, has introduced the Knowledge, Learning and Information Management Toolkit – KLIMT, for short (Knight, 2001). This contains assessment activities, workshop materials, questionnaires, white papers and measurement tools, designed for use by teams to get them started on their knowledge management journey.

Communicate, communicate and communicate

Communications is often a much under-estimated and under-exploited tool in change programmes. And yet communications is a vital way of building relationships with key stakeholders during times of change. It is the means by which individuals are helped to engage at the intellectual and emotional level.

Q: Why do you need to communicate and keep on communicating? A: Because as individuals there is a limit to how much information we can take on-board at any one time; much of what gets communicated gets screened out by other background noises.

When communicating change managers, and HR practitioners, need to consider what is the most appropriate communications medium given the type of change being introduced. Often a large percentage (around 80 per cent) of an organisation's communications resources go into communications approaches that fall into the formal/conscious category. However, the biggest impact (again

80 per cent) falls into the informal/unconscious category, indicated in Figure 5.1.

One of the areas to be considered, and one where HR can be particularly influential, is helping managers understand the relationship between the medium and the message, thereby ensuring that the right communications vehicle is selected.

As Figure 5.2 shows, in situations where the level of complexity of what is being communicated is low and the level of emotion is low, then communicating via notice-boards and e-mails is probably OK. However, as the level of complexity increases and emotions are likely to be higher, more personalised communications approaches are required, such as team briefing and one-to-one conversations.

What we need to remember, however, is that these are 'rules of thumb' and that we should not forget the person-situation factor, such as individual preferences for the way things are communicated. However as Kotter and Cofen (2002) argue, it is only by acknowledging and working with individuals' feelings that organisations can bring about change. It is important then to appeal to their hearts, not their minds. As Kotter and Cofen point out some individuals will only change when presented with

Formal	Agenda priorities Promotion policies Appointments Pay policies Perks	Emails **80% of the effort!** Press releases Speeches Videos Road shows
Informal	Behaviour and body language Who you value How time is spent Interest **80% of the impact!**	Chats Newsletters Attending social events Corridor greetings
	Unconscious	**Conscious**

Figure 5.1 Relationship between communication resources and impact (Source: Oxford Group, Consulting & Training. Reproduced with permission)

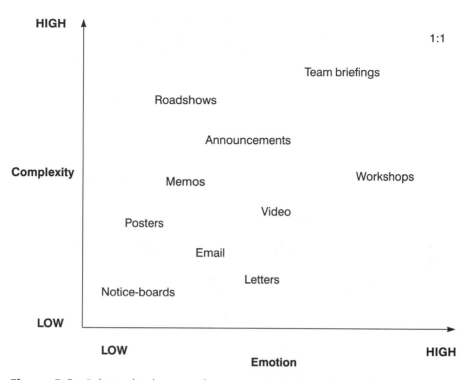

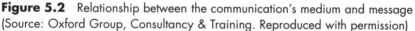

Figure 5.2 Relationship between the communication's medium and message (Source: Oxford Group, Consultancy & Training. Reproduced with permission)

extreme examples of real-life problems. This reinforces the need for organisations, seeking to bring about change, to see communications as a strategic tool in the change process.

Moving forward – Developing organisational capabilities

Ensuring the right leadership

Leadership was at the heart of the model, Towards a Blueprint for a Knowledge-Centric Culture, introduced in Chapter 2. Both knowledge management practitioners, and writers, see leadership as being key to organisations capitalising on their knowledge assets.

Peter Senge, for example, points out that:

In a learning organisation, leaders' roles differ dramatically from that of charismatic decision makers. Leaders are designers, teachers and

*stewards . . . In short, leaders in learning organisations are
responsible for building organisations where people are continually
expanding their capabilities to shape their future (Peter Senge,
1998:587).*

So what competencies do leaders need to have if they are to help
the organisation's overall capabilities?

As a practitioner I have worked with many organisations over
the years, helping them develop their competency frameworks,
particularly behavioural competencies. From this work, combined with what is emerging in the literature, it seems that
organisations require leaders who can:

Think and act strategically
- Able to work in partnership with others to create a vision for
  the business
- Able to inspire trust and motivate others
- Always alert to change, both inside and outside their own
  business
- Takes a broader perspective
- Spots and act on opportunities to grow the business and the
  people within it
- Understands and applies the principles of systems thinking
- Use difference as an enabling force for change

Build and mobilize knowledge
- Knowledge aware – recognises knowledge as being a critical
  business asset
- Incorporates knowledge capital into strategic management
  processes
- Ensures that lessons learnt from successes and failures are used
  in future organisational planning
- Creates a climate for learning and experimentation
- Develops a knowledge ecology, i.e. creating an environment to
  support knowledge building and sharing
- Manages the generation of new knowledge
- Well-connected, both inside and outside the organisation
- Understands the social architecture of the organisation

Lead change and innovation
- Inspires, engages and supports others through change
- Understands the emotions associated with change
- Demonstrates respect for other people's ideas
- Creates the right amount of turbulence to foster creativity
- Helps others to see things (i.e. problems, situations) through a
  different lens

Build effective teams
- Creates an exciting and challenging work environment
- Builds alliances with internal and external teams
- Adopts a consensual approach to decision-making
- Demonstrates a willingness and self-discipline to listen
- Makes time to get to know individual team members and what makes them tick
- Demonstrates trust by regularly sharing information, insights and ideas with team members
- Values difference, in its many forms
- Demonstrates multi-cultural awareness

Raise performance and deliver results
- Focuses on what is important and ensures that others understand why what they are doing is important too
- Challenges embedded assumptions
- Sets stretching targets and standards
- Has a continuous improvement mindset
- Creates a context for collaborative working
- Links dispersed knowledge and skills
- Creates a sense of fun and playfulness at work
- Breaks down organisational barriers
- Addresses the things that get in the way of people doing their jobs effectively

Develop self and other
- Has regular coaching conversations with others
- Willingness to make time to exchange ideas with others
- Develops others through a variety of approaches
- Helps others to learn from their mistakes
- Uses feedback as a means to improve performance – invites feedback, rather than waiting for it to be offered
- Draws on a broad range of learning resources and opportunities
- See every task, every project, and every event, as a learning opportunity

In order to be able to deliver on these broad areas of competence, some of the 'soft skills' that need to be developed include:
- Self-awareness
- Self-regulation
- Personal motivation and energy
- 'Metaskills' (Hall, 1991): adaptability, tolerance of ambiguity, and identity change
- Risk-taking
- Emotional resilience

- Holistic view of self and the world around them
- Generous in spirit and time
- Non-egotistical – willing to help others to shine

Leaders in knowledge-businesses – 'knowledge experts' or 'knowledge facilitators'?

If leaders are to focus on developing the capabilities outlined above, this leaves a question mark as to the extent to which they also need to invest in developing their own technical specialism. Should the leader of an R&D team, for example, be the leading expert in a particular discipline, or should his primary responsibility be that of bringing on and nurturing future experts? To what extent then do leaders need to be 'knowledge experts' in their own right?

There are mixed views on this subject. The English Nature case study (see Chapter 11) suggests that leaders of communities who act as facilitators add value by focusing their energy on encouraging and facilitating multi-directional knowledge exchanges. This helps to ensure that knowledge is spread across the organisation, rather than remaining localised.

However, a study of how leaders develop creative potential in their teams (Whatmore, 1999), identified that unless leaders are recognised as being the best in their field they are unlikely to have the necessary qualities to make them good leaders. The research also found that having a knowledgeable leader added to the leader's credibility, from the team's perspective. What we have here though is an inherent paradox; the demands of the leadership role today suggests that leaders need to move away from their technical specialism so that they can focus on developing the knowledge, skills and behaviours needed to become a first-class facilitative leader. However, organisations need to provide some reassurance that in making this shift, leaders will not be moving down a path of obsolescence.

Getting the right leadership – selecting and developing leaders

Given the range of leadership competencies discussed above, it is no wonder that organisations have difficulty in getting the leadership element right. However, having defined and agreed the competencies relevant for your organisation this makes the job of selection and development a little easier.

Increasingly organisations are aspiring to make the selection and development process more transparent. Indeed, if one of the critical leadership qualities is that they should be self-managing and self-regulating then it is important that prospective leaders have an opportunity to self-assess themselves against the competencies needed for their role. Providing leaders with access to Development Centres is one of the formal approaches used within organisations to help them develop. The big question though is whether organizations should wait until someone has been appointed to a leadership role before giving them the opportunity to attend a Development Centre, or should this opportunity be provided earlier? There isn't a clear-cut answer to this. But looking at the list above, commonsense shows that waiting until someone is in post is leaving it too late.

However, someone, i.e. HR, needs to be keeping an eye on the talent pipeline so that those with high potential are given the right development opportunities at the right time. It could be that individuals need to be moved, or helped to find an 'out of the box' development opportunity, which gives them the chance to develop/refine some of the competencies outlined above.

Developing the organisation's leadership needs constant attention. Leaders need regular feedback, both formal and informal, as well as someone to help them interpret and decide what to do with this feedback. Who should be responsible for nurturing the organisation's leadership? Should this be a key deliverable for senior managers? If so how much of their time should they allocate to this task? What should HR's role be? Where can external developers add value?

Getting the right people, in the right place, at the right time

One of the essential building blocks for building a knowledge-centric culture is defining and developing the core competences needed by those in non-leadership positions. To be able to operate effectively in the knowledge society individuals need:

Basic skills, including . . .
- Questioning – our ability to ask good questions enhances and deepens our knowledge
- Observation – given that people know more than they can tell, observation can be a way into other people's 'know how'
- Listening – this means applying all of our senses
- Communicating
- Problem-solving
- Information handling – research/investigative skills
- IT literacy – adept in keyboard skills, using the intranet and internet and basic tools such as word processing and database packages
- Active learner – curious, seeks out learning opportunities for self

- Creative thinking
- Collaborative working
- Sociable and networked
- Experimenter – 'try it and see' and 'what if' mindset
- Making connections – between ideas, insights and people
- Knowledge aware – recognises and understands the critical importance of building knowledge for the organisation and own career
- Working with change

Soft skills, including . . .
- Self-managing – sets and works within high-performance standards
- Self-reliant
- Critical reflection
- Comfortable working cross-boundaries
- Hunter-gatherer – willingness to seek things out for themselves
- Honesty – able to be trusted to give credit to other people's ideas and not to abuse relationships
- Generous
- 'Mindset' flexibility
- Risk-taker

Of course for individuals to optimise their performance they need to combine their knowledge, skills and attitude, which means engaging the head, heart and hands. In practice this means individuals need to develop:

The **Knowledge** to know and understand
The **Will and Attitude** to apply their knowledge and skills, and
The **Skills** to apply the knowledge that they have to everyday tasks and situations

Training and development

Helping to build informal learning environments

Learning is a crucial ingredient for success in knowledge building organisations. While formal learning programmes, such as training programmes and qualification programmes, are important sources of learning, the value of informal learning in the workplace should not be underestimated. Around 70 per cent of what we learn occurs in informal contexts. There is now more of an acceptance of the importance of the social context for learning and how much of what we learn occurs through social interaction (Wenger, 1998).

This next case study from Oxfam GB shows how the Corporate Learning and Development team are taking the lead in helping the organisation move towards becoming a learning organisation.

Learning and Knowledge Management – The challenges and experience of Oxfam GB

Organisational context and knowledge management challenges

Oxfam GB is a development, relief, and campaigning organisation dedicated to finding lasting solutions to poverty and suffering around the world. The organisation works with communities, local partners, volunteers and supporters to help overcome the injustices of poverty and suffering. The organisation works internationally as part of a worldwide movement to build a just and safer world.

The organisation employs around 3,000 permanent staff and approximately 23,000 volunteers working in various roles throughout the organisation in Great Britain.

The organisation is structured into five major divisions:

Marketing Division: which is responsible for fundraising, communications, campaigns, and work to raise awareness of development issues in formal education in Great Britain.

International Division: which is responsible for implementing Oxfam's relief and development programme overseas; for the GB Poverty Programme; and for research, lobbying, and publications about the causes and relief of poverty.

Trading Division: which is responsible for shops (with sales of donated goods and fair trade products) and recycling, in Great Britain.

Finance and Information Systems Division: which is responsible for organisation-wide finance and information systems.

Corporate Human Resources Division: this leads on the work carried out with Human Resources teams in all Divisions on delivering Oxfam's HR strategies.

Although the organisation prefers to use the term Learning Organisation rather than Knowledge Management, Knowledge Management is one of the key strategic areas featured in Oxfam's five-year strategic plan. The organisation sees Knowledge Management as

> *... creating, managing, applying and sharing explicit knowledge (that exists typically in documents, databases and as part of processes) and tacit knowledge (embedded in people and their experience) in order to 'make a difference' in overcoming poverty and suffering.*

Through its Knowledge Management approach the organisation is aiming to transform behaviours in a number of key areas:

- The way in which knowledge is applied to decision-making and choices
- The value placed on creating, managing, disseminating and utilising knowledge
- The attention given to 'packaging' knowledge so that it can be effectively applied
- Expectations that individuals within the organisation have of each other in terms of preparedness to maintain a learning posture and also a willingness to collaborate and share

While the organisation sees technology as being an important enabler for Knowledge Management it recognises that effective Knowledge Management requires more than a technological solution. It views technology as being there to facilitate communication, help embed practice ('know how') into systems and to enable mangers quickly to extract the information that they need to do their jobs effectively.

Oxfam GB's approach to knowledge management can best be described as being emergent, rather than following a co-ordinated strategic approach. To-date this approach has encompassed the following areas.

Responsibilities for Knowledge Management

The organisation has chosen to adopt a 'light touch' to introducing Knowledge Management rather than launch a large-scale Organisational Development initiative. One of the key messages that the organisation has tried to communicate to its staff is that managing knowledge is central to the work of everyone within Oxfam and hence everyone needs to be responsible for managing the organisation's, as well as their own, knowledge. The focus has been getting people to think of Knowledge Management as 'the way we do our work' rather than it being a separate activity, or initiative.

Some of the underpinning principles of Oxfam's Knowledge Management approach include:

- Activities need to be clearly linked to organisational priorities, so that learning informs key decisions and debates
- Integral to the design and implementation of day-to-day activities
- Uses simple tools that make effective use of what is already known, rather than generating more information
- Helping the organisation become more skilled at seeking out and sharing learning

Despite wanting to adopt a 'light touch' to its Knowledge Management approach some key changes have been introduced to ensure that the organisation is structured effectively from a Knowledge Management perspective.

Having defined its core Knowledge Management goals and underpinning principles the next task for the organisation was to introduce a new management structure thereby ensuring that responsibilities for Knowledge Management are shared across significant parts of the organisation. There are three main strands to the organisation's Knowledge Management approach and senior managers have been assigned specific responsibilities within these three areas:

Culture: The organisation is aiming to become a learning organisation. It is striving to build a culture in which Communities of Practice and Storytelling techniques are valued. The use of Storytelling as a Knowledge Management tool is seen as having a strong cultural fit given that Storytelling is a natural communication tool used in many of the Southern world countries that Oxfam works with. Because of this learning focus the cultural strand of Oxfam's Knowledge Management work is being led by the Corporate Learning and Development Manager.

Processes and content: Responsibilities here fall to senior managers from the main business divisions (International, Marketing and Trading).

Technology: While this aspect of the organisation's Knowledge Management approach is headed up by a senior manager from the Information Systems department, other key players have a responsibility to input to and validate the design of information systems to ensure that they are consistent with the organisation's Knowledge Management goals. Many of the IT tools needed for effective Knowledge Management are already in existence, these include the corporate Internet, intranet and the use of Lotus Notes.

In addition to these areas of responsibility the organisation has also established two Knowledge Management Reference Groups. These are basically forums in which people within the organisation who have an interest in Knowledge Management can meet to exchange ideas, thoughts and stories about Knowledge Management.

A Knowledge Management Core Group, consisting of the key senior managers taking knowledge management forward, meet once every few months to discuss projects and share progress, and agree next steps.

A wider Knowledge Management Reference Group normally meets over lunch, every couple of months, and has become known internally as 'the brown bag' group, since people generally turn up with their own lunch. The format and discussions that take place at 'the brown bag' sessions are fairly loosely defined. Staff from different parts of Oxfam including those who work as volunteers, are encouraged to attend 'the brown bag' sessions. Visitors from overseas, and occasionally external KM practitioners, are encouraged to come along to share their Knowledge Management stories.

Approaches to encourage and support knowledge building and sharing

Enhancing communications across organisational boundaries

Communications is seen as a critical ingredient of the organisation's Knowledge Management approach. The geographical boundaries of Oxfam's work however can make communications and cross-boundary learning difficult. This difficulty is compounded by the fact that many people within the organisation tend not to shout about their successes. Culturally there is a tendency for people to hide their light under a bushel. One of the priorities then for the organisation has been to develop a more joined-up approach to its communications activities (e.g. published/unpublished, electronic/paper-based and internal/external communications).

The organisation draws on a number of different communications approaches as a means of ensuring that its people get to hear about the different projects that are taking place in different geographical locations and hence have an opportunity to learn from the experience of others. The main communications tools include:

Internal magazines and journals – the organisation produces a regular in-house newsletter known as VOX (The Voice of Oxfam) and Division specific journals, such as 'Shoptalk' in the Trading Division.

Storytelling – Storytelling is now a critical tool in the organisation's communications approach. Most external and internal communications start with a real story as a way of reinforcing the key message that the organisation is trying to communicate.

The use of narrative in different forms of communications is becoming more and more common. For example, real stories are being incorporated into Monitoring, Evaluation and Impact Assessment reports. Including real stories in these types of reports help to illustrate the real impact on individuals' lives of the work carried out by Oxfam and other agencies.

Video technology – Video technology is increasingly being used so that stories in the organisation can be videoed. These videos are then duplicated so that Team Leaders can use them as part of their team meetings. Examples of stories of successful projects include: A waste recycling project in Datcha, Trade Fair, Rice farming in the Caribbean. Showing videos during Team Meetings is viewed as a key medium for learning and hence is seen as a legitimate use of time.

Intranet – There is a separate area on the organisation's intranet dedicated to Learning and Knowledge Management. Within this area there is a section known as 'Talking'. Here staff can read stories of various projects that are taking place in different Oxfam regions. The topics range from 'HIV/AIDS: Impact on livelihoods in Southern Africa' to 'Evaluation: How do we measure up to the job?'

The organisation has also considered introducing a travelling minstrel, whose role it would be to travel around different Oxfam regions gathering and telling stories about different projects.

Encouraging Communities of Practice

Given the geographical scope of the work that Oxfam does the organisation is keen to encourage its staff to participate in Communities of Practice (COPs). An internal document promoting the use of COPs stresses that '*Communities of practice are not just "one more thing to do", but are how people do their work.*' In the future more emphasis will be placed on developing COPs and collaboratives, i.e. groups of practitioners who meet to share their learning as they take practical steps to solve practical problems.

Training and development

The Learning and Development function within HR see their role as being very much one of helping others in the organisation to build and enhance their knowledge-building capabilities. They do this through:

- Facilitating learning within teams
- Helping teams learn how to tell good stories so that they provide clear messages
- Helping teams unpack stories told by other teams within the organisation
- Helping individuals and teams unpack what they know
- Developing strategic leadership
- Helping line managers build their questioning, communication and visualising skills

Given that Storytelling is a crucial element of the organisation's Knowledge Management approach a Storytelling component was added to the organisation's Strategic Leadership Development Programme, which 200 members of the senior management team took part in.

A developmental opportunity available to all individuals within Oxfam (permanent staff, as well as volunteers) is something known as the 'Tours'. This is an opportunity to go on an extended tour of Oxfam to learn more about its work in different regions. Each tour lasts for between 3 and 6 weeks and involves a group of 6–10 people.

Although not initially envisaged as a knowledge-building tool, the structure and requirements of the 'Tours' programme is knowledge enhancing. One of the criteria for being selected to go on the 'Tours' programme is that individuals agree to give around 30 presentations to colleagues on their return, thus helping to bring the work of Oxfam alive for others in the organisation.

To help individuals meet this requirement they are provided with cameras and tape recorders so that they can capture what they have seen and learnt. On return individuals are offered one-to-one coaching on presentation skills and storytelling so that they are equipped to deliver informative and knowledge-rich presentations.

Revisiting evaluation

Evaluation and impact assessment is an important part of the work carried out within the organisation. It is seen as crucial for ensuring accountability, legitimacy and learning. Part of the learning that has taken place within the organisation is that of learning how to become more effective at carrying out monitoring, evaluation and impact assessments.

Drawing on the lessons learnt in recent years the Programme Policy unit has produced a set of good practice guidelines for Impact Assessment programmes. These include:

- Keep monitoring systems simple and user friendly and ensure that they build on what people know and can do
- Embed Impact Assessment in all phases of the Project/ Programme cycle
- Focus on key questions
- Recognize the diversity of different groups views and conditions and where possible tailor reports to take into account their needs
- Ensure that monitoring systems evolve and are adapted over time
- Ensure organisational coherence and alignment, e.g. in incentives, rewards and other organisational practices

HR has a pivotal role to play in building a culture where informal learning is valued and supported. This requires paying attention to the way in which different learning resources are positioned, as well as the physical spaces within which learning can take place. Coaching, mentoring, job shadowing, secondments, back-to-the-floor, participation in Communities of Practice and cross-boundary team working are all practices that are being revisited and/or adopted within organisations to build their knowledge base. Equally, priority needs to be given to providing all employees with training in the key knowledge management skills: information management, problem-solving, creative thinking, working with change, collaborative working.

Another role for HR is to help the organisation experiment with, and learn from, new ways of working, such as cross-boundary team working. Cross-boundary team working is one way of tapping into the organisation's diverse talents. It is also a means to help individuals develop a broader perspective of problems/tasks. Cross-boundary team working can also help individuals build their social capital (i.e. their network contacts).

To some extent there is a potential clash of interest here for trainers whose natural reaction when presented with a learning need from the business is to offer a training programme. However, many organisations are now beginning to re-visit their learning offering, drawing on broader learning approaches including: formal learning programmes; self-directed learning programmes, as well as utilising new technologies for learning.

An organisation in the financial services sector that I came across while carrying out background research for this book has taken a strategic decision not to offer a structured skills development programme for its managers. Instead it is helping to develop its managers through the use of Self-managed Learning. Adopting this approach is enabling managers to focus on their specific learning needs. Learning in Self-managed Learning Sets has the added advantage that it helps managers to develop their 'soft' skills (e.g. listening, questioning, offering feedback); skills which can then be applied when working with their teams, colleagues and other stakeholders. This approach can also help to bring about more collaborative working in the future through the trust that is established when working with colleagues in learning sets.

Some factors to consider when creating a learning and sharing environment are:

Make learning and sharing easy by . . .

- Providing time and mental space, e.g. scheduling time for thinking and learning
- Create public and private spaces for learning, e.g. open space areas, coffee areas, quiet areas
- Provide learning resources, e.g. libraries, information centres, special learning laboratories, virtual university
- Drawing, on expertise from outside, e.g. regular talks from external people, and

Make learning and sharing worthwhile by . . .

- Giving recognition to the sharers
- Publicising best practice
- Providing awards for sharers (particularly at annual conferences, thus maximising publicity)
- Rewarding the learners, for example through introducing a time matching scheme for learning

People movement plans – Co-ordinating plans for the free movement of people (and hence knowledge)

In knowledge businesses succession planning needs to have a different emphasis. Instead of thinking of succession planning purely in terms of the upward movement of staff, as is the case with traditional succession planning, there is a need to consider the lateral movement of staff. This is crucial for knowledge to circulate freely around an organisation.

HR has an important role in re-educating managers on how to plan for and manage lateral career moves, as well as helping co-ordinate plans for the movement of people around the organisation.

People moves, however, do not have to be on a permanent basis. Other ways of working that can enable knowledge to flow across departmental boundaries include: secondments; cross-boundary team working; work shadowing, as well as coaching and mentoring.

Where HR can add value is to make it easier for these knowledge-building opportunities to occur. The Workforce Development team within Berkshire NHS Shared Services, for example, has introduced a KM Sharematch Scheme, providing a way of connecting staff who wish to build their knowledge through work-shadowing other professionals, in different healthcare roles. The availability of technology means that this does not need to be an administrative burden for HR. However, there is an important role for HR in terms of promoting such schemes, as well as evaluating the outcomes.

Help people develop a sense of community and belonging

As organisations and cultures become more fragmented this can become a source of tension for individuals as it conflicts with one of Maslow's five basis needs, i.e. to be able to identify with a social group that is close to them. Social isolation, or the fear of feeling socially isolated, is one of the known difficulties with teleworking and home working. Yet individuals can also feel socially isolated when working in organisations that are more loosely structured, i.e. in virtual organisations, or where the organisation is moving towards more mobile working.

As the employee champion, HR has a role to play in ensuring that practices exist to help individuals feel part of a bigger community. This may be something as simple as engineering informal gatherings where people can come together to chew the fat about whatever is meaningful for them. A voluntary organisation that I have been working with holds 'Air and Share' sessions. These provide a forum to let off steam and also work through some common problems with colleagues. However, as many of these individuals work autonomously, one of the main drivers for holding these sessions is to help bring people together.

With fun being high on the wish list of what employees today want out of a satisfying career, creating opportunities for them to let their hair down seems important. Club Med in Nice was the chosen venue for staff at Electronic Arts European Head Office as a venue to get together to exchange ideas, share experiences and also let their hair down.

Keeping the momentum going

Monitor how you are doing

Evaluation is often one of people's least favourite activities. But if your organisation wants to move towards and/or remain knowledge-centric then it is crucial that you monitor how you are doing on your journey. This process should cover:

Reviewing the initial KM goals

How are you doing? In what areas have you made most progress? What has been the most significant learning points? What has happened to that learning? Are the initial goals you set still relevant, or is it time to set some new goals?

Taking the pulse of the organisation

It would be difficult to give a blueprint for what to include here as this would depend upon the organisational values, KM goals, or areas that the organisation is striving to improve on. However, some suggested areas for a KM pulse check include:

- My manager is supportive of me participating in Communities of Practice, allowing me to schedule time for this work, alongside other deliverables.
- My manager really listens to my ideas for enhancing performance.
- Team meetings are used as a way to proactively share knowledge and for learning through joint problem-solving.
- I regularly get the opportunity to hear about future business plans directly from senior managers.
- I have a career plan which addresses both my own and the organisation's future knowledge needs.
- I feel supported in trying out new ways of working.
- There are enough spaces (both time and physical) for me to have learning conversations with others.
- I am encouraged to network with others, both within and outside the organisation.

What seems crucial is to focus on a few key indicators that can be easily tracked, rather than trying to monitor too much. As part of their commitment to enhancing employability Motorola have introduced an 'Individual Dignity Plan'. This contains six key indicators that managers discuss quarterly with individuals in their team. A negative response to any of these six items is treated as a quality failure and is dealt with in the same way as other quality failures.

If these types of indexes are communicated and discussed alongside other business indicators (such as sales, profits, external customer feedback scores) this can be a powerful way of reinforcing the message that the organisation is taking knowledge management seriously.

Revisit existing HR practices to ensure knowledge aligned

Chapter 10 sets out a model for linking HR and KM practices, thus providing a framework for ensuring that a knowledge focus is added to current and future HR practices. The model encompasses steps that can be taken to ensure that a knowledge focus is maintained in the recruitment, induction, reward and recognition, career management and performance management systems.

Communicate, communicate and communicate

Build effective approaches for communicating and sharing success stories, bearing in mind the points made earlier about choosing the right medium for the message that needs to be communicated.

Summary

There is a growing consensus that HR has a key role to play in helping their organisation move forward on their knowledge management journey, particularly by helping the organisation develop an organisational culture that supports knowledge building and sharing.

While HR cannot change an organisational culture itself, it has the 'know how' to support the transformation process. This chapter has discussed the steps in the process, which include: agreeing strategic priorities and areas for change, helping demystify knowledge management by linking knowledge management activity to established business processes and HR practices, and engaging others in the knowledge management dialogue.

Specifically HR can add value by developing a knowledge awareness programme, either as a separate development activity, or by integrating it into existing development programmes; communicating how the organisation is building its knowledge management capabilities; ensuring that the right leadership is in place and receiving the relevant developmental support: as well as building a culture where learning from day-to-day practice is valued, encouraged and supported.

Pause for reflection

- What do you see as the strategic priorities in your organisation, from a knowledge management perspective? How do these map against those identified by your business colleagues?
- To what extent do the leadership competencies discussed in this chapter mirror those in your own organisation?
- How are leaders perceived in your organisation, as 'knowledge experts', or 'knowledge facilitators'?
- Do you see communication as a strategic tool? What steps is HR taking to enhance the quality of the communication processes within the organisation?

6

Re-visiting learning in the knowledge economy

Developing a learning-centric organisation

The need for understanding how organisations learn and accelerate that learning is greater today than ever before. The old days when a Henry Ford, Alfred Sloan or Tom Watson learned for the organisation are gone. In an increasingly dynamic, independent and unpredictable world, it is simply no longer possible for anyone to figure it all out at the top. The old model 'the top thinks and the local acts' must now give way to the integrative thinking and acting at all levels (Peter Senge, 1998: 586).

The learning and change spiral

There aren't many certainties in today's business world, but one certainty is that change is the norm. This includes a change in the language associated with organisational change. Recent work by Herriot, Hirsh and Reilly (1998), for example, shows that organisational change now seems to consist of a series of overlapping transitions, some more profound than others, where one transition is often not completed before another transition starts. This phenomenon of overlapping transitions has led Herriot, and his co-writers, to suggest that the stabilisation phase, present in more traditional transition models, is possibly now outdated, give that many organisations no longer reach that stage.

Edie Weiner, President of Weiner Edrich Brown, an American consultancy, suggests that in today's business world we need to think about the concept of 'transitioning' i.e. of changes where there are no clear beginnings or endings, as opposed to the concept of transition singular[1].

One of the implications of this new phenomenon of 'transitioning', is that organisations need to be constantly learning. Change requires learning and indeed learning leads to change: the bigger the change the greater the need for learning. Thus a key strategic task today is developing the organisation's capability to learn from each transition experience, so that the organisation can be better prepared for subsequent transitions.

The key career development task in organisations then, according to Herriot and his co-writers, is to help individuals make effective transitions by helping them learn from these, so that they are better prepared for making even bigger transitions in the future. This requires providing the right kind of support at each of the three distinct transition phases: preparation, encounter and adjustment phases.

As facilitating learning and change map directly onto HR's core capabilities, HR has an opportunity significantly to add value, from a knowledge management perspective. However, there is a view that if HR wants to develop a learning-centric culture there is a need to re-educate themselves, and their business partners, on what we mean by learning and how best to encourage and facilitate learning in the modern workplace.

Etienne Wenger (1998), a leading researcher and writer in the field of learning, believes that one of the assumptions that many institutions hold about learning is that of learning being an individual process that occurs through teaching in locations held away from the workplace. It is for this reason, Wenger argues, that many of us find learning irrelevant, boring, and end up believing that it is something that we are not cut out for.

Alred and his co-writers (1998) suggest that we have adopted a very linear view of learning up until now, one that is reinforced through some of the language associated with learning. For example, we refer to 'key stages' in the national curriculum, and learning levels in the National Vocational Qualification system. However, in the case of adult learning, learning isn't always linear as it doesn't always involve learning something new. Instead, learning can involve 'finding new ways in old truths', i.e. developing new perspectives on the ways things have always been done.

So is there an alternative way of thinking about learning? Wenger argues that there is. He has developed a theory of learning, which he refers to as a social theory of learning, based on the assumptions that (a) learning is as much a part of human nature as eating and sleeping and (b) learning occurs naturally through our active participation in the practices of different social communities. It is Wenger's view of learning that has fuelled the renewed interest in Communities of Practice, as we shall see in the next chapter.

As Edie Weiner points out, individuals today suffer from 'Educated Incapacity', i.e. knowing so much that they have difficulty seeing things differently anymore. To overcome this phenomenon, she suggests that there is a need to create learning forums that enable individuals to see things through a different lens.

Learning, I would argue, is fundamental to the process of seeing things through a different lens. However, one of the key challenges for organisations is to let go of some of their traditional ways of thinking about learning and to encourage and help teams and individuals experiment with new ways of learning.

While it is acknowledged that formal learning has an important role to play in developing knowledge, the value of informal learning and learning by other means should not be under-estimated. Formal learning only represents the tip of the iceberg when it comes to learning; around 70 per cent of our learning is informal. Thus it is important that organisations build and encourage environments where informal learning is as valued and supported as formal learning.

Ghoshal and Bartlett (1998) suggest that training programmes alone cannot develop employees to their maximum potential in environments where the knowledge base for people's jobs is changing rapidly. In their book, *The Individualized Corporation*, they refer to the experience of General Electric (GE) who, despite investing extensively in formal training, acknowledge that only about 10 per cent of a manager's knowledge comes from this type of training.

A survey by Reg Revans[2], a leading expert in the field of Action Learning, identified that many organisations find it helpful to make distinctions between training and development. Revans's survey identified these distinctions as:

Development involves:
- Self-motivation and people thinking for themselves
- A more holistic approach, taking into account the whole situation
- Addressing longer-term needs
- No right or wrong answers

Whereas training:
- Is more specific as it is related to identified current learning needs

- Produces an extension of existing abilities
- Is done for you and to you (i.e. it is less learner-directed)

But what about formal education, what is its role in the knowledge economy? Traditionally education, particularly higher education, has provided the means for opening up peoples' minds, exposing individuals to new thinking, thus helping them see things through new lenses. In a world where change is a constant, formal learning is important, and indeed continues to form an important part of many organisations' Learning and Development strategies, particularly for those in senior roles. Corporate sponsorship for MBAs is an example of the value placed on this particular type of learning activity. In addition, in recent years we have seen a trend towards organisations setting up their own workplace university, where individuals can gain exposure to ideas, theories and practices, which are not necessarily related to their immediate role.

Other strategic questions relating to learning in the knowledge economy include:

- Should the organisation focus on providing 'just-in-time' or 'just-in-case' learning solutions? and
- Who should be responsible for developing generic human capital (i.e. skills and knowledge which enhance the worker's productivity irrespective, of where he or she is employed) and specific human capital (i.e. skills and knowledge which only apply to current employer)? Should this be the organisation's responsibility, or should this be a joint responsibility between employers and employees?

Where there is a recognised shortage of skilled workers and the pool to be drawn from is getting smaller and smaller it seems that organisations have to become adept at managing the paradox of helping individuals build their employability, but at the same time provide a stimulating and enriching work environment so that individuals want to stay. This is part of the changing psychological contract of employment.

That said, it seems that not all organisations are prepared to invest in building their employees' human capital (generic or specific). A survey by KnowledgePool[3], a worldwide training provider, identified that less than half of the workforce surveyed had received any training in the past year. Wearing their strategic hat, HR should be prepared to question and challenge statistics like these. Questions that spring to mind include: What category/levels of workers are not receiving training? Is it possible that these categories/levels are being developed in other ways? What skills need to be developed? What is the best way of developing these skills? How can we turn statistics like these to our advantage?

Developing organisational 'know how' – the need for an integrative approach

Given the renewed interest in the social dimension of learning, organisations need to consider adopting '. . . *an integrative training approach which focuses on practice and seeks "points of leverage" to support learning'* (Wenger, 1998). These leverage points, according to Wenger, can come from learning through everyday practice, as well as by encouraging shared learning through communities of practice.

In the race to get a handle on managing knowledge many organisations have come unstuck by investing too much energy in developing formal systems to encourage the dissemination of knowledge, at the expense of capitalising on the benefits that come from informal processes. What seems to have been over-looked is that knowledge creation doesn't always flow from formal structures and systems, but instead is often the by-product of day-to-day interactions.

Dave Snowden, Director of the Cynefin Centre for Organisational Complexity, IBM Global Services, argues that organisations need to consider the dimensions of space and time when choosing appropriate learning approaches to maximise opportunities for knowledge transfer.

In his learning and knowledge transfer model[4], Snowden sets out four different learning approaches together with their relationship with the knowledge transfer process. The first of these he refers to as the *Apprenticeship Model*. This is where individuals learn by working alongside a knowledge expert, observing first-hand how a particular task is carried out. The opportunities for knowledge transfer in this learning scenario are high as individuals are proximate in both time and space to the knowledge expert. In addition to building skills needed in the modern workplace and passing on 'know how' from generation to generation, the Apprenticeship Model is increasingly being seen as a way of building the 'reflexive capacity of the workforce' (Fuller and Unwin, 1998).

A variation of the Apprenticeship Model is that of *Virtual Observation* where, facilitated by technology, individuals can observe an expert in action where the expert is in a different geographical location. So although the learner is spatially separate the opportunity for real-time leaning is high because of the proximity to the knowledge source. The third learning approach involves the use of *Manuals and/or Online Learning*. Here the learner is separate in time and space to the knowledge source, making it difficult for an individual to ask questions to check out his or her understanding. The fourth learning approach is that of the traditional *Training Course*. While individuals may be closer to the knowledge source on training courses the opportunities for immediate knowledge transfer can be limited, as there is often a lead-time between knowledge acquisition and application.

So when it comes to developing organisational knowledge, it seems that organisations need to adopt a broader perspective of learning, ensuring a balance between formal learning (i.e. learning that leads to a qualification), training (either in-house or external), development (i.e. through practices like coaching, or learning sets), as well as capitalising on the learning that occurs through everyday practice. Each of these approaches can help in developing existing knowledge, as well as helping to build new knowledge and skills for the future.

Opportunities for learning through everyday practice

There are numerous approaches that come under the umbrella of learning through everyday practice. Some of these approaches are discussed below.

Team meetings

In many Japanese cultures daily communication meetings are the means by which firms, such as Matsushita and Honda, ensure continuous improvement. The Japanese management philosophy is one of ensuring that all of its employees are integrated through open communication, job rotation, consultative decision-making, team working, as well as through the sharing of information across departmental boundaries (Thompson, 1993).

From my consulting work with organisations I am aware of the lost opportunities for knowledge sharing from everyday practice, such as team meetings. So often team meetings are used as forums for communicating down, rather than opportunities for knowledge-building and sharing. In addition, too much emphasis is given to formal meeting structures. While these are important, we shouldn't underestimate the power of informal structures. A colleague of mine recently recounted how, in a former role as a Lecturer in a College of Nursing, knowledge was built through the daily informal interactions between lecturers and nurse practitioners in the coffee lounge. In these impromptu meetings, colleagues discussed some of the questions (and answers) posed in lectures. Often the nurse practitioners would add in observations from the wards, or pose questions based on their observations on the wards. The interactions provided a forum for developing new knowledge, and for raising questions for further research. Through this daily ritual, those in practice, as well as those learning about practice, were able to exchange ideas and raise questions that enhanced their own knowledge, as well as that of the organisation.

By re-visiting the purpose and practice of team meetings, organisations can benefit from:

- Regular forums for sharing best practice and for questioning the assumptions upon which operational routines are based
- Opportunities for identifying solutions to common operational difficulties through joint problem-solving
- Opportunities for sharing intelligence (gathered internally, or externally)
- An exchange of operational highs and lows, together with an opportunity to discuss the lessons learnt, as well as discuss where existing processes need to change
- Shared information to help with the 'know why'

Informal meetings and conversations

Another consideration when building a learning culture is that of revisiting our assumptions about what counts as productive work, as these can get in the way of developing a knowledge-centric culture. As part of the research that I have been conducting into how organisations are developing a knowledge-creating and sharing culture (Evans, 2002) I have uncovered numerous stories of lost opportunities because managers seem to have a narrow perspective on what constitutes productive work. One example comes from a consulting firm where managers were critical of the time consultants spent in conversation with colleagues in other teams, as this was perceived as time taken away from 'real work'. Another story, told in Chapter 4, is that of the Utilities company where the management team decided to cancel the service engineers' weekly team meetings because it was felt that bringing the engineers together once a week was not productive use of time. What had been overlooked was the importance of these weekly get-togethers from a knowledge-building and sharing perspective.

What lessons can we draw from these stories? A key lesson is that time spent in conversation with others sharing insights, discussing solutions to common operational problems, and exchanging ideas, needs to be seen as productive work. If they are not then organisations will struggle to develop a high performance culture. Research into the factors that can affect participation in e-learning reinforces this view. Attempts to introduce e-learning often fail because of the assumptions held by managers that learning and development is something that takes place away from the office, or away from an individual's desk. For some managers, learning is seen as an extra-curricula activity, rather than something that is an integral part of daily work routine.

Cross-boundary team working

In the quest for high performance, many organisations are realising the benefits of learning from difference, whether this be learning from difference within their own organisation, or learning from difference outside (i.e. through benchmarking, study tours, secondments, or community-based projects).

In the late 1990s the Ford Motor Company launched a business leadership initiative, based around cross-functional team working, as a way of developing ideas for improving the way the company runs its business[5]. This Organisational Development initiative was based on a simple assumption that through the casual conversations that individuals have in their day-to-day work there is the spark of an idea of how to improve the business; however, day-to-day responsibilities mean that these ideas often remain untapped. This company-wide leadership initiative brought together managers from different functional areas to develop working propositions. So why has this approach worked? First, those involved believed that well-thought ideas would be adopted, or at least given a trial run. Second, each team is sponsored by a senior executive who is charged with ensuring that the team have access to the necessary resources to develop their ideas into workable business solutions.

But it is not just in the private sector that learning through difference is perceived as a valuable source of learning. In the public sector partnership working is increasingly being seen as a way to bringing about radical change. An example here being the innovative approach adopted by the London borough of Lewisham when they conducted a Best Value review of its entire customer interface. Rather than follow existing approaches, the elected members and council officers adopted a new approach. This involved bringing together a team of independent thinkers from different business backgrounds, to work alongside elected members and officers. One of the lessons learnt cited in the end of project learning review included '*This new model of partnership and review had avoided the passivity and other "baggage" traditionally encountered in Council committees and released people from playing pre-ordained roles, so that they could instead challenge each other.*[6]'

Learning throughout the project management cycle

There are many opportunities for integrating a learning focus into the project management cycle. At the *Project Initiation Phase*, learning can be facilitated through planning time for experimentation and prototyping, or by locating teams that have been in a similar terrain before and asking them to share their 'war stories' and 'major leaps forward'. Learning can also arise by bringing together resources from diverse backgrounds and experiences.

As you move on to the *Development Phase* consider assigning someone on the project team the task of capturing the lessons learnt as they emerge, rather than trying to capture these at the end of the project when many of the key players have moved on. In addition it is important to allocate time to reviewing process issues, as well as outcomes. This is definitely an added-value role that learning and development practitioners can offer project teams and are being started by the Training and Development function of the BBC. Also as new people join the project team ensure that they have an opportunity to share their know how; new starters have a valuable role to play in helping an existing team separate out the wood from the trees.

At the *Post-project Review Phase* learning can come through individual and team level reflection, thereby closing the learning loop. For individuals this is the time for them to revise their Personal Development Plan and update their Yellow Pages entry, so that it reflects the experience gained on the project, as well as to log new learning needs.

Communities of Practice

Communities of Practice are seen as an essential ingredient in successful knowledge cultures. Communities are self-forming groups that have a shared interest in developing knowledge about a particular topic. Because communities are self-forming, organisations may not be aware of their existence, a situation that can make some managers feel uncomfortable because of the feeling of loss of control. A cynical view of communities is that they have become the new label for the self-directed work groups that organisations tried to introduce a few years ago. This cynicism aside, there does seem to be benefits for organisations and individuals from working and learning in informal learning communities. The next chapter goes into more detail about the benefits of Communities of Practice and also how HR practitioners can support these learning communities, ensuring a win–win situation for the organisation and individuals.

Attending to the physical spaces within which learning occurs

Attending to the physical spaces within which knowledge is created and shared was one of the components in the model – Towards a blueprint for developing a knowledge-centric culture – introduced in Chapter 3.

While some organisations are developing their knowledge base by paying more attention to the physical environment within which work and learning naturally co-exists, others have created separate environments that allow learning to occur through experimentation and play.

These approaches suggest that organisations are beginning to pay attention to what other writers refer to as the 'knowledge ecology', i.e. the environmental factors which influence how knowledge is developed and shared. So how are organisations doing this?

Facilitating learning through informal thinking and learning spaces

In creative organisations the importance of paying attention to the physical work environment within which creative work thrives is well understood. Research carried out by John Whatmore (1999), into what makes a successful leader of creative teams, illustrates the importance of paying attention to the environment within which creative work flourishes. Some of the practices uncovered in this research include having big toast and coffee rooms on every floor to encourage team members to eat and drink together and creating spaces for informal meetings, away from the regular work areas.

The legacy of the downsizing era of the 1990s has led to a much tighter view of what counts as productive work. Organisations have become much more results focused. As a consequence the time available for activities such as informal learning conversations is increasingly being squeezed out.

However, there are signs that more and more organisations are beginning to see the value in paying attention to the physical surroundings within which teams work and learn. Pearl Assurance, for example, has experimented with different work environments designed to help staff be more effective at work[7]. The experiment, designed with the help of its advertising agency, involved creating three new workrooms which have a 'funfair quality'. The three rooms include:

The Pit Lane – this is a meeting room with no door or chairs, but with a large clock which starts ticking away as a soon as a meeting begins. This room has proved most popular as it encourages people not to 'waffle on' in meetings.

The Sanctuary – this room is designed to help people when they have to make difficult calls, so it has a calming decor including pictures of idyllic water and fish-tanks.

Customer room – this room resembles a family kitchen, including all of the clutter one might find in a family kitchen. The idea behind this particular room design is to encourage staff to focus on customers' needs when they meet in it.

In an article in *Harvard Business Review*, Jacqueline Vischer[8], cites the approach adopted for managing workspace within Microsoft's R&D headquarters. The philosophy adopted there is that 'the nature of a person's work dictates decisions about space'. This reflects the view that no single type of workspace fits all knowledge workers. So while software developers have private offices, as they need quiet spaces to work, marketing teams have big open meeting spaces as most of their work gets done in meetings. Microsoft believe that paying attention to the work environment of knowledge workers, particularly where they are in scarce supply, is crucial for attracting and retaining these workers.

My own earlier research (Evans, 2000) identified that organisations are beginning to reap the benefits of planning informal learning spaces into their office building layouts. In one pharmaceutical company, for example, one of the regional teams had created a 1960s style café area. This area includes a coffee machine, whiteboards and also PCs with Internet access. What this team has created is an informal meeting area where individuals want to meet with colleagues to exchange ideas and solve problems together. The success story from this changed environment is that two product developers were chatting over a coffee one day, while scanning the comments on the whiteboard. One of the two individuals happened to mention to the other that he was currently struggling with a particular aspect of a project and that he didn't know who to turn to for help. A third person in the café area happened to hear this conversation and joined in the discussion. This third person contributed *'I had a similar problem when working on product x, what I did to resolve it was . . .'*. Armed with this insight the individual was able to move forward with his project. This chance conversation is reputed to have saved the organisation the cost of setting up the informal meeting area.

Building learning environments to facilitate experimentation and play

One of the biggest areas of learning and change for individuals in today's workplace is that of keeping up-to-date with changing technologies. Changes in technology are affecting all individuals' working lives, not just those working in the IT industry. It is this area of change that has led organisations like the BBC and The Post Office to invest in learning environments where managers and teams can experience and interact with new technologies and together with colleagues learn about the capabilities and impact of these technologies on the business. Some of the background to the introduction of these new environments, together with how they are working in practice, is discussed below.

The introduction of digital video (DV) camcorders represented a particularly new challenge to organisations within the TV production industry. DV camcorders are capable of producing pictures that can be used directly in broadcasting, for some types of programmes. The surprisingly low cost of this equipment meant that producers could make direct purchases. Once the BBC had begun to see the opportunities which this new technology could bring, they created a new team, DigiLab, to help others within the organisation become aware of the potential of new technologies like DV camcorders (Semple, 1999).

The DigiLab team was given a brief of '. . . *looking at consumer convergent, low-cost technology, to assess its functionality and potential usefulness and then make as many people as possible aware of its potential'*. The DigiLab team have created a relaxed environment where people from different parts of the organisation can come together with colleagues to experiment with new technologies and discuss its capabilities, in a non-pressured way. DigiLab is a unique learning environment that provides what the Head of Knowledge Management refers to as the organisational spaces between departments within which real learning can take place.

Users of facilities with DigiLab come from all parts of the organisation, including programme makers, IT specialists, producers, as well as training and development practitioners.

Even those who do not make direct use of this type of technology in their work have an opportunity to learn about its capabilities, in this way they have some of the language and terminology in order to be able to participate in general discussions about digital technologies. This is important given that participation in the knowledge-economy is very much dependent upon having a common language base.

It was the recognition of the importance of technology and innovation to the future success of The Post Office, that was the driver behind the launch of the Innovation Lab[9]. This is a purpose-built learning environment, located within The Post Office's Management Training Centre. It provides managers with a different type of learning environment, away from their everyday workplace. Here managers can experience and interact first-hand with new technologies and also discuss the impact of these new technologies on the business with colleagues.

The Innovation Lab has three linked areas: an experiential area where managers can see and experiment with new technologies; a development area where prototype technologies can be built with the help of strategic technology partners and finally a creativity space, known as the Creativity Zone.

Within the Creativity Zone managers have access to networked computers, supported by various groupware products, a range of creativity tools and toys, as well as several business planning tools to help them work through real-life business problems. There are experienced facilitators on hand to help managers make the best use of all of the different tools and products available. A particular feature of the Creativity Zone is its floor-to-ceiling whiteboard walls. Individuals can use these to note their ideas, or re-draw a problem, at any time while working within the Creativity Zone.

As part of my own learning I took advantage of the opportunity to experience the learning facilities within the Creativity Zone, together with a group of colleagues brought together by The Centre for Leadership in Creativity. We used our half-day session to explore the topic of '*What are the blocks to creativity within organisations?*'. We found that the groupware enabled us quickly to capture individual thoughts about this topic, and for these to be swiftly collated and sorted with those of others. This enabled us to identify one or two key themes that we were able to explore further using some of the other facilities within the Creativity Zone, including the whiteboard walls, as well as the 'thought provoking toys' provided by the facilitators. We found the environment very thought provoking and stimulating. It also helped to surface and build-on ideas in a non-threatening and collaborative way.

Building a coaching culture

As discussed earlier in this book, the role of managers has changed significantly in recent years. Managers are increasingly being expected to take on the role of facilitator and coach, helping to create a climate within which individuals and teams perform at their optimum, rather than necessarily being seen as 'subject experts' themselves. In many organisations, coaching has become an essential management skill and forms part of the core development for managers.

Through coaching, individuals develop job-specific skills, as well as skills in learning how to learn. In the coaching relationship individuals can learn and refine many of the essential skills required for operating in a knowledge-enabled culture. These include questioning skills, what-if type thinking, problem-solving, creative thinking, as well as assessing and managing risk-taking. The coaching relationship can also provide an opportunity to help individuals develop their ability as reflective practitioners.

Reflection, as a way of learning, is again not a new phenomenon. It is a process that has been used by many eminent philosophers and critical thinkers. Sadly, despite its link with learning, very few organisations use the reflective practitioner model as a way of learning. Some management writers (Daudlin, 2000), think that this is because organisations place a higher value on action rather than reflection; a situation that is reinforced through the adoption of short-term management rewards and incentives. That said it seems that some of the larger organisations in the USA, according to Daudlin, such as Motorola and Hewlett-Packard, are starting to incorporate the reflective practitioner philosophy into their management development programmes.

Daudlin has introduced tools and learning interventions to facilitate learning through reflection among managers within her own organisation, the Polaroid Corporation. One tool, The Reflective Workbook, outlines the different stages in the reflection process: articulation of a problem; analysis of the problem; formulation and testing of a tentative theory to explain the problem and deciding on what action to take to address the problem. The tool also incorporates the use of learning logs, as a way of capturing an individual's random thoughts about the learning that occurs throughout their day-to-day work. Individuals can use this tool on their own, with the help of a coach, or as part of a more formal learning process with a community of fellow learners. One of the benefits of learning with a community of learners, as we shall see in the next chapter, can open up the learning terrain, providing the opportunity to learn from other people's knowledge.

One of my colleagues, David Lines, suggests that as practitioners we can add value by helping people find different ways of reflecting. Often in the reflective process individuals start with questions like What did I do wrong? or Where did I go wrong? A different way of reflecting would be to start asking questions about the situation the person and/or team find themselves in. Where are we? Where did we intend to get to? Where did we actually get to? How do we feel about that? What are the implications?

I was reminded of the importance of reflection in the learning process when I met with the head of a Montessori school in London to talk about the Montessori approach to learning. From this discussion I learnt that the underlying principles behind the Montessori approach include:

- Observation – in the first few days when a new child joins the nursery the teacher simply observes the child's behaviour to get a sense of what interests them most and what areas they are naturally drawn to, rather than directing the child into a particular activity. From there, the teacher then knows where best to channel his/her energy to help the child's learning.
- Adopting a holistic approach – of the child itself and also the child within its learning environment.
- Helping children become reflective practitioners – i.e. working out for themselves why one way of doing something brings a different result than another.
- Helping children develop their identity and self-esteem – this is crucial if a child is to engage in learning in the future.

Some questions that comes to mind for me then are: How could we transfer this type of thinking into the workplace? and How can HR help managers develop their ability of helping people to learn?

The 'softer' side of knowledge management – linking knowledge management and career development Insights from KPMG

Organisational background

KPMG is the global advisory firm whose purpose is to turn knowledge into value for the benefit of its clients, its people and its communities.

The firm prides itself on its reputation for being a respected professional service provider, something which it acknowledges can only be achieved through the quality and commitment of its people. This in turn requires the firm to demonstrate commitment to its staff by creating an environment within which they feel fulfilled and able to develop and grow and build the capabilities to operate within a knowledge business.

Building blocks in the firm's knowledge management approach

Defining its values

In 1998, KPMG defined its three global values: Clients, People and Knowledge. As a means of accelerating the adoption of the global values, the UK firm developed its Values Charter to explain what the values meant in terms of people's behaviour. The Charter included the following:

- We will respect all of our people and the contribution they make to the firm.
- We will listen to and aim to understand alternative perspectives.
- We will openly and proactively share knowledge.
- We will respect our own and our people's need to balance personal and business lives.
- We will support our leaders, encourage our peers and develop our people.

In terms of the implementation of these values within the UK one of the ways in which the firm has proceeded is by using these as a base for development, the partner admission process and for assessment (and hence reward). Since the introduction of the Values Charter the firm within the UK has been working on a number of changes to help bring these values alive, to ensure that they inform and become embedded in day-to-day practice.

The firm has continued to revise its practices to reflect its values, particularly those relating to knowledge creation and sharing. Knowledge is seen as a highly valuable asset within the firm and all staff are expected to apply and share their knowledge. It is for this reason that there has been a strong emphasis on developing a coaching culture. One of the firm's aspirations is to facilitate individuals' learning, and hence build their knowledge assets, through encouraging more movement around the firm. Thus a link is being made between career development and knowledge management.

Some of the initiatives introduced to help equip individuals with the skills and tools needed for knowledge sharing, as well as to manage their own learning and development, are set out below.

Culture change

To succeed in business today the firm recognises that it needs to offer a more responsive and flexible service to clients, but at the same time provide a fulfilling environment for its people, and pay attention to its longer-term future and overall sustainability.

Early in 2001, the UK firm launched 'darwin', its most significant culture change programme. The name for this culture change programme was chosen carefully to encapsulate the themes of evolution, growth and sustainability. The ideas arising from 'darwin' have their origins in complexity theory and the principle of self-organising systems. The firm has focused on five strategic levers for change:

- *Thought capital* – the ability for ideas to surface and for intellectual capital to circulate freely around the firm. This is a key element in the firm's knowledge management approach.
- *Mindset* – having an ability to deal with complexity, being comfortable with ambiguity and having the courage to act despite uncertainty.
- *Diversity* – to provide a richer tapestry of varied approaches and perspectives to business problems.
- *Coaching culture* – a quality of helpfulness demonstrated in the way people relate to one another and the way the firm's systems and processes work.
- *Joined up accountability* – having the right emphasis on controls while providing the freedom for people to experiment and develop, in consultation with others.

The way in which 'darwin' was designed, planned and launched represents a new approach for the firm. The project has been managed by a 'nerve centre' consisting of a changing core group, drawn from different parts of the firm, thus very much taking a multi-disciplinary team approach. But it is the way in which the firm chose to communicate this culture change programme to its people that marks a significant cultural shift. Instead of using traditional communications approaches e.g. powerpoint presentations, or memos, to launch the culture change programme, a more creative and open communications approach was adopted.

Over a four-day period everyone in the firm had an opportunity to observe video streamed clips of pre-filmed discussions at their desktops. These discussions were very similar in style to those in the television programme 'Big Brother' and involved colleagues discussing a topic linked to each of the five strategic change levers. Staff who participated in these discussions were encouraged to be as open as possible. The series of videos were named Galapagos. They gave everyone in the firm the opportunity to observe colleagues dealing with significant cultural change issues in real time.

One of these topics was about how individuals manage their career within the firm, including the difficulties they encounter. Those participating in the discussion exchanged their own career stories, as well as those of colleagues. The stories included: the difficulties encountered when trying to make lateral career moves within the firm; the difficulties encountered by those who want to work more flexibly, such as home-working, or working part-time; the tensions experienced by support workers, such as secretaries, who want to broaden their career opportunities, as well as the experience of colleagues who have left to go and work for other consultancies. Each of these discussions surfaced valuable insights into some of the existing restraining factors experienced by individuals when managing their own careers, thus providing insights into where change is required.

Supporting career development

Individuals within the firm have always been encouraged and supported with managing their own careers. An additional resource, introduced in the late 1990s, to help individuals manage their own career was the career broker service (see Holbeche, 1999).

One of the key strands emerging from 'darwin' relates to people and career development. A key theme of the people and career development work is that of helping individuals manage their careers within a broader eco-system. Here the firm is aspiring to help its people learn and grow through developing a career that involves moving around its eco-system. In this way individuals will be supported to develop a successful career within a knowledge business.

In essence the firm is adopting a much more grown-up stance on career development, even to the point of acknowledging that it may be appropriate for some individuals to look outside the firm for a career move, at some point in their career. Equally it may be appropriate for an individual, who has made a career move outside, to return to the firm at a future point in time too. In career terms a stronger emphasis is being placed on valuing diversity, adopting modern ways of working, facilitating relationship building, as well as the development of skills through building a coaching culture.

The firm recognises the learning opportunities that can occur through involvement in community programmes and actively encourages its people to participate in its community involvement programmes, which have five themes: mentoring, leadership, enterprise, employability and team building. The 'Community Bank' programme enables employees to allocate half a day a month to various community projects. During 2001, around 1,500 people within the firm participated in one or more community projects (KMPG UK Annual Report, 2001). There is also the opportunity for some people to work on more substantial projects within a community organisation.

Developing a coaching culture

Coaching is seen as one of the firm's strategic change levers and hence an integral part of its culture, i.e. the way in which individuals work with, and learn with and from each other. The firm stresses that everyone in the firm has a right to expect coaching from others and that its people have a responsibility to provide coaching to others when requested.

There are two key aspects to the coaching culture being developed within the firm. First, in terms of the way in which individuals operate and relate to one another, for example:

- having a leadership style which helps individuals to realise their full potential;
- encouraging and enabling coaching and mentoring processes;
- encouraging and supporting an environment where people feel motivated and encouraged and receive timely and constructive feedback;
- continuing to enhance the quality of our performance management processes.

Second, in terms of accessibility and availability of more structured help, for example:

- the accessibility of coaching following specific development activities;
- having learning and knowledge management tools which provide intelligent information and help people to make the right decisions.

The firm has invested, and is continuing to invest, in a number of resources to help build a coaching culture. These include: access to internal and external coaches to support personal development; skills training to develop the skills used in a coaching relationship; leadership support for coaching; information and access to appropriate coaching support through the firm's people portal (*MyLife@KPMG*), as well as learning and development resources and contacts.

In addition there are a number of structured development processes that can lead to a specific coaching need. For example: 360-degree feedback; performance management review; senior management development programme; senior management assessment centre and the Director and Partner Panel Interview. Guidance on how to gain access to coaching support following any of these development processes is again available via the firm's people portal.

The Nerve Centre, set up as part of 'darwin', regularly tracks initiatives and progress being made in different parts of the firm on its coaching journey. Its role is one of identifying and connecting different players within the firm so that lessons learnt can be shared across the firm.

Bridging the gap between formal learning and workplace learning – The rise of corporate universities

The Chief Executive of the Japanese organisation the Kao Corporation insists that '. . . *learning is a frame of mind, a daily matter*'. He refers to the KAO Corporation as '. . . *an educational institution*', rather than an organisation. Does this sound like your organisation?

Over the past decade an increasing number of corporate universities have been established. A FT Survey[10] indicates that over the past decade the number of corporate universities in America has increased from 400 to 1,600. These universities are bringing together traditional bricks and mortar learning facilities, with newer online learning facilities. The survey cites examples of IBM Learning Services and the Swiss-Swedish company ABB, which has recently launched its Academy. There are some who believe that corporate universities are the solution to encouraging life-long learning in organisations. On the one hand organisations are realising that learning is key to their competitive edge, and individuals are realising that their initial qualifications are no longer enough to see them through their entire work career.

Formal learning can often provide a bridge for individuals who choose to make a career change (see Chapter 7).

What these new educational institutions offer, unlike traditional universities, is 'know why' – the opportunity for top managers to share information on where the organisation is going, and also discuss the issues and challenges that the organisation is likely to face on the journey. As ABB is in the process of transforming itself from a heavy engineering company into an agile knowledge-based company, the Chief Executive's vision for the ABB Academy is a forum where the organisation's 165,000 strong workforce can join together to share ideas. The Academy also addresses feedback from employees about their needs to help them manage better during this change process. This includes a forum where employees can get strategic messages directly from top management, have opportunities to build networks with peers and also have access to tools, ideas and project management techniques to help them manage better.

In this country, Anglian Water for example, has created a University of Water as an integral component of its knowledge management strategy. The vision behind the launch of the University of Water was to create a learning environment that would enable the creation and dissemination of knowledge about sustainable water management. The University operates on a federal structure, with a Learning Council advising on what format the learning should take across the Group. Each operating company is then responsible for setting up its own learning communities. To ensure this happens, each business appoints its own learning champion.

In 1994, the company set up a number of networks designed to exchange knowledge and best practice across the group. These included executive management networks, technology networks and learning networks. This was followed in 1996 by knowledge network colleges covering areas like creativity, open learning and international learning. These colleges operated horizontally, thus ensuring cross-company knowledge sharing. In 1997, the structure of the university was developed again when four new knowledge faculties were established. These were headed up by senior directors. These faculties reflect the knowledge capabilities that the organisation identified as being crucial for success. These include project management, mentoring, treatment technology and pipeline technology.

Anglian Water has also developed a reciprocal learning approach with several of the leading technology universities. Anglian Water employees lecture on the academic courses and students are encouraged to make visits to Anglian Water sites to get real-life experience. In addition, the company sponsors research projects and studentships, in this way benefiting first-hand from the knowledge developed by these academic institutions.

BAe is another UK company that has introduced a corporate university: a decision that was taken to ensure that all training was linked to the organisation's strategic plan. Its overall aim is to bring education, knowledge and training for its entire workforce into the workplace. In addition to enhancing its learning facilities, the BAe corporate university has its role in helping to spread best practice and ensuring that the organisation is making the most of its own research capabilities. The organisation has entered into a partnership arrangement with a number of academic institutions to help deliver the range of courses that it is looking for: masters programmes, leadership development programmes, as well as modern apprenticeship programmes.

Learning from the outside world

To what extent is your organisation open to learning from the experience of other organisations, even where there may not seem natural synergies?

Benchmarking activities

Many companies see benchmarking as a way of building their knowledge base and enhancing their overall level of performance, not just as a metrics and measurement activity. It is a way of moving from 'doing more of the same' to doing something better, even doing different things. Benchmarking is a discovery and learning process. It involves taking a systematic look outside your own industry, or sector, in search of practices that occur elsewhere, and questioning why and how these practices could be applied within your own organisation. Benchmarking can also be used as a way of helping the organisation stay ahead of its competitors – recognising that no matter how good you are there is always room for improvement.

Some of the steps in carrying out a successful benchmarking activity include:

- Identify an area of the business that requires improvement – this could be a business process or an HR process.
- Identify a network of people willing to share information on this process – this could be personal contacts, external consultancies, customers, strategic partners and business schools. Other sources of information include business libraries, company reports, business databases and websites and research companies.

- Make direct site visits – this enables you to gather data about actual practice, but also to explore lessons learnt on the journey. Both sorts of data are important for developing your own organisation.
- Develop a metric for assessing best practice – here what you are looking for is a way of quantifying best practice in the area that you are investigating. This may require working with business colleagues to identify and agree on performance criteria which are appropriate for your organisation in its current state.

Learning directly from specialists in other organisations

'Borrowing' is one of the five strategies for building employee competence (which includes knowledge) advocated by Dave Ulrich (2000). One innovative practice, adopted by some organisations is that of finding ways of learning from companies in totally different business areas[11]. Some examples include:

British Airways, for example, often pay for a day of a specialist's time from a different field in order to help them get a new perspective on operational problems. On one occasion, faced with the problem of how to stop grease trails developing along the floor-covering on the aircraft's galleys, an expert on the lay-out and equipping of surgical theatres was invited to come and help them work through a solution to this problem.

A group of cardiac surgeons at Great Ormond Street Hospital concerned about the dangers involved when an infant is handed over from Surgery to Intensive Care, because of having to disconnect and reconnect feeding lines, asked MacLaren, the Formula One racing company, to help them because of their expertise in pit stops!

A variation of this practice comes from the experience of Matsushita when they were designing a new home bread-making machine (Nonaka, 1998). When the product developers were experiencing difficulties getting the new machine to knead the dough in the way that they wanted, a member of the design team went to work alongside an expert bread-maker in a top international hotel. After observing how this expert bread-maker set about kneading dough, the designer then transferred this knowledge to the design of the electronic home bread-making machine.

Volunteering

Despite continuous change, some organisations struggle to provide the sort of development opportunities that individuals need to develop their skills, knowledge and behaviours. One solution to this intractable problem, and one that seems to be gaining momentum, is providing developmental opportunities through volunteering to work on community-based projects.

Companies like Barclays Bank and Abbey National operate a 'Matched Time Scheme' scheme whereby the company matches the amount of personal time that individuals are prepared to give up to work on community projects[12]. The Boots Company has taken their volunteering scheme one step further, through the introduction of a national qualification – Certificate of Recognition as a Community Associate – which recognises volunteering activities in company time. Through the certification process individuals and line managers have a means of recognising and valuing the skills and behaviours developed through volunteering.

There are a number of benefits of volunteering from a knowledge management perspective (Evans, 2002).

At the individual level:
- Exposure to different cultures and different ways of working, thus helping individuals see things from a different perspective.
- An opportunity to apply existing skills in new environments. While this may not seem particularly developmental, applying existing skills to a new area can help individuals re-visit their assumptions about why things are done in a certain way within their own organisation. This can then lead to suggestions for improved practices back within the workplace.
- An opportunity to stimulate innovative thinking and learning in unfamiliar territories.
- For some, an opportunity to 'try out' more senior roles before an internal career move.

At the organisational level:
- Enhanced opportunities for knowledge building by learning from the experience of other businesses.
- Used as part of a strategic approach to development, volunteering can lead to enhanced skill-sets e.g. strategic thinking, project management, team working, creative thinking, influencing and negotiating. It can also provide important 'out of the box' developmental experiences for certain groups of employees. The importance of volunteering then, from a learning and development perspective, should not be underestimated.
- More motivated, energised and committed employees.

One final thought about the dangers of not being open to learning from the outside world comes from the lessons learnt from the Space Shuttle Challenger project.

Lessons from the Space Shuttle Challenger Project
(*Source:* John Bank, 1999)

The disastrous launch of the Space Shuttle Challenger on 28 January 1986 is attributed, in part, to the homogeneous company culture of the decision-makers – male engineers with identical engineering backgrounds and similar personality profiles. The NASA managers were so hell-bent on reaching their objectives that they ignored safety warnings from outside contractors Rockwell (about ice on the launch pad) and from Morton Thiokol (about the cold temperature and rubber O-rings) and their own engineers who opposed the launch.

Because the NASA managers were too similar in type and backgrounds they easily developed a 'group think' mentality and a management style that let programme objectives override good judgment. Since research indicates that individuals cannot be made to change their management profile drastically in the long run, the way to change the aggregate profile of NASA managers is to bring in a small but significant number of managers from the outside, who would add the desired diversity to the team.

Does this example have any resonance with the way people behave in your organisation?

Where does 'group think' get in the way of your organisation moving forward?

What success have you had in getting others to value the knowledge that can be gained from outsiders?

How can you ensure that those who think and act differently to others are heard and feel valued?

So what can HR do to help their organisations benefit from learning through everyday practice? Some options to consider include:

- Review your training and development portfolio to identify whether it reflects the different approaches for maximising knowledge transfer discussed in this chapter.

- Re-educate managers on the importance and benefits of informal learning, providing them with options and examples.
- Offer to facilitate team meetings and project reviews to help teams focus on learning outcomes.
- Encourage and support managers who are prepared to trial new ways of working, such as cross-boundary team working.
- Introduce a knowledge exchange slot at your own team meetings then, once embedded and benefits realised, share the lessons learnt with others in the organisation.

Summary

With change being the norm in today's business world there is an increasing interest in developing the organisation's ability to learn. Facilitating learning and change maps directly on to HR's core competencies, however, what is now needed is for HR to re-educate others, possibly even themselves, on what is meant by learning and how best to facilitate learning in the knowledge era. This chapter has discussed how, for organisations to enhance their knowledge base, they need to select their learning approaches carefully, thereby maximising the opportunities for knowledge creation and transfer.

Increasingly organisations are looking for ways of creating new learning spaces, as well as maximising opportunities for learning in everyday practice through making more use of cross-boundary team working, learning through the project management cycle, facilitating learning through different working spaces, building environments that enable experimentation and play, as well as developing a coaching culture.

Notes

1. Weiner E., Global Trends in the Way That Work and Jobs are Organised. International Association of Career Management Professionals (IACMP) 2000 Global Conference, Brighton, 6–9 July 2000.
2. Survey findings reported in C. Pearce (ed.), *The Effective Director: The Essential Guide to Director & Board Level Development*. Kogan Page Limited. 2001.
3. Survey: 12 million British workers did not receive any training in the last year. www.knowledgepool.com/news/press/britain2002
4. Snowden, D., Storytelling: an old skill in a new context. Unicom Seminar. May 2000.

5. White, D., Focusing on the value of teamwork. *The Guardian*, Saturday 27 March 1999.

6. Citizen First. Putting citizens first in Lewisham. A 'Best Value' strategic review. Lewisham Council – Directorate for Resources. 2000.

7. Giving staff rooms for improvement. Management Section. *The Guardian*, Saturday 9 May 1998.

8. Vischer, J., Will This Open Space Work? *Harvard Business Review*. May-June 1999.

9. Wright, H., *Free to be Creative. Harnessing Technology Yearbook 1998/1999*. Post Office Research Group.

10. Companies get bitten by the learning bug. www.ft.com.ftsurveys/spa.htm

11. J. Whatmore, *Ideas via Intermediaries*. The Centre for Leadership in Creativity.

12. See *www.volunteering.org.uk*

Note: This chapter has been developed from articles produced by the author for Croner.CCH, available as part of a subscription service to Croner.CCH British Personnel Management. The articles were: 'A fresh look at knowledge management', *CCH Personnel Management Newsletter*, Issue 85, 26 October 2001 and New approaches to learning in the knowledge economy', *CCH Personnel Management Newsletter*, Issue 59, 15 August 2000.

7

Understanding the motivation for learning amongst knowledge workers

The previous chapter looked at the learning component of a knowledge-centric culture, particularly the importance of organisations re-visiting the theory and practice of learning in today's knowledge-intensive world. Learning is crucial if organisations, and indeed individuals, are to address the issues of obsolescence and avoid the phenomenon of 'Educated Incapacity', also discussed in the previous chapter.

This chapter is concerned with the motivational aspects of learning, particularly the motivation for learning amongst knowledge workers. It is based on the findings from some of my own research conducted among independent HR professionals (Evans, 2001).

Motivational factors associated with learning

Cross (1981), suggests that participation in a learning activity, whether formal or otherwise, is the result of a chain of reactions, linked to an individual's evaluation of where he or she is at in relation to their environment. Some of the factors that influence voluntary participation in learning among adults include: an individual's self-view; their attitude towards learning, based upon their previous experiences of learning; personal goals and expectations; opportunities and barriers to learning, as well as access to information about what learning opportunities exist.

An alternative view of the motivation for learning, particularly amongst knowledge workers, is that their learning is fuelled by the need to manage the issue of obsolescence. Addressing the issue of obsolescence, according to some writers, means that professionals should spend around 20 per cent of their working time learning about recent developments in their field; a big commitment than in terms of people's time.

In my own research I discovered a number of drivers for learning amongst independent HR professionals. These fell into two main categories:

'Self-identified' learning needs – these were learning needs that surfaced either during the process of critical reflection (either on their own, or facilitated by others), or some form of strategic planning for their future career, or direct comparison of their own knowledge relative to that of other professionals in a similar situation.

'Other identified' learning needs – this included learning linked to meeting the legal requirements of running a small business, and clients' expectations regarding the level of formal qualifications that independent consultants should have.

One particularly interesting finding from my research was how learning had become such an integral part of these individuals' lives; work and learning are blended in together, rather than being compartmentalised. Indeed personal growth was one of their four key career success criteria. This manifested itself in behaviours such as 'In any situation I try and get out of it what I can learn' and 'I no longer think anymore in terms of this is the career for me. I do have a purpose though. To me the jobs that I do are stepping stones towards my development.'

Closely related to the success criterion of personal growth, was that of being free to choose enjoyable and challenging work. For some individuals there was a strong overlap in the interests between their work and non-work activities projects/activities. This often meant that the line between what individuals considered as work and non-work was somewhat grey.

How independent HR professionals manage their learning

My research identified that the learning strategies of independent HR professionals involved six distinct approaches, many of which fall into the category of informal learning.

Learning with and from other professionals through specific work assignments

Many of these individuals reported how working alongside other professionals was an important source of learning for them. Opportunities for learning in this way occurred either by direct collaboration with others in their network, or through their work as an Associate.

Some explained how, having worked mainly on their own for a number of years, they reached a point where they actively sought work that involved working closely with other professionals. One individual, for example, became an Associate Trainer for a public sector organisation where the training is delivered purely through Associates rather than in-house trainers. A key factor in taking up this Associate role was to minimize the effects of social isolation that he was beginning to experience, having worked largely on his own since becoming self-employed. However, he discovered that this work arrangement had benefits for his development too.

In this particular Associate arrangement trainers worked in pairs; an arrangement that provided opportunities for him to enhance his knowledge and skills as a trainer. This arose through the review process that he and fellow trainers conducted at the end of training programmes. In addition to reviewing the training programme to meet the formal evaluation process (as specified by the client), the trainers often allocate time to reviewing their own contribution and learning. As he explained, this work arrangement provides him with an incredible amount of learning, none of it formal, but instead facilitated by the informal personal contract between himself and fellow professionals through the giving and receiving of feedback.

Learning by observing other professionals at work

The process of learning by observing 'experts in action', often referred to as the apprenticeship model in the knowledge management literature (see Bird, 1994), is an approach that several of these independents adopted as a valuable learning model. One individual, for example, developed the skills needed to work as a career counsellor by adopting what she described as the 'sitting next to Nellie approach'. The learning process involved working alongside an experienced counsellor in a firm of careers counsellors, learning first hand from this 'subject expert' (who in this case was also one of her clients).

However, in her case the 'sitting next to Nellie' approach had mutual benefits for both parties. She was able to build the knowledge needed to develop a new area of business. The client benefited too, as she was able to introduce the client to tools and techniques, developed in her earlier HR career. This again was part of the 'contracting'.

Where it wasn't possible to learn directly through observing other professionals at work some of these individuals learnt through setting up a peer-coaching relationship, thus getting others to help them with the process of critical reflection.

Learning with and from other professionals through networking

Several of the independents that participated in the research reported that one way in which they build their Knowledge Assets in a cost-effective way is through participating in a learning set. The learning set model, similar to Revan's Action Learning Model, involves a group of people contracting with other set members to provide support and challenge for each other's personal develop-ment. Participation in a learning set helps individuals prioritise their learning needs, review the progress being made, as well as gain support and challenge from others in the set on how to address the issues encountered with their learning plan. One individual described the benefits of participating in this learning process as '*It helps me focus more and prioritise things [to do with learning] . . . having something arranged makes me more con-scious of the things I said I was going to work on. It acts as a kick, so I actually get something done.*'

Another individual reported several benefits for him of this particular learning approach. First, listening to others in the set talking about their learning experiences helps him think more objectively about his own development, particularly the gaps that he needs to consider addressing. Second, it helps him take a longer-term view of his career, and what his future learning needs might be; something that he finds difficult to do on his own.

However, in order to participate in this particular learning approach, individuals recognised that they needed to have built up the right contacts in their networks. They referred to the importance of having relationships based on trust, as being an important enabler for this type of learning.

Learning through 'explicit' knowledge-generating activities

A number of individuals reported how reading professional journals and management books, as well as attending conferences, provided valuable learning resources, for example:

At the moment I am not terribly strong on negotiating skills and I am going to be doing a course on this quite soon, so this afternoon I am off to the bookshop to buy some books on negotiating. I spend at least a £100 a month on books (Female, self-employed for 7 years).

I do a lot of reading. I probably read a book every couple of days. I have got a study with about 4000 books in it, but that doesn't stop me buying more (Male, self-employed for 5 years).

I like new ideas and I do a lot of reading as a way of getting new ideas. I do tend to flit about a bit though. I read something and I think that sounds interesting, but then I move on to something else (Female, self-employed for 3 years).

Despite the amount that individuals invest in these particular learning resources, several reported that they do not invest as much in developing their knowledge through reading professional journals and management books as they feel they should. Here then we have an example of one of the other tensions that individuals can experience when building their knowledge assets, that of having easy access to key learning resources, such as professional journals and management books. Some rely on the goodwill of others in their network to point them in the direction of articles and other learning materials that they feel may be of interest to them. However, this goodwill takes time to nurture and it also requires a reciprocal arrangement, something that can be a drain on individuals' time.

Learning through non-work-related projects/activities

Some individuals used their non-work-related interests as opportunities to develop their knowledge. One individual who participated in the research spoke of how his role as Chair of Governors at his children's school had been a significant source of learning for him. His learning came from applying his existing knowledge about recruitment, mentoring and managing people, to a new contextual environment.

Learning through critical reflection

Learning through critical reflection was an important source of learning for many of the people who participated in my research. One individual, for example, spoke of '*A lot of it [what I need to know] I am picking up as I go along. Learning for me is about doing it for myself, reading about it, deciding what is important and trying things out . . . all you need is a strategy for trying things out and working out where you are going wrong.*' Another individual had developed his training style by applying Kolb's 'learning cycle' so taking feedback from others, reflecting on this, changing his style of delivery and then reflecting further on the impact of the changes made.

Another individual reported that a pattern that he has noticed about his own learning, since becoming independent, is that whenever he wants to learn something new he seeks client work in the area that he wants to learn about. However, not all of the individuals in my research adopted this same self-confident approach. Two of the women, for example, reported how they only sought work that was within their existing capabilities, as they worked on the assumption that clients expect them to 'turn up with the knowledge'. One pointed out how holding on to this assumption causes her difficulties at times, as it means that she doesn't always get work that is stretching enough.

Despite making use of these six different informal learning approaches formal learning, i.e. learning that leads to some form of qualification, had also played an important role in these individuals' lives at strategic points.

Overall their level of educational achievement was high. Most had a first degree and around half (fourteen out of the twenty-six) had a higher degree too. Ten were participating in some form of formal learning activity at the time when I was carrying out the research. This included studying for a degree, Masters or PhD. Indeed for eight of these individuals it was their formal learning career that had provided a bridge between their earlier work career (which often hadn't been in Human Resources) and their independent career. Their experience is consistent with the view among educationalists that those individuals with the largest capital investment in learning, because of their previous learning experiences, are likely to be the biggest purchasers of learning in the future (Edwards, 1993).

What broader lessons can be drawn from this piece of research?

First, the research findings reinforce the point discussed in the previous chapter about the many opportunities for learning that occur naturally within the workplace, if only individuals could see them and be prepared to take them up. Of course one of the big differences between these independent knowledge workers, and those following traditional careers within organisations, is that they are totally self-managing. This means that they are able to make decisions about how to apportion their time, between work and learning, without having first to agree this with someone else.

Their decision about what work to take on can be based around expected opportunities for learning and growth. How often do employees get to make similar decisions?

Second, we have seen further evidence to support the benefits of volunteering from a knowledge management perspective, discussed in Chapter 6.

Third, networking is crucial for the learning process. These independent professionals are often very dependent on others in their network to help them manage their learning; trust is a critical ingredient of the relationships that they form.

But how does the learning experiences of independent HR professionals map against that of knowledge workers within organisations? Research by John Whatmore, from the Centre for Leadership In Creativity[1], has surfaced a number of tensions encountered by trainers when working with knowledge workers, such as scientists and technologists. These are shown below.

Learning styles of scientists and technologists and the issues and opportunities trainers can encounter

- They prefer to learn their leadership skills directly from other leaders/managers, rather than go on training courses. But they also tend to expect leadership to be mastered like other intellectual subjects – by reading the latest material and discussing and/or arguing with the latest experts.
- They crucify anyone who is intellectually inferior and play games to demonstrate their intellectual capabilities.
- They make excuses just before training courses about why they cannot attend.
- Topics associated with intellectual property are important to them.
- They prefer to listen to outsiders than insiders and to those whom they respect, or whom they regard as having wider experience.
- They value and seek learning events that are exclusive.
- They are more adept with facts and theories than with people and feelings.
- They like focus and structure and like being given articles to read.
- They do not like flowery, waffley, or airy-fairy approaches (such as music or meditation), or apparently irrelevant happenings (e.g. outward bound courses).

Both of these pieces of research help to build better insights into what motivates knowledge workers, insights which can then be used, as Wenger points out, to create the conditions within which learning can really take place.

Drucker has suggested that the behaviour of knowledge workers resembles more that of volunteers than employees, given their strong belief in what they do. A critical task for leaders then, according to Drucker, is to maintain the sense of purpose that keeps knowledge workers alive.

Summary

This chapter has set out some of the motivational factors associated with learning amongst knowledge workers, drawn from my own research into the learning approaches adopted by independent HR professionals. It has also discussed the different learning strategies that these independent professionals adopt. Informal learning, for a number of reasons, is often their more preferred learning approach. This includes: learning by observing other professionals at work; learning with and through other professionals through networking; learning through 'explicit' knowledge-generating activities; learning through non-work-related activities, as well as learning through critical reflection.

Pause for reflection

- To what extent does the research discussed in this chapter map onto your own personal learning experience? What is your own preferred learning style and strategy?
- Do you think that others in the organisation are aware of the benefits of informal learning? How might you use these research findings to help educate colleagues?
- Can you identify with any of the issues that trainers can encounter when working with scientists and technologists, outlined in this chapter? If so, how do you deal with these?
- What support does your organisation provide to help knowledge workers maintain the 'sense of purpose' that Drucker argues is crucial for them to be fully engaged?

Note

1. Further details about The Centre for Leadership in Creativity can be obtained by e-mail from *john.whatmore@btinternet.com*

8

Working and learning in Communities of Practice[1]

In the days before formal education learning came not from teachers or textbooks, but from one's social networks.
(Daniel Pink, author of Free Agent Nation)

Re-visiting assumptions about learning

The need for organisations to adapt and change in today's ever-changing and complex business world has led to a focus on continuous learning. 'We need to become better at learning' and 'We need to learn faster than our competitors' are some of the common mantras among today's business leaders.

But what do these business leaders understand learning to be? What assumptions do they, and indeed HR practitioners, hold about learning? Often when organisations refer to learning they have a narrow view of learning, one where learning is perceived as an individual process, which occurs through teaching in locations held away from the workplace.

---

[1] I am indebted to Elizabeth Lank, independent consultant, and previously head of ICL's Mobilising Knowledge Programme, for helping me develop this chapter by sharing her experience of building and supporting Communities of Practice within organisations.

Etienne Wenger (1998), a leading researcher and writer in the field of learning, believes that this is an assumption that many institutions hold about learning. It is for this reason, Wenger argues, that many of us find learning irrelevant and boring, and end up believing that it is something that we are not cut out for.

So is there an alternative way of thinking about learning? Wenger argues that there is. He has developed a theory of learning, which he refers to as a social theory of learning, based on the assumptions that (a) learning is as much a part of human nature as eating and sleeping and (b) learning occurs naturally through our active participation in the practices of different social communities.

Wenger points out that communities exist naturally within the workplace and, over time, these communities develop and shape their own practices. In his book, *Communities of Practice*, Wenger illustrates this point through a vignette on the lives of individuals in the Claims Department of a large medical insurance company. He refers to the Claims Department as being a natural community of practice, as:

- Individuals share the same environmental conditions.
- They also share the same assumptions about work, its good and bad points.
- Members collude, conspire and conform to make the Claims Department what it is.
- Individuals within the community make their job possible by inventing and maintaining ways of squaring institutional demands with the shifting realities of their work.
- Individuals operate within a communal memory that enables them to do their job without having to know everything.
- Newcomers are helped to join the community.
- Collectively they make their job liveable by creating an environment where the monotonous nature of their jobs is woven into the rituals, customs, events and dreams of community life.
- They have a developed a practice – a way of doing things and getting things done – that is set within a historical and social context, and which gives structure and meaning to what is done.

Engaging in practice, Wenger argues, involves the whole person – both acting and knowing – it involves doing, working out relationships, inventing processes, resolving conflicts and producing artefacts.

The social perspective on learning encompasses the principles shown in Table 8.1

Table 8.1: Principles associated with adopting a social perspective of learning (source: Wenger, 1998)

Principles relating to a social perspective on learning	Description
Learning is inherent in human nature	Learning is integral to our lives, not a separate activity.
Learning is the ability to create new meaning	Involves the whole person, and shouldn't be reduced to pure mechanics. Links knowing and learning and the processes by which competence is developed.
Learning creates emergent structures	Requires structures for continuity but sufficient discontinuities for meanings to be renegotiated.
Learning is experiential and social	Involves our own experience as well as the competencies within learning communities.
Learning constitutes trajectories of participation	Builds personal histories, connecting an individual's past and future. Practice involves shared learning.
Learning is about engagement	Requires opportunities actively to contribute (i.e. by adding value) to learning communities and make creative use of learning repertoires.
Learning is about imagination	Requires reflection and orientation to place practices into a broader context.
Learning cannot be designed	Learning is a living experience – it cannot be designed, only designed for.

Communities and communities of practice – what are they?

Communities of practice, according to Wenger, are characterised by three dimensions: mutual engagement, joint enterprise and shared repertoire.

Mutual engagement

One of the characteristics that distinguishes a community of practice from a community, such as a local residential neighbourhood, is the level of coherence among community members brought about through the mutual engagement of members in achieving what needs to get done. So membership is grounded in practice. In addition, being included in what matters is an essential ingredient of participation in communities of practice. This may involve being included in routines and rituals, or it may mean simply being included in the particular memos, or the latest gossip. Work is another defining feature of a community of practice, it is not simply a case of building different social relationships. However, these do inevitably form through engagement in practice.

For mutual engagement to work, it doesn't mean that there needs to be homogeneity amongst community members – many communities are characterised by diversity and difference. Despite their differences, community members work together, exchanging ideas and opinions, and in doing so influence each other's understanding. In belonging to a community of practice, it is just as important to give and receive feedback thereby contributing to the overall knowledge of the community, as it is to know everything yourself.

From an organisational perspective it is important that communities have access to the resources that they need to help them learn what it is that they need to learn, so that they can refine and develop existing practices.

Joint enterprise

The second characteristic that distinguishes a community of practice is that of being part of a joint enterprise. The community invents its own practices in order to achieve its goals. While external forces can influence this process they have no direct power, as it is the community itself that negotiates its overall enterprise.

For communities to flourish not everyone in the community needs to see things in exactly the same way, or agree with the practices that occur within the community. Instead what is important is that practices are communally negotiated. Whatever the practices that community members are involved in they share a common purpose of making these real and workable. In addition there is mutual accountability for the practices within the community. This does not just relate to getting things done, but also about how things get done. For example, treating information and resources as something to be shared, being personable to others and not acting in a way that makes life more difficult for others.

Shared repertoire

The final characteristic that distinguishes a community of practice is the development of a shared repertoire. This includes routines, use of language, tools, ways of doing things, stories, symbols, actions or concepts that the community itself has developed, or taken on board, over time and thus have become part of its accepted practice. These repertoires become a resource for building shared meaning, which themselves are subject to discussion and negotiation.

What are the implications of this theoretical perspective on learning for organisations? Wenger argues that communities of practice represent fundamental elements of an architecture of learning in organisations, and are key to an organisation's competence, as well as the evolution of their competence. Communities of practice are different to other entities in organisations, e.g. groups, or project teams, since they: negotiate their own enterprise; they are self-forming and they shape their own boundaries. In addition they are driven by doing and learning, as opposed to institutional politics.

Their importance to organisations include:

- Negotiation of meaning – in communities of practice participation is rooted in a history of practice, which in itself is a resource for continuing the community history. This is vital for the negotiation of meaning, as every action is based upon a wealth of past interpretation and negotiation.
- Preservation and creation of knowledge – because communities are concerned with developing and sustaining meaning through shared practice, they are the ideal context for the acquisition and creation of new knowledge. Communities of practice are living entities that enable new generations of the community to develop the necessary competence to participate in practice. As Wenger points out, they are privileged entities for the acquisition of knowledge. However, as they are informal structures, they can easily be overlooked and thus their benefit, from an organisational learning perspective, can be overlooked too. Organisations then need to foster the communities that occur naturally within the workplace, or at the very least, work at removing the institutional practices that can get in their way. Equally, communities

provide a context for exploring new ideas and concepts that can lead to the creation of new knowledge. For this to occur the tension between the interaction between experience and competence needs to be maintained, in order to keep the community alive and alert.

- Spreading of information – the mutual accountability of participation in a community of practice necessitates the sharing of information among community members. Information sharing and communication are synonymous, as they are both tied in with the process of developing meaning. It is for this reason that communities, particularly in organisational contexts, cut across organisational boundaries thereby enabling knowledge to flow more freely. Wenger suggests that multi-membership of communities of practice ought to become a core organisational principle.

- Source of identity – Wenger points out that, as individuals, we function best when our knowing is steeped in an identity of participation. This occurs when we can contribute to shaping the community that we belong to. What Wenger is referring to here is the notion of engagement. Creative work, he says, relies on the personal investment and energy of community members, more so than institutionalised compliance. As communities straddle the boundary between work and learning in encouraging communities of practice, organisations are effectively enabling them to take responsibility for some aspects of organisational learning.

From theory to practice – the role of communities of practice in knowledge building

One of the ways in which organisations are enhancing their learning capabilities is by encouraging communities of practice (COPS). These are self-forming groups who have a shared interest in developing their knowledge and expertise about a particular topic area. The topic areas are wide-ranging, encompassing anything from new technologies to developing expertise in particular business processes and even HR processes.

An important feature of these learning communities is that they cut across organisational boundaries, allowing groups of individuals from different parts of an organisation to come together to work on common areas of interest and resolve common problems. Entry to these communities is limited solely by an individual's willingness and commitment to participate.

In many organisations, particularly technology-based or tech-nology-related organisations, it is not a question of do you support COPS but how many are there. A review of the knowledge management literature indicates that in some organisations there are hundreds of COPS operating at any one time. So what is their value? In an article in *Harvard Business Review*, Wenger and Snyder summarise the value that COPs can bring to organisations as:

- Driving an organisation's knowledge management strategy forward.
- Generating new lines of business.
- Solving problems faster – community members know who to ask for relevant information and they also know the right questions to ask.
- Transferring best practice – these forums are not just problem-solving groups. They are invaluable in spreading best practice across organisations.
- Assisting in the development of professional skills – the least experienced can learn from those who have more experience.
- Helping with the recruitment and retention of talent – the opportunity to become a member of a prestigious community of practice can provide a useful retention strategy.
- Self-perpetuating – new knowledge leads to new questions, which leads to further opportunities for knowledge creation.

When the conditions are right some of the benefits which COPS can bring in terms of organisational learning include faster problem-solving, opportunities for sharing best practice and development of professional skills (those with less experience can learn from those with more experience). In addition, they enable a self-perpetuating learning cycle to form – new knowledge leads to new questions, which leads to further experimentation and hence opportunities for new learning and new knowledge creation.

The use of COPs, however, as a vehicle for learning and change is not new. It was a technique used by hunter-gatherer cultures, and among craftsmen, as a way of passing on knowledge to the next generation. The learning that took place in these earlier forms of communities occurred through storytelling. Ralph Stacy (1993) argues that communities are essential learning mediums in situations where there is high ambiguity and uncertainty; situations where traditional procedures, rules and regulations are not appropriate. Through the community, however, individuals can engage in double-loop learning, where individuals challenge existing ways of doing things.

Conditions within which communities thrive:

- *Focus on problems that map directly onto individuals' work* – in this way community members can get an immediate pay-back for the time they invest. So instead of struggling with problems on their own, individuals can tap into the community's knowledge base to solve day-to-day operational problems.
- *Voluntary participation* – while Wenger and Snyder point out the importance of ensuring that participation in communities of practice should be voluntary, some of the examples they draw on are from organisations where individuals are either invited, or have been specially selected to become a member of a particular community group. These are often groups that have particular strategic importance. Within IBM Global Services, for example, admission to community groups is '. . . *limited to those who can be trusted.*'
- *Getting the scope of the group's work right* – this is a key task when groups first come together. However as time passes, groups may find that the scope is too narrowly defined, or that it doesn't match their interests. When this happens sub-groups or new communities should be formed.
- *Support from senior management* – although self-forming, COPs need support from senior managers. This support can take many forms. First, ensuring that individuals know that what they are doing is a legitimate use of time, recognising the value of talk. Second, providing high-level direction, not about the content or format of discussions, but sufficient for individuals to ensure that what they focus on is aligned to the organisation's knowledge management strategy. Third, providing access to funding for equipment, materials, or even to spend on bringing in experts from outside the organisation to help build the communities' knowledge base. Fourth, making time to listen to members' stories about what they have achieved, as well as what new areas they are exploring.
- *Time* – this is again where management support is essential, ensuring that all of the 'slack time' isn't squeezed out as a result of successive business re-engineering.
- *Clear ground rules regarding entry, exit and acceptable behaviours* – these are the norms within which individuals in the community operate. A high degree of trust is essential. Communities rely on the underpinning values of trust, honesty and reciprocity. Community members need to be aware of the consequences of betraying the trust of others within the community.

- *Ease of access to information* – this could be both internal and external information necessary to help inform, or direct, the work of communities.
- *Technologies to connect communities who are geographically dispersed* – where it is not practical for communities to meet face-to-face then appropriate ICT technologies can help virtual communities operate just as effectively.
- *Addressing multiple WIFMs* – Organisation, line manager and individuals.

Factors that can lead to communities failing include:

- Lack of trust among members.
- Needs of members ignored.
- Too much control, i.e. they are over-engineered. Communities seem to be different in terms of size and structure, leadership, frequency of meetings, as well as the format of meetings. What seems crucial, however, is that participation should be voluntary. It is not something which management should force individuals to participate in. However, in some organisations participation in a community of practice is one indicator used to monitor an individual's willingness to share his/her knowledge. Having monitored individuals' involvement in COPs, this is then linked to the organisation's reward system.
- Lack of focus and/or disconnect with real business needs.
- Lack of resources and/or support.
- Lack of recognition from senior management for the work that communities do.

Practitioner tips for introducing, facilitating and supporting communities of practice

For communities to work successfully it is important to give some consideration to the following areas:

Getting started
1. Assess and prepare the ground
- Identify what types, and how many communities already exist in the organisation.
- What sort of knowledge-building activities are they engaged in?
- How do the communities operate? What works well? What do they struggle with? How might you, HR, help?

2. Establish 'buy in' from senior management
- Be aware of the politics relating to the work of communities.
- Gain commitment for team members to spend time on community activities.
- Pre-empt some of the questions that senior managers (and indeed individuals) will ask, e.g. How much time should individuals allocate/be allowed to allocate to this knowledge-building activity? Should participation in COPs be recognised in an individual's role description? How will the organisation know if the community is working? How will the organisation know if this way of working and learning is bringing real business benefits? How will the learning that emerges from the work of communities be disseminated? How much money should an organisation invest in learning communities? Should it be assumed that communities will run themselves and hence not require any additional resources?

3. Clarify roles and responsibilities
- Make sure that there is a senior level sponsor, someone who recognises how COPs can benefit the business. This needs to be a senior person with a vision of what can be achieved in communities and who can use their influence to secure the necessary resources. This person needs to have strong influencing skills, and be willing to invest time in promoting the work of communities to other senior managers. They need to be strong enough to manage the blocks and the blockers.
- There also needs to be someone in the organisation who is keeping a watching brief on how many COPs exist within the organisation and that these are all serving a useful purpose. It is all too easy for COPs to mushroom and get out of control without some overall sense of direction and focus. A balance needs to be struck between encouraging COPs, because of the benefits that his can bring in terms of breaking down organisational barriers, and as a vehicle for building the organisation's knowledge.
- Gap Gemini Ernst and Young suggest the need for a Innovation Council, the role of the Innovation Council being to sift out ideas being proposed by COPs and provide guidance on whether or not these are consistent with the strategic goals of the business. The Innovation Council, together with the senior level sponsor, can thus help to ensure that communities work on areas that are helping to develop the business.
- Community facilitator/leader/advocate. Each community will need a facilitator who has a vision of the possibilities and outcomes for the community. They need to be passionate about the work of the community, as well as being able to put the work of the community into a broader context. The facilitator

also needs to work at keeping the momentum for the community going, so has to deal with the issue of sustainability.

- Coordinator/administrator. These people can help the community be more productive by dealing with all of the administrative aspects associated with the smooth running of the community, e.g. booking meetings and meeting rooms, organising travel, arranging speakers, as well as carrying out other administrative tasks linked to the community.
- Community members. These are the people who make the community what it is. They define the common areas of learning, as well as sharing out the learning tasks. As participation is voluntary the level of involvement is understandably going to vary too. One of the messages that needs to be got across is that it is OK to lurk, rather than be an active participant. However, it needs to be common practice that whenever people use material developed by the community, or stored on the community site, this is properly acknowledged.
- Community associates. These individuals are not actual members of the community, but instead are people who have expressed an interest in the work being carried out by the community. They can be an extremely important resource none the less in that they are very often active supporters and useful 'knowledge connectors'. It is important then that community members keep these people in the communications loop.
- Facilitators to help get the community off the ground, as well as help them keep focused. This could be a role that HR is well equipped to take on.

4. Establish budget and secure necessary resources
Some of the costs that need budgeting for include: time for meetings, travel expenses for meetings, payment of external speakers to come and talk about topics related to the work of the community, as well as the cost of the coordinator/administrator. There may also be technological resources needed too, for example, a new intranet for communities, or at least a separate area on an existing intranet. Other technologies might include Lotus Notes, Video Conferencing facilities, as well as software to facilitate on-line discussion groups. A question here though is whether these resources should be centrally, or locally, resourced.

Case study – The Institute of Electrical Engineers (IEE)

The IEE is the professional body representing electrical engineers. It has a membership of around 130,000 worldwide. Its role is to encourage and support the professional technical development of its members. It also supports members with their career development. The Institute has always played an important role in helping its members develop their knowledge. Historically it has done this by bringing members together through the branch meeting structure, as well as at centrally organised events.

However, recognising the growing importance of the Internet, and electronic communications tools, the organisation has introduced the concept of Professional Networks (PNs). These are effectively knowledge communities consisting of members with a shared interest in a particular area: industrial structures, academic discipline, even management.

The organisation felt that the PN structure would enable them to build global knowledge communities. It also felt that the PN structure was more congruent with the changing nature of where and when work takes place, enabling members to keep in touch and up-to-date without having to invest time in travelling to branch meetings.

It is envisaged that these PNs will help build a community spirit among members, as the PNs would share the common aim of keeping up-to-date with new developments in their field. The PNs are not just online knowledge communities, they offer more than this:

- Interactive community websites – providing easy access to key information relevant to their profession
- Tailored news
- Events – physical and virtual
- Library of information resources
- Links to relevant websites
- Survey information about their industry sector
- Interviews with gurus
- Development of products and services to enhance the knowledge of the profession
- Networking facilities with community members

The organisation seems to have recognised the importance of providing the relevant central resources to help get PNs started, as well as helping them grow and develop. One of the ways in which it is doing this is by creating a new role – On-line Knowledge Communities Manager. This is a full-time role based at the organisation's central offices. What is interesting is that the Institute envisages a number of people working in these roles in the future.

5. Possible ways of gaining funding for CoPs
Some options include:
- Sponsorship by a senior executive, for example in the form of a SEEDCORN fund.

- The Knowledge Manager allocating some of his/her budget to the work of communities.
- The central learning and development department allocating some of their budget to learning through communities.

Preparing for and running the first meeting

- Decide who should be invited – remember the politics involved. Having the sponsor present at the inaugural meeting would send out a powerful message. Consider inviting an external speaker.
- Organise and publicise the venue.
- Open up a dialogue on how to set about gaining the necessary resources.
- At the first meeting: clarify the community's focus/scope; discuss and agree scope of involvement, outcomes and responsibilities; decide on frequency of contact; plan next steps and discuss and agree how the learning will be disseminated.

Developing and sustaining interest in the work of communities

- Communicate what communities exist and how to join.
- Disseminate findings from the work and learning that is emerging from COPs.
- Education – run some KM road shows to help others get a better understanding of what communities do and how they work.
- Produce some guidelines on how to get the best out of working and learning in COPs.
- Help COPs manage the peaks and troughs in their energy levels, perhaps by balancing face-to-face with on-line meetings. Face-to-face meetings are important too. ICL's Mobilising Knowledge community has been organising a physical meeting of a subset of its 150 members every two months or so. Community members present to the group on the KM work that they are doing with customers and receive input from other members. The personal networking element of communities should not be underestimated.
- Remain focused on the needs of members.
- Tempt people into discussions by posting interesting snippets of information on the community's intranet or posing some interesting questions.
- Review the reward and recognition element. Start a debate about whether or not the work of communities needs rewarding, or is recognition on its own enough? If communities should be rewarded what form should that take (extrinsic versus intrinsic

rewards)? There is a view that there should be some form of recognition for publishing papers on behalf of the community, or for use by community members. Often this recognition comes from regularly circulating a list of new content to group members and to members of the management team.

- Promote the benefits to individuals. Participation in COPs can help individuals develop a sense of identity and belonging; something that is particularly important where individuals work in fairly autonomous roles, or are location-independent.

Monitoring and evaluating outcomes

Despite the importance of not over-managing COPs there is a need for some form of evaluation, given that COPs consume both organisational and individual resources.

Some questions that could be considered in the evaluation process include:

How will you know whether the work being done within COPs is helping the business move forward? Here then organisations will need to monitor the extent to which the work carried out in communities is leading to action and change.

How will you know whether working in COPs is an effective way of working? What indicators might be used?

- Regular attendance at community meetings, or involvement in online community discussions.
- Participation in COPs respected, as opposed to being challenged and questioned by others, particularly line managers.
- Good judgement of use of time by community members.
- Commitment to ensuring lessons learnt are shared outside the community.
- Community members regularly consider who else might need to know and/or might be interested in what the community has discovered.
- Low attrition rates among community members – if the attrition rate of community members is high, this could be an indication that the community is not functioning effectively.
- Enhanced social capital – individuals' contacts within the organisation grow and strengthen as a result of working in COPs.
- Enhanced career and personal development – working in COPs helps individuals to develop knowledge that enhances their future career opportunities.

And finally, what broader organisational learning is emerging from the work of communities? The English Nature case study in Chapter 11 provides an example of this.

Summary

This chapter has discussed the role of Communities of Practice (COPs) as a vehicle for knowledge building and encouraging shared learning in the modern workplace. Although not a new medium for learning, COPs have a number of advantages from an organisational learning perspective: they help with knowledge creation and preservation; they provide a way of integrating work and learning; participation in communities can help people develop a greater sense of identity, something that can be difficult in geographically dispersed teams, as well as enabling individuals to take responsibility for some aspects of organisational learning.

The chapter has provided a number of practitioner tips, drawn from the experience of an established learning and knowledge management practitioner. These include: How to help communities get started, How to develop and sustain interest in communities, and How to monitor and evaluate the outcomes of communities.

Pause for thought

- What communities exist within your organisation? How are they supported? How many have active sponsorship from a senior manager?
- What new learning needs have been identified from the various communities? How have these been addressed?
- How is the knowledge created by communities disseminated across the organisation?
- What communities do HR practitioners participate in, either internally, or externally?
- What broader organisational learning has emerged from the work of communities within your organisation?

Part Three

Building HR's KM Credibility and Capabilities

9

Aligning HR and KM practices

By now you will, hopefully, have had an opportunity to reflect on how influential a role HR can play in helping to build the organisation's capabilities in the area of managing knowledge. The earlier chapters have looked at the various roles and responsibilities associated with building a knowledge-centric culture, including the role of the HR function itself.

One of the themes that emerged in the earlier chapters is the importance of ensuring that managing knowledge becomes an integral part of day-to-day organisational life, rather than it being a separate managing activity, or initiative. The endpoint is to move people away from thinking 'I need to do some knowledge management now' to a point where they automatically consider the implications for the organisation's knowledge, and their own, of the decisions, actions and projects that they are involved in.

This chapter looks at some of the ways in which HR can revise its own systems and practices to ensure that they have a knowledge focus and reinforce the organisation's overall knowledge management goals. Given that there are so many interdependencies amongst HR practices it is important to adopt a systems perspective, ensuring that each HR practice complements the other from a knowledge management perspective.

Aligning HR and KM – start by getting some of the basics right

When asked about HR's role in developing a knowledge-centric culture one of the HR managers that I interviewed spoke about HR needing to start by getting some of the basics right. Getting the basics right in his opinion meant:

- Start with good old-fashioned recruitment. Focus on getting the right people and be sure that you know what knowledge they are bringing.
- When people join make sure that they are exposed to as many people in the organisation as possible. The view being that 'People don't join an organisation just to form a relationship with their immediate team. They want to work with the whole company. So make sure that there is maximum interaction with others.'
- Focus on building the skills that people need to perform well.
- If your organisation thrives on the free-market principle then ensure that you develop information systems that enable the free-market system to work.
- Make sure people have access to the basic information that they need to do their jobs.
- Create opportunities for people to be physically located and/or work closely with people from different parts of the organisation, so that they can interact and learn more about the work of the organisation as a whole.
- Communicate what HR is doing to help the organisation develop its knowledge base.
- Make sure HR is in the know. 'Our HR team writes the monthly briefing to staff. This way we get to find out what is going on in different parts of the business as we have to go and seek out the information.'
- Work in partnership with your business colleagues, e.g. IT, Marketing, Finance.

In these pearls of wisdom, we can see the importance of ensuring that the various HR practices are integrated from a knowledge management perspective, if an organisation is to capitalise on its knowledge assets. So having attracted individuals with the right skills and knowledge it is important to ensure that they are then managed, developed, valued and rewarded such that they will want to continue building their knowledge, preferably with your organisation, and in doing so continue to add value to the organisation.

In adopting a strategic approach to managing knowledge HR practitioners will need to ensure that each of the practices shown in Figure 9.1 are aligned with the organisation's knowledge goals, in this way maximising the opportunities for acquiring, building, sharing, reusing, developing and retaining the organisation's knowledge.

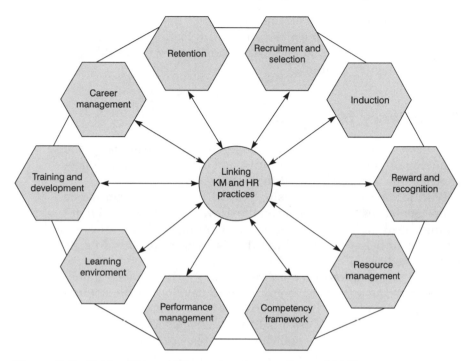

Figure 9.1 Linking KM and HR practices (source: Evans, 2000)

Where to start?

The initial area of focus in any single organisation is likely to be different given the organisation's start point and desired endpoint. If, for example, knowledge retention is a key concern for your organisation then the initial focus of attention will no doubt be on enhancing practices that relate to staff retention. A first step might involve gaining as much detailed information as possible about current staff turnover figures: What types of people are leaving? Are they the ones you want to lose? What are the stated reasons for leaving? What are these people going on to do? Is turnover higher in some business areas than others? What is the impact on customer service? What is the impact on the business's ability to deliver? Does it mean that new ideas are not coming forward? Does it mean that new products are not being developed, or taking longer to develop? Is more time being spent re-inventing the wheel? How are managers addressing the issue of retention, short, medium and longer term? The initial answers to these questions will determine which of the HR practices in Figure 9.1 than need more immediate attention.

The rest of his chapter discusses some of the ways in which each of the core HR practices shown in Figure 9.1 could be developed to ensure that these are consistent with building a knowledge-centric culture.

Competency framework

The need clearly to define the competencies, particularly the behavioural competencies, to build and maintain a knowledge-centric culture was discussed in Chapter 5.

With jobs becoming increasingly more fluid, and performance management systems focusing on the 'How', as well as the 'What', people need to have a clear understanding of how they are expected to behave in a culture that is focused on building its knowledge base.

Where organisations do not already have a competency framework, adopting an inclusive approach to developing the competency framework can be a positive way of demonstrating the cultural values that are essential in knowledge-centric cultures, i.e. openness, fairness, collaboration, respect for individual contributions. In other organisations, it may simply be a case of revising an existing competency framework to include knowledge-creating and sharing behaviours, and to reflect the organisation's overall knowledge management aspirations and goals.

Once defined the competency framework should then inform, or certainly not conflict with, other HR practices such as recruitment, performance management, career management, as well as learning and development practices.

Recruitment and selection

As well as using the competency framework to guide the recruitment and selection process, organisations need to take some time to consider the best way of filling an identified knowledge gap. Some of the options that could be considered, according to Dave Ulrich (2000), include:

- Buy – acquire new talent by recruiting individuals from outside the organisation, or from other areas within the organisation, or
- Borrow – develop a partnership with other organisations/ people, e.g. consultants, vendors, customers, suppliers.

There are of course variations within these two broad options. Depending on how critical the loss of knowledge, a decision could be taken not to take on a full-time replacement, but instead take someone on on a short-term contract, thereby buying time until another team member can be developed to fill the knowledge gap. The need to provide some training/coaching could perhaps be negotiated as part of the contractual arrangement with the temporary worker. What is crucial is to address those aspects of the 'psychological contract' that relate to managing knowledge during the recruitment process. In the knowledge economy, individuals want to know what the opportunities for developing their own knowledge are likely to be.

Another option would be to consider re-recruiting a former employee, possibly someone who is now running his/her own business, on a project, or short-term contract basis. Some organisations now make a point of keeping in touch with former employees, recognising that there can be mutual benefits of this arrangement, particularly given the speed of change within organisations today (the section on Retention Management covers this point).

Other organisations, such as NHS trusts, are starting to take a more strategic approach to recruitment and retention in what is now a particularly difficult sector for attracting and retaining employees. Some are experimenting with a process known as the Skills Escalator. This involves identifying different entry points for staff, what the organisation needs to do to attract people at these different entry points and also what specific support individuals at each entry point might need, to help them with their continuing development.

This approach has led to some trusts putting different training schemes in place to support staff at the different entry levels. These range from basic skills training for individuals targeted from the long-term unemployed sector, to sponsorship through higher education for individuals wanting to move from a support role into a professional role.

One final point on the actual recruitment process, from a knowledge perspective, is to ensure that it embraces the principles of diversity discussed in Chapter 3. These include opening up the recruitment process to attract individuals from diverse backgrounds, building the organisation's reputation within the local community as an employer that values difference, as well as promoting the fact that the organisation is receptive to experimenting with different ways of working.

The selection process will need to address the best person fit, from a knowledge management perspective. This may mean revising interview and selection processes so that they gather evidence about individuals' knowledge-building behaviours, such as:

- How well networked is the individual? What role does he/she play in the networks they belong to? How does he/she contribute to these networks?
- What types of Communities of Practice do they belong to? What specific contributions have they made?
- How have they helped develop their colleagues?
- How do they keep their own knowledge and skills up-to-date?

Induction

The induction process is often the first opportunity for individuals to get a formal introduction into the organisational culture. Thus it is important that the induction process is designed to give new employees a sense of what managing knowledge means in the context of your specific organisation, including the behaviours that are most valued. Some good stories at this point will help reinforce this message. This will help new recruits develop a common understanding of how knowledge management practices are incorporated into day-to-day practice within the organisation. Without this individuals may work on assumptions drawn from their experience in other organisations.

As networking is so important for knowledge acquisition and sharing, the induction period should be used to enable new recruits to get as much exposure to as many different people as possible, e.g. key personnel, their own team, other functional areas and departments, suppliers, strategic partners. In this way they can start to build their network base, getting a sense of who is who, who knows who and also who knows what. Given the increasing shift towards more flexible ways of working, particularly mobile working, providing new employees with the opportunity to start to build these working relationships is crucial. People are more inclined to share what they know with people whom they have met in person and have had a chance to identify areas of mutual interest. Once this mutual area of interest has been established individuals are more likely to work as part of a virtual community, at some future point.

Some organisations believe that the induction process should also include exposure to customers, particularly for those individuals whose work would not normally involve having direct contact with customers. Novo Nordisk, a major healthcare and pharmaceutical company with one of the broadest diabetes product portfolios in the industry, ensures that every new employee gets the opportunity to meet at least one customer face-to-face, as a way of helping them build an understanding of what the organisation is really about.

The induction process is also crucial from the point of gaining further insights into the knowledge base of new employees – what their interest are (both in and out of work) what they know, as well as who they know – and also to start the discussion process about development needs.

As a way of reinforcing the importance of keeping one's CV up-to-date, new employees should be encouraged to input further details about themselves onto the central skills database and/or Yellow Pages, in their first week of joining. In this way they can quickly become a known entity to those whom they have not yet been able to meet in person.

Performance management

On the basis that what gets measured normally gets done it is important that organisations address the knowledge component in their performance management system. Equally if employees are to see that the organisation is taking knowledge management seriously a balanced-scorecard approach needs to be adopted, ensuring that an individual's 'knowledge contribution' is evaluated alongside delivery of Key Results Areas.

When discussing an individual's overall 'knowledge contribution', managers will need to take into account the different ways in which individuals might do this. They will need to consider:

- Knowledge acquisition – What knowledge has the individual brought into the organisation?
- Knowledge sharing – How has the individual applied their knowledge to help others develop?
- Knowledge reuse – How frequently has the individual re-used existing knowledge and what has been the outcome?
- Knowledge development – Has the individual actively developed his/her own knowledge and skills? What different approaches have been adopted? How well has the individual applied his/her learning?

Reward and recognition

There are mixed views as to whether organisations need to introduce separate rewards to encourage knowledge building and sharing. Where organisations have introduced a competency framework that includes knowledge building and sharing behaviours, and this is linked to the performance management system, then in theory there doesn't seem to be any need to have a separate reward system. However, where the performance management system does not allow for equal weighting to be given to the 'How' as well as the 'What' element of an individual's performance, then this can run counter to building a knowledge-centric culture. In environments where individuals are under pressure to meet revenue/sales targets there is a danger that performance reviews focus purely on 'hard' targets, rather than taking into consideration an individual's knowledge contribution.

Another school of thought, however, is that rewards for knowledge sharing and reuse, in particular, should be more immediate, and be of a more public nature, as this acts as an incentive to both the receiver, and perhaps more importantly to others, that this type of behaviour is important to the organisation.

The experience of R&D organisations suggests that a mixture of rewards are needed to motivate knowledge workers, such as scientists and engineers. These include: equitable salary structures; profit-sharing or equity-based rewards; a variety of employee benefits; flexibility over working time and location, as well as being given credit for significant pieces of work (Jain and Triandis, 1997). Where organisations expect their knowledge workers to participate in Communities of Practice it may also be appropriate to consider some form of reward for individuals who are prepared to invest considerable amounts of their own time in building the community's knowledge base and/or keep the community alive.

Bearing in mind the factors that motivate knowledge workers, discussed in Chapter 7, non-financial rewards, in the form of 'free time' to work on knowledge-building projects, may be more motivating for some, than monetary rewards. Within DERA, for example, individuals who are widely recognised as being a leading expert in a particular area, can be awarded up to £15,000, to spend on conferences, purchasing a particular piece of equipment that could enhance their work, or buy some time to spend working on a project which is of personal interest to them (Evans, 2000).

What seems important from these different examples is having a flexible reward strategy that provides a balance between organisational and individual needs, and where individuals have some element of choice over the rewards and benefits they receive. Some technology companies, for example, make it possible for employees to trade salary for extra holiday. This approach enables individuals to invest more time in knowledge-building activities, such as research and writing, going on a short study tour, attending an international conference, or to create much needed thinking time. Why would individuals want to do this? – because they see the importance of investing in their own intellectual capital.

As the demand for certain categories of knowledge workers intensifies organisations will need to become more creative in their approach to rewarding these individuals. How many organisations, for example, would allow one of their knowledge workers to take up an opportunity that allowed them to combine their love of athletics with applying their existing technology skills by providing IT support at the Commonwealth Games[1]?

As Richard Scase (2002), points out, if organisations want to nurture creativity they need to reward employees in such a way that they have a stakeholder interest in the innovative outcomes, for example through part ownership of patents, or ensuring professional recognition. The new Enterprise Management Incentive (EMI) schemes may be another way of motivating and rewarding knowledge workers, or indeed any employees who contribute to enhanced business performance. EMI schemes provide employees with the opportunity to acquire share options, which can be cashed in if the organisation floats at some future point. This type of scheme seems to offer real potential in the SME sector, where the business has strong growth potential.

Given the critical need for learning today, another reward option could be to consider introducing a 'Learning Time' scheme, similar to the 'Matched Time' scheme that some organisations have introduced as part of their commitment to supporting community work (see Chapter 6). This type of scheme would enable individuals who demonstrate a commitment to continuous learning to be awarded extra learning time, which they could use to invest in further learning activities. This would be one way of addressing the generic versus specific intellectual capital dilemma discussed earlier.

Another area to consider is that of discretionary, or one-off rewards, which managers, or teams, could use to acknowledge specific knowledge contributions as a way of encouraging others to make similar contributions. The HR community within BT Global, for example, award a bottle of champagne each month to the person in the team who is the most prolific user of other people's ideas (fully accredited of course). BP runs a 'Thief of the year' award, which goes to the person who has stolen the best ideas in applications development. Allied Domecq, a national drinks company, makes a point of promoting and rewarding good examples of knowledge re-use at its annual staff conference.

Resource management

In a business world where change is a constant and thus it is not always possible to know what skills are likely to be needed in the future, there is a need to adopt diversity in thinking with regard to resource planning. Dave Ulrich (2000) suggests five different strategies for building organisational and employee competence:

- Buy – acquire new talent by recruiting individuals from outside the organisation, or from other areas within the organisation.
- Build – train or develop existing talent through further education, formal job training, job rotation, action learning.
- Borrow – develop a partnership with other organisations/ people, e.g. consultants, vendors, customers, suppliers.
- Bounce – remove individuals who are under-performing.
- Retain – retain the most talented employees.

Does your organisation draw equally on each of these strategies, or does it tend to rely on one tried and tested resourcing approach? Does your organisation consciously build its knowledge base through encouraging different ways of working, e.g. cross-boundary team working, virtual team working, or through strategic partnering? Are managers encouraged to think creatively about how to resource a need in their area, or do they automatically think that recruiting from outside is the only way?

If you have a central skills database, who monitors and reports on its usage to ensure that it is bringing the benefits that it was designed to bring? Who promotes case studies of good practice? What form does that take, e.g. feature in internal newsletters and/ or bulletin boards, line managers communicating stories at team meetings?

Do managers and individuals give sufficient priority to keeping the central skills database up-to-date, so that the right people can be quickly located for projects, or to help resolve operational difficulties? Do managers spend time with individuals helping them review, refine, even discard, details in the skills database? Is this practice linked to regular feedback and/or performance review sessions?

Addressing the changing psychological contract of employment

The changing psychological contract of employment has important implications from a knowledge management perspective. With few employers today able to guarantee life-time employment, and indeed some employees no longer looking for life-time employment, there is a need to think more strategically about how to address the area of developing and retaining 'know how'.

This is not a new phenomenon, it is an area that organisations that have introduced flexible work contacts, such as the media, healthcare and higher education, have had to address for some time. It was also a theme that I identified many years ago when I was conducting some research for the Employers Forum on Age on the practices adopted by organisations for managing an age diverse workforce[2]. At that time, the early 1990s, many large organisations were pruning their workforce as a way of increasing organisational efficiency. In the majority of cases it was older employees who were losing out. These were often the ones with valuable knowledge that in hindsight the organisation found that it really could not afford to lose.

What did stand out in my mind from that piece of research was the way in which the more enlightened organisations were addressing the tensions of having to come to terms with the fact that guarantees of life-time employment were no longer feasible. Some of the organisations that participated in the research ran workshops and focus groups where employees were able to talk about the broader changes taking place in the economy and society, the implications for employment and careers, and thus the importance of focusing on employability.

One major retail organisation had adopted a multiple strand approach to addressing the issue of employability. This included helping employees assess whether they had the skills to run their own businesses, helping individuals apply and/or broaden their skills through working on community projects, as well as providing training that led to a nationally recognised qualification.

Other organisations were considering phased retirement options. If used in a strategic way, phased retirement can have benefits from both the organisation's and the individual's perspective. The transition period could be used to help transfer skills and knowledge between the retiring employee and other employees within the organisation. But as we know knowledge transfer only takes place in situations where the individual who shares his/her knowledge gets something back in return, so what would the 'WIFM' factor be in this scenario?

- Some space in their lives to start to explore and build other interests before reaching retirement age.
- An opportunity to develop/enhance their 'softer' skills through coaching and mentoring.
- A sense of feeling valued.
- An opportunity to build new networks in preparation for the transition into retirement.

Learning environment

Chapter 6 discussed at length the importance of re-visiting our assumptions about learning in the knowledge economy and what is needed for organisations to become learning-centric. The key points from that chapter include:

- Work on developing people who are hungry to learn.
- Ensure that there is a balance between formal and informal learning practices and that managers understand and utilise the options that come under each of these categories.
- Ensure that training and development solutions maximise opportunities for knowledge transfer.
- Help people draw out and value the learning that comes from day-to-day experiences.
- Make learning and sharing easy – several organisations have introduced 'Learn and Share' sessions as a way of enhancing opportunities for individuals to develop their knowledge base. Often these sessions are held at lunch-times, thus reinforcing the social dimension of learning. In organisations that do not have a restaurant area 'Learn and Share' sessions are often one of the few forums where people from different parts of the organisation can physically get together to learn with and from others.
- Make learning and sharing worthwhile.
- Ensure that the organisation taps into every possible learning source, e.g. suppliers, customers, associates, individuals working on short-term contracts, strategic partners, as well as its volunteer workforce.
- Build informal learning spaces (both physical and virtual) where individuals can exchange ideas, share insights and problems.
- Listen to what is getting in the way of the organisation becoming learning-centric and develop joint plans with line managers and their teams to address the blocks and barriers.

Training and development

- Develop generic and specific human capital

One of the questions raised in Chapter 6 was to what extent should employers be responsible for helping employees develop their generic human capital (i.e. skills and knowledge which enhance the worker's productivity irrespective of where he or she is employed) and specific human capital (i.e. skills and knowledge which only apply to their current employer). However, in practice the boundaries between these two categories of human capital are not always so clear cut.

Case study: Introduction of a Business Skills Development Programme in a small technology-based company

As background to writing this book I interviewed the HR Director of a small technology company. The company employs around 250 people. The nature of the work that the organisation does means that its people are highly marketable. The average tenure is around two years. Most of the people in the organisation are educated to a high level: many have higher degrees, e.g. masters degrees, or a PhD. Technically then, many of the employees are very able. However, the organisation felt that some of its more junior staff lacked the necessary business awareness needed to survive in what is a highly competitive marketplace. There is a strong focus on entrepreneurialism within the organisation and all employees are expected to initiate and follow through ideas for new products and services.

To address the identified knowledge gap the HR team approached the management school at a local university to help them design and deliver a short Business Awareness Programme. The programme consisted of formal lectures, held at the university, covering areas such as: developing an understanding of the supplier–customer relationship model (thus building an understanding of what makes customers tick); corporate finance; economics; as well as how financial markets work.

Selecting an academic institution to deliver this type of development activity was felt to be particularly important given the backgrounds of employees who would be the main recipients. Many of those attending the programme were familiar with the academic learning environment, having previously spent a significant amount of time in higher education. Thus they also had a respect for the knowledge generated in these learning environments.

The programme seems to have helped these highly capable technical specialists get a better understanding of the range of factors that influence management decision-making, such as the link between share price and business performance and the economic arguments behind hiring and firing people.

This broader development activity has helped these individuals develop their 'know of' and 'know why', helping them to put their own work into a broader context. It has also exposed them to the terminology and language associated with running a business, thereby providing a common language for discussions with business leaders and senior decision-makers.

What this case study illustrates is how technical skills and knowledge is often not enough to succeed in today's business world. With a greater emphasis on customer service, technical specialists need to be business aware, i.e. able to apply their knowledge to create business solutions that the customer actually wants. Tesco.com, for example, claims that much of the success of its online shopping service stems from the fact that each of the technical staff in its online operations area regularly spends time in a store doing basic retails tasks so that they can get closer to the customer and their shopping habits and needs[3].

● Ensure that your evaluation process addresses the transfer of learning.

Does your evaluation process encourage individuals to consider questions like '*Who else would benefit from the insights developed on this programme/learning event?*' and '*How will I communicate this to them?*' Are these questions posed on the 'happiness sheet'?

● Experiment with new approaches to training delivery.

As part of the background research for this book I discovered one or two organisations that were experimenting with different forms of skills-building workshops. One organisation, for example, had introduced a programme of short workshops designed to address gaps in specific skills areas, such as report writing and presentation skills. Instead of planning a one or two-day workshop, a series of short learning sessions, held over a three to four-week period, were held for each of these topics. These shorter sessions have proved to be more popular with managers and staff. Staff find it easier to fit the shorter learning sessions around their other work commitments. It has also made it easier for individuals to apply and build on what thy have learnt in the workshops. Equally the short time-span between workshops means that individuals can bring 'live problems' to the workshop, providing more valuable learning opportunities.

● Build basic IT skills training into the organisation's overall training strategy.

Even in technology-intensive companies technophobia can prevent individuals from participating fully in knowledge creation and sharing. The Ford Motor Company, for example, has introduced a scheme that enables staff to lease a PC, printer and modem for a nominal monthly charge. The scheme is intended to help international staff, in particular, develop the skills needed to be at the cutting edge of e-commerce.

● Encourage 'best practice scouring'.

Speaking at a Knowledge Management conference, the former Deputy Managing Director of Anglian Water, spoke of the need for membership of external networks and attendance at conferences to be seen as 'intelligence gathering' rather than academic jollies[4]. However, individuals need to develop the habit of summarising the key learning from conferences and sharing with colleagues.

Career management

In the introductory chapter I outlined the broader economic, technical and social changes that have occurred over the past twenty years and the effect that this is having on work, employment and careers.

The career landscape does appear to be changing, partly as a result of structural change within organisations, and partly through individual choice. Work–Life balance has risen up the political, corporate and personal agenda for individuals. Providing ways of helping employees achieve the Work–Life balance that they are looking for is seen as a key way of attracting and retaining skilled employees, particularly women, who are still very much under-represented in some business sectors.

However, from my own research (Evans, 2001), the policies that organisation have introduced are not yet hitting the spot for some individuals. They are considered too inflexible and are often-based on a narrow definition of Work–Life balance. These are individuals who have chosen to develop an independent career. A career choice that enables them to 'blend', as opposed to balance, the different aspects of their lives, e.g. work, family, learning, health, and community work.

Irrespective of whether individuals choose to develop an organisational career, or an independent career, one of the areas that they need to address is how in knowledge economy the half-life of an individual's skills is now a few years, not a few decades. It is crucial then that employers and employees develop plans for keeping their knowledge and skills up-to-date.

In the opening presentation of a Women in Management conference, Valerie Hammond, the Chief Executive of Roffey Park Institute, spoke of how, in the world of the free agent, we need to regularly review our skills, identifying which ones are currently in demand, which ones are likely to be in demand in the future, and which ones to let go of[5]. However, as we have seen a lot of evidence in the knowledge economy of old skills being dusted down and applied in different contexts, e.g. storytelling and social network analysis, perhaps there is a need to consider archiving these skills, rather than abandoning than for good.

What can HR do to help individuals build meaningful careers in the knowledge economy?

● Help people reframe their view of a career

My experience of running career workshops is that individuals are often unhappy with the career options on offer within organisations, yet they do not have any other models to work with. Providing examples of different ways of thinking about a career, like those set out in the introductory chapter, can help to shift people's thinking. This is particularly important for individuals working in more flexible ways with the organisation. Individuals who opt to work part-time can often feel excluded from career discussions, as it is often assumed that they are no longer interested in pursuing a career. However, this assumption is based on a particular view of a career.

● Provide career workshops

These provide opportunities for individuals to take stock of where they are, connect, or reconnect, with their own personal values and career drivers, take stock of their current skills-set, carry out a stock-take of their existing knowledge, and likely future demand, as well as make some tentative plans for how they would like their career to take shape in the future.

● Help people prepare for roles, not jobs

Flexible and adaptable organisations need people who can be flexible and adaptable too. For this to happen individuals will need help in thinking through how they might apply their skills and knowledge to different roles, either within the organisation, or possibly outside, albeit temporary. They may also need some space to 'try out' different roles, to assess the fit.

● Provide dual career tracks

This will enable technical specialists to develop a career that fits with their model of career success, without feeling that their only career option is to pursue a management career (Holbeche, 2000). Without this, organisations are in danger of facing the 'Peter-out Principle', i.e. where individuals rise up until such point as they stop having fun and then, when that happens, choose to walk out (Pink, 2001).

● Help people learn from transitions

One of the key career development tasks in organisations, according to Peter Herriot and his co-writers (1998), is that of helping individuals make effective transitions so that they are better prepared for making even bigger transitions in the future. The manager's role is crucial in providing the right support, particularly that of helping individuals learn from different transition phases, which they define as preparation, encounter and adjustment. In the future it is likely that individuals will need to become more adept at 'transitioning' as careers become more fluid and 'boundaryless', e.g. employment, time out to build new skills and knowledge through full-time education, employment, followed by self-employment, prior to retirement.

● Make it easy for people to move around the organisation

This is crucial if the organisation wants to ensure that existing knowledge is shared and reused. Lateral career moves can be more motivating for some individuals, provided that the role that they move into provides scope for challenge, knowledge building and personal growth.

● Ensure that career management systems do not give mixed messages

If you have a skills database make sure that this is used for matching individuals with posts and/or career opportunities. In one former public sector organisation there was a conflict between using the skills database as a vehicle for matching resources to projects, and the open job-posting system (introduced under the umbrella of Equal Opportunities). As the skills database wasn't being used in the way that staff anticipated, they could see no personal benefit in keeping their skills entry up-to-date. In this example neither the organisation nor individuals were deriving the full benefit from the system.

● Develop managers' ability to hold meaningful career discussions

Increasingly line managers are expected to provide career support and coaching for individuals within the organisation, both direct reports and others, and yet few receive any formal training for this task. Equally HR needs to play its role in providing independent and skilful career guidance. Research carried out by Wendy Hirsh and colleagues (2001), on behalf of NICEC, identified that in order for line managers to provide effective career discussions at work they need support and back-up from HR. The research concluded that HR can make a valuable contribution by acting as a 'career lubricator', advising some individuals directly, particularly in situations where line managers had recognised that they were dealing in areas outside their own comfort zone.

Retention management

'Data and information live in systems, but knowledge resides in people. Much of the logic behind knowledge management lies in ensuring that when valuable employees walk out the door, they leave some value behind' (*People Management*, August 1998).

In his book, *The Talent Solution*, Edward Gubman suggests that in today's workforce one of the things that gets in the way of retaining talented individuals is having a command-and-control culture which demotivates employees. An important part of any organisation's retention strategy therefore, according to Gubman, requires maintaining a focus on engaging employees, as excited and engaged employees are more likely to continue to deliver, and stay with the organisation longer.

So how can you help your employees feel engaged? Gubman and his colleagues at Hewitt Associates have identified a simple framework:

Explain – Help people to see the big picture so that they know where the organisation is going and what it is doing to get there, how they can contribute and what the rewards will be if they help you get there. So the 'know why' talked about earlier.

Ask – Gubman argues that this is where many organisations go wrong, as they operate from a telling management style, rather than adopting a consultative style. He points out that it is far better to ask people what they think they can contribute to the business, along with what their needs are. The process of asking questions engages people's thought processes. However, having asked for ideas or feedback from employees, it is of course very important to listen, and follow through.

Involve – Once people know where the organisation is going and what they can do to contribute, the next step is to let then get on with some of the implementation tasks without interfering. One thing that needs to be established is what level of freedom and autonomy is appropriate for employees to have. This needs to be balanced against the risks involved. Line managers need to ensure that they are seen as a resource to help people make the right decisions, not make decisions for them.

But what can HR do to help the organisation retain its talent, and hence knowledge assets?

- Help line managers identify who their most vulnerable team members are, i.e. the ones that they would least like to lose. Here managers will need to consider the different roles that individuals play in building, communicating and sharing knowledge. Losing central connectors, boundary spanners and information brokers, could be just as catastrophic as losing particular knowledge experts (these roles are discussed in more detail in the section on Social Network Analysis in the next chapter). Work with managers to develop a specific retention plan for vulnerable team members, or at least a transition plan, where it is inevitable that particular individuals will move on at a future point. Where HR can particularly add value here is in spotting knowledge gaps, overlaps and opportunities, because of their broader knowledge of resources in different business teams.
- Work with line managers to help them categorise their team members along the lines of Needs Attention, Watch this Space, Key Contributor and High Potential, so that they can then focus on the most appropriate development plans.
- Encourage line mangers to hold 'anniversary chats' with team members, using this as a time to reflect on most enjoyable projects/experiences, least enjoyable projects and experiences, critical learning moments, treasured secrets, as well as who their key supporters have been and why. Armed with this information, managers will then have a better understanding of personal motivators, how best to help an individual to develop going forward, as well as building an insight into the networks that individuals belong to.
- Provide managers with tools to help them manage the transfer of knowledge, which they can use at the end of major projects, or as individuals join/leave the team.
- Use Exit interviews as a way of gathering information to improve HR practices and also identify where HR practices are not aligned.
- Share Exit interview data with line managers, so that they can use this to reflect on, and then change, their own behaviours.

- When facilitating change programmes think through the implications and opportunities for building and retaining knowledge.
- Find ways of keeping in contact with former employees, so that their expertise can be tapped into at some future point if needed. A concept that seems to be gaining interest in the United States is setting up an Alumni scheme for former employees[6]. The benefits of an Alumni scheme include: keeping the door open to re-employ certain employees in the future (often a more cost-effective way of recruiting than traditional routes); a source of intellectual capital; ambassadors and retention of investors (good Alumni relations can increase the odds that ex-employees will retain their stock holdings).
- The events of September 11th will have brought home the importance of considering the people implications of major disasters. Many organisations invest large sums of money in developing Disaster Recovery plans for their IT systems and yet a similar concept doesn't necessarily exist for the organisation's intellectual capital. What seems to be needed is a co-ordinated approach to IT and human resources disaster recovery planning, where plans are regularly tested out, as is the case with good IT Disaster Recovery plans.

Summary

This chapter has looked at some of the core HR practices and how these can be enhanced from a knowledge management perspective. As a start point, HR needs to focus on getting some of the basics right: recruiting the right people who have the knowledge and skills to meet an identified gap, ensuring that new recruits get maximum exposure to others in the organisation when they join, provide people with the information and tools that they need to perform at their optimum, make sure that individuals are working in roles in which they are fully engaged, as well as helping them develop their skill-sets. Delivering on these basics will require investing in developing line managers' capabilities so that they can play their part in ensuring that these basics are delivered. Equally important is ensuring that each of the core HR practices are aligned so that changes in one practice do not have a negative effect on others.

Pause for reflection

- Thinking about each of the HR practices outlined in Figure 10.1, which ones are more developed from a knowledge management perspective within your own organisation?

- Where there are gaps, what do you think would be a priority area for change? What would others see as being a priority area for change?
- How does HR keep itself 'in the know' in your organisation?

Notes

1. A day in the life of a Games technology volunteer. *Computing* 25 July 2002.
2. For further details about the work of the Employers Forum on Age see *www.efa.org.uk*.
3. Skills Section, *Computing*, 24 January 2002.
4. Knowledge Management Conference. Strategic Planning Society. October 1999.
5. 21st Century Women's Voices. Women in Management Conference. London. November 1998.
6. Cultivating ex-employees by Sem Setoglu and Anne Berkowitch. *Harvard Business Review*, June 2002

10

Knowing what we know: language and tools for knowledge mapping

This chapter has been written by Dave Snowden, Director of Cynefin Centre for Organizational Complexity, IBM Global Services.

The over-zealous pursuit of efficiency at the cost of effectiveness lies at the heart of the many failures in otherwise well-intentioned management initiatives to deliver against expectations. This pursuit, with its emphasis on process improvement has dominated management thinking either side of the millennium. It attempts to use (and abuse) human agents as if they were components in a machine, capable of categorisation, deployment and replacement. Human resource or personnel management has not been exempt. They have frequently served as the impersonal agent of financially driven organisational downsizing; or perpetuated the mechanical metaphor of efficiency through attempts at categorisation such as competence modelling and the ascription of empirical prescriptive truth to a variety of psychometric instruments.

The understandable, if unacceptable, intent to render the human aspects of an organisation into something that can be managed without ambiguity, in part originates from a desire for control, but also from a discomfort with uncertainty: efficient systems require control and the repeatability of function, something to which humans are not naturally inclined. In this chapter strong emphasis will be placed on sense-making achieved through models based on viewing a subject from different perspectives, rather than by categorisation. Categorisation assumes that the whole is the aggregate of the parts, each of which can be understood in its own right. Perspective modelling argues that by looking at a thing from many perspectives new patterns of meaning will emerge. In knowledge management, as in all human systems, the whole is never the sum of its parts, it may be more, is frequently less, but it is never the same thing.

Conceptual problems with early knowledge management practice

Knowledge management to all intents and purposes took off as a management discipline with the popularisation of the words 'tacit' and 'explicit' by Nonaka and Takeuchi (1995) through the SECI model that identified four transitions of knowledge: tacit to tacit through socialisation in the form of conversation, observation and the like; tacit to explicit by the codification or externalisation of personally held knowledge; explicit to explicit through the combination of codified forms of knowledge; explicit to tacit following the internalisation of documents by human agents. The deficiencies of the language of tacit and explicit as a way of understanding knowledge will be discussed later in the context of the perspective model of knowledge ASHEN and there are more general issues with the model (Snowden, 2002a). The effect of this model was to launch a technology-based emphasis on the disembodiment of knowledge from its owners, be they individuals or communities on the basis that knowledge was not a corporate asset unless it was held by the organisation independent of human agency. This simplistic popularisation of the SECI model largely determined knowledge management practice, resulting in a restricted approach to knowledge. As a description of the process of knowledge creation in the context of product design in the manufacture of consumer goods in Japanese industry the SECI model was sound, as a general model of knowledge flow in organisations, including the service sector and government, it is inadequate.

Another major issue was the proximity of the knowledge management movement to business process re-engineering, the growth of which had coincided with and partially fuelled the growth of management consulting. Re-engineering is focused on efficiency, in removing waste, in optimisation achieved by ensuring the repeatability of prescribed best practice. This was ideally suited to the growth of recipe-book consulting. Indeed the consultancy firms themselves pioneering knowledge management as the codification of recipes based on past projects allowing larger teams of inexperienced consultants to use the knowledge of their more experienced predecessors. For systems and practices where order exists, can be discovered and is repeatable the disciplines of recipe-based consulting are ideal, for the dynamics of human communication, organisational change and knowledge management it proved not only inappropriate but just plain dangerous. In the case of knowledge management the models and practice of re-engineering were inappropriate, but they were the dominant model of the day and as such were applied. Rather like the scientific community of the eighteenth century attempted to apply the dominant disciplines of astronomy to the measurement of longitude and in consequence ignored or simply failed to see that accurate clocks were a more effective solution[1].

The nature of human acts of knowing reflects a complex and inherently unknowable (in the sense of being empirically verifiable and repeatable) space. It is a quantum shift away from process management, quality management and the like. We can understand this through three rules or heuristics of knowledge management practice.

The three rules of knowledge management

The use of rules, supported by anecdotes or stories, based on a succinct encapsulation of common sense or common values has a strong tradition in human thinking and communication. The Sermon on the Mount and the American Declaration of Independence are both examples of a set of rules or principles against which events in an as yet uncertain future can be tested. The form is useful but it is always in danger of trivialisation through over-simplistic formularisation, or the codification of a flexible principle into a doctrinally rigid commandment. The following rules are offered in the spirit of gaining understanding while acknowledging the danger of such formulation. Each rule has implications for the design of knowledge management systems, and for the process of knowledge audit or mapping; an organic approach to which, will be described later. The rules arise from the author's experience, have been validated with other practitioners and have not been substantially challenged since their formulation in 1998.

Knowledge can only be volunteered, it cannot be conscripted

In practice we can enforce compliance with a process or quality standard because the outcome is measurable. We may have difficulties with motivating people, but we know whether something has been done or not; in contrast we can never know if people have used their knowledge. Attempts to enforce or mandate knowledge sharing result in two types of behaviour that, from a manager's perspective are inseparable.

Camouflage behaviour in which knowledge is shared, but in a form which is unintelligible or unusable without reference to the knowledge holder. This ensures that the trustworthiness of the requestor can be validated before knowledge exchange takes place. Camouflage behaviour is often linked with knowledge retention-based on fear of abuse, rather than power. For valuable knowledge, fear of abuse is more significant, in that the knowledge holder is afraid that their knowledge will be abused or misused if they do not maintain control. Such behaviour is often justified by past history, and exhortations to the contrary will not be listened to.

Conformance; pressed to share knowledge, people do the minimum required to satisfy the formal requirement, but do no more. If fear of abuse is a more powerful reason for knowledge retention than power, then time is the most important of all. The volume of e-mail, collaborative requirements and the like create time pressures on employees, which mean that difficult or complex tasks get insufficient attention. Conformance is more dangerous than camouflage. With camouflage interested parties can gain access to human validated knowledge, with conformance they may think that the recipe is complete, but may be missing a vital ingredient, or more likely important context. Best practice schemes are particularly prone to this, as they are dependent on sufficient disclosure of context to understand applicability of the relevant practice.

We always know more than we can say and we will always say more than we can write down

Writing is a reflective process; it is more time consuming than oral forms and less spontaneous. The time delay between event and codification also results in modification: all humans have a natural tendency to alter history to conform to the requirements of the present. The volume of knowledge that can be captured in oral format is much higher than can ever be written down, but even this only provides a partial representation of the knowledge that I know, or am capable of knowing in the right context.

Most knowledge management practice, with its focus on tacit to explicit knowledge conversion, only ever manages a partial representation of what is known, and often the least valuable. This has led the author to separate knowledge management into three separate activities.

Context management, which is all about creating linkages and connections between people and communities in order to handle the Knowledge that is 'not a "thing", or a system, but an ephemeral, active process of relating' (Stacey, 2001). Here we focus on managing the channels and connections through which knowledge flows and by which it is created, rather than making any attempt to manage the knowledge itself. Social network stimulation is an example of one of the emergent techniques in this important area.

Narrative management is the use of stories and story telling, including oral history techniques and narrative databases to store knowledge that people can easily speak, and which can be accessed through the process of serendipitous encounter that is natural to the human knowledge-sharing process. Given a choice between drawing down best practice and hearing the stories of five or six trusted individuals, most opt for the latter not the former (Snowden, 2002b). Narrative databases are particularly useful in lessons learnt environments and the capture and distribution of knowledge held by retirees.

Content management comprising document management systems, search engines, best practice systems (although worst practice using narrative can be more useful) and the like, which has been the main focus of knowledge management practice, but which is at best a partial view of the full richness of the potential of knowledge management.

We only know what we know when we need to know it

Human knowledge is deeply contextual, triggered by circumstance, requiring the stimulus of events to remind us of what we know, or to stimulate the creation of new knowledge. The very human phrase 'I'll sleep on it' illustrates this. For a human to sleep on something is to engage in a complex knowledge process; if a computer is sleeping on a problem it has to be rebooted. Serendipity is a powerful human knowledge process, it's about multiple encounters with people, ideas, concepts, data or whatever, from which knowledge can be recalled or created.

The other major aspect of this rule is the nature of human knowing, while experts when interviewed tend to explain the process of their knowing as a rationally constructed and logical series of steps, direct observation of knowledge in the field generally results in knowledge being displayed in the application of heuristics or rules of thumb which are rarely articulated and often lie below the level of conscious awareness.

The nature of stimulus and attention gaining behaviour in human systems is generally underestimated in organisational design and theory. Clark (1997) emphasises 'the need to find very close fits between the needs and lifestyles of specific systems (be they animals, robots, or humans) and the kinds of information-bearing environment structures to which they will respond'. He makes an interesting reference to the sense-making capability of a tick, which will sit on a branch in a forest responding to no stimuli until the presence of butyric acid on the skin of a passing mammal allows her to drop and feed. This form of focused attention to specific stimuli is replicated in human knowledge behaviour and over-efficient models will tend to narrow the range of stimuli that will trigger a response. Pattern entrainment is a common aspect of human decision-making, in that we tend to respond to a first fit pattern match with prior experience rather than make a rational evaluation between carefully considered alternatives. We even go beyond that and 'imagine contradictory evidence away' (Klein, 1994).

The consequences of this for knowledge management are twofold:

First, we need to manage the stimulus either to trigger existing patterns, when appropriate, or to disrupt the triggering of inappropriate patterns when the context has changed.
Second, the standard approach to enquiry, namely structured interviews and the like will not work when it comes to knowledge. To ask someone what he or she knows is to ask a meaningless question in a meaningless context.

Creating a meaningful context

The ideal context for the disclosure of knowledge is at the moment of its creation or use. At this time the environment has stimulated the subject and there is a greater chance of awareness of the nature of the knowledge in use. Of course this is not always possible and we may have to rely on recollection, or fiction to create the context. One of the ironies of knowledge work is that fiction can be as important as fact in revealing the context of knowledge use.

A key learning from fieldwork is that the preliminary search is not for knowledge itself, but for evidence of knowledge use. Accordingly we create the context in which a knowledge question can be asked. Accordingly the purpose of initial enquiry is to identify knowledge disclosure points (KDPs) through observation of the moment of creation or use. The most common KDP is a decision as we always use knowledge in decision-making consciously and unconsciously. KDPs can also be acts of judgement, problem resolution, learning points, solution discovery, conflict resolution or any combination or permutation thereof. Various techniques serve to 'surface' KDPs in an organisation, most of which are orientated to the stimulation of story telling.

Stories are the means by which humans communicate and recall experience and through which they communicate knowledge. Elicitation of stories provides one of the most effective means by which evidence of knowledge use can be identified. An interesting feature of this practice is that fiction is as valuable as fact, the speculations of what could have been and might have been reflect the knowledge assets of an organisation to the same or greater degree than fact. Methods for the elicitation of story include:

Field Observation drawing on techniques from anthropology. Here the investigator becomes a part of the environment, an unseen observer. Critical is not to act as a consultant either external or internal, but to undertake labour or service in the organisation as a new, and junior member of staff. The author in carrying out this work has stacked shelves in supermarkets, been plunged into sewers, swept metal scarf from a factory floor and acted as a bag carrier for a merchant banker. The essence of this approach uses the human obligation of gifting; by providing service we create an obligation for openness.

Story Circles are effective for groups of people with a common experience and history. They work on the natural human tendency to reminiscence and to a certain degree, the desire to tell a better story than someone else in the circle. Story telling stimulates the memory; it provides the contextual stimulus to recall specific events and experiences. Story telling is not a natural process in some cultures and it cannot be forced but it can be enabled. Scenario planning or alternative history techniques can create an environment in which people will tell stories without being asked to. The essence of a story circle is to replicate the natural process of story telling that takes place around the water cooler, over a meal or in the mess.

The Naïve Interview utilises the naturally occurring social networks that exist in all organisations. For example, issuing

250 tape recorders to 250 randomly selected staff asking them to find two or three people based on different selection criteria (normally opposites such as youngest–oldest, most and least experienced etc. The interviewers are then provided with indirect questions designed to stimulate the recall of relevant experience. This technique is more likely to tap into open disclosure than a formal interview conducted by third parties: the naïve interviewer will utilise the social obligation of their own trusted networks.

Virtual Story Capture is not as rich as the above techniques; the nature of human communication and trust is not best served in a virtual space where social clues are restricted. For example, in a physical story circle it is not possible for anyone to lurk without other members of the group being aware of their non-participation, whereas lurkers are common in virtual discussion groups. The value of virtual story telling is that it can reduce cost, which is legitimate, provided the limitations are acknowledged and validated by other techniques, but the main value is the ability to create anonymity in a virtual space which can enable disclosure of core material which would not be revealed in other environments.

Life-cycle Interviews focus the interviewer on the natural cycle of decision-making. What decisions are made on a daily, weekly, monthly or annual cycle? The process of walking through past experience provides a stimulus for recall and can be combined with a story circle. As a one to one interview it is the least effective of the techniques as the interviewer can too easily influence it. There is a tendency for an interviewer who has conducted two or three interviews to form a hypothesis and then to only see evidence that supports that hypothesis in subsequent interviews. This is a variation of the pattern entrainment referenced earlier.

All of the above techniques are designed to create a rich body of anecdotes that can be used to reveal knowledge disclosure points. This can be done by review of recorded material from the above exercises, or by a review period with participants in each process. The intent is to generate as many knowledge disclosure points as possible over multiple versions of each process and then to cluster and group the results. It is then possible for each cluster of knowledge disclosure points to identify individuals or groups who make the decision, exercise judgement, resolve the problem or whatever. We can then conduct a more structured and traditional interview process with those individuals or groups asking them in the context of the KDP cluster, a meaningful question about the knowledge they use, have used or might use.

Asking a meaningful question: the ASHEN model

The language of knowledge is of importance both in discovery and in use. Aside from the question of creating a context in which a person or community are able to recall the nature of what they know, the language of the question has to both provide additional context, and stimulate a way of thinking which is seen as sensible to the subject being questioned. The question must provide a way in which the subject matter is seen from different perspectives in such a way as to stimulate the recall of knowledge and also to describe that knowledge in a manner that can lead to action. The ASHEN question is designed to achieve that, but it should be emphasised that ASHEN is about seeing things from different perspectives to elicit a response; it is not a categorisation model in which knowledge is, for example, either an artefact or a heuristic, but a means of eliciting a response.

art'ĕfăct, art-, *n. A product of human art and workmanship*

These comprise the processes, documents, filing cabinets, databases and other constructed 'things' that encompass the codifiable knowledge of an organisation. The management issue here is the removal of duplication and the general optimisation and ready distribution of such artefacts to communities that need them. The artefacts will ideally be in the right place at the right time, even though most people may be unaware of their existence most of the time. This is a non-trivial management challenge for which technology can only support, but not provide, answers.

Many artefacts exist but are not known. They may be notebooks of past exceptions events in the drawer of a staff room of a supermarket; a diary in a café frequented on a regular basis by field engineers or a web site using the free space in Hotmail used by individuals in competitive companies who shared a common interest. All three of these examples come from the author's own experience, and in each case were probably one of the most valuable assets identified in a knowledge mapping exercise. It is important to respect naturally occurring artefacts and to separate the creation and capture of knowledge from its analysis and distribution. It may not be neat and tidy to do so and appears to be anti-rational and sub-optimal; but it works.

skĭll, *n. Expertness, practised ability, facility in doing something, dexterity, tact.*

In this context skills are those things for which we can identify tangible measures of their successful acquisition. If I employ a plasterer then I can measure the deviation from a vertical plane of his work and the time taken to complete. Customer relationship is a more different thing to measure and although it has aspects of 'skill', the term is not enough in its own right. The time element is an important aspect of the skill measurement. The author is a reasonably accomplished carpenter, but a skilled chippie can accomplish in one hour a task that is a weekend's work for the amateur.

Skills are something that organisations know how to manage. Both training needs and skills analysis are well-known techniques. Training courses, moderated work experience; the gambit of techniques available is wide and well proven. However, there is always the danger of the codification heresy: the belief that once something is written down, then it is shared. Most of the published 'success' stories of Intellectual Capital Management often suffer from this. While skills can be structured and trained, time has to be taken to internalise them. The management task is to catalogue the skills, understand the time horizon and resource requirements for their acquisition and plan accordingly.

heuris'tic *(hur-), a. & n. serving to discover*

Heuristics or rules of thumb are one of the most valuable of assets and may be articulated without the need to render them fully explicit. They are the effective way by which we make decisions when the full facts are not known or knowable in the time available. A good example is the CEO looking at a range of investment proposals without sufficient time – or the inclination – to go through the detailed case. The decision criteria often take the form of a simple rule set: Has someone I trust checked this out? Will it impact on my targets for this year? Will it distract key staff from other more important targets? They are also the means by which experts and/or professionals make decisions in conditions of uncertainty. The essence of heuristics is that they have fuzzy edges and therein rests their power. They allow greater consistency in conditions of uncertainty but follow the Pareto principle that 80 per cent is good enough. Over time they may become fully explicit and become artefacts, or they may remain tacit – only available to an expert community.

exper'ience, *n. Actual observation of or practical acquaintance with facts or events; knowledge resulting from this*

Experience is the most valuable and most difficult of the tacit assets of an organisation. It is difficult for two reasons: (i) the experience may be collective rather than individual, and (ii) replication of the experience may not be practical or sensible. One case will illustrate this; a major UK company knew one of their key assets was the ability to manage cash but they didn't know why. Using the ASHEN model the artefacts were readily identified in the form of management reports. Skills were a mix of accountancy training and, interestingly, a common training course in negotiation skills. The heuristics in contrast were clinically paranoid in their attention to detail, but made sense when the experience was identified: two members of the finance team had lived through a bankruptcy in a previous employment. That collective experience had given them an ability to spot trends, and take common-sense actions faster and with more effect than others, no matter how intelligent or how well trained. The issue was twofold: (i) the experience was collective – they were a team and, (ii) although it could be repeated it does not make sense to plunge a company into bankruptcy every two years as a training exercise for the finance department! Over time narrative and other techniques can mitigate this problem, but organisations should be under no illusion – mitigation is possible, but there is no full substitute for the experience itself. Key then is to understand the dependence – and the consequent vulnerability in the event of change.

nătural (-cher), n. *Existing in or by nature, not artificial, innate, inherent, self-sown, uncultivated.* **tăl'ent,** n. *Special aptitude, faculty, gift, (for music etc., for doing; see Matt. XXV. 14–30), high mental ability, whence ~ED², ~LESS*

Like it or not, some individuals are simply better at doing things than others. Whatever the reason or origin of that talent, from an organisational point the retention and attraction of natural talent is a key aspect of knowledge management at all levels of the organisation. It doesn't matter if it's the problem-solving ability of a software engineer, the welcome of a receptionist or the entrepreneurial capability of a divisional director. In all cases there is something other than artefacts, skills, heuristics and experience that provides an 'edge'. In knowledge mapping we improve our ability to spot it and in consequence we can foster its development and attempt to prevent corporate politics from stifling its realisation, but we cannot manufacture or transfer it. We can build the skills necessary to spot it, and foster the experience that will allow us to use it. Like non-repeatable experience we need to understand our key dependencies, measure the risk and vulnerability to loss and take appropriate action.

ASHEN – a different perspective

The ASHEN model is powerful in that it uses commonplace, or slightly unusual words (artefacts and heuristics) and invests them with common-sense meaning. It provides a different perspective, or creates an awareness of a required change in attitude. By asking the ASHEN question in the context of a KDP we can achieve a meaningful answer which itself leads to action. *When you made that decision, what **artefacts** did you use, or would you like to have? What **skills** did you have or need and how are they acquired? What **heuristics** do you use to make such decisions quickly, what is the range of their applicability? What **experience** is necessary and what experience do the people you respect in this field have? Who are the people who just seem to get this right, who have something special (**natural talent**) how exclusive is it? Who else has it?* Such questions allow the questioned to produce meaningful answers with minimal interference from the questioner.

Both ASHEN and the process of identifying KDPs from the stories of current and past experience are means by which we can gain new perspective on the issue. It is important to emphasise that ASHEN is not a set of categories into which knowledge can be allocated, but a means of gaining perspective; the questions get the interviewee to see things from different perspectives and is more likely to stimulate them into remembrance.

Most importantly ASHEN helps create a key shift in organisational thinking from key-person dependency to knowledge dependency. This essential step of depersonalisation is critical to effective knowledge practice. It is the shift from *Only Linda can do X* to *X requires this combination of artefacts, skills, heuristics, experience and natural talent and at the moment, only Linda has them.* The former statement has only crude solutions, the latter permits greater sophistication and the potential for long-lasting solutions and sustainable management action. It achieves this by using language that describes the situation at the right level of granularity to permit action without excessive analysis.

Critically, the nature of the language we use determines the actions that we can take. The crude description of knowledge as either tacit or explicit encourages the tendency to focus on codification of knowledge. The language represents thinking of knowledge as a 'thing' that can be either tacit or explicit, and thus the presumption, all too common in knowledge management, that tacit knowledge can, and should be made explicit before it can be regarded as an organisational asset. The ASHEN model on the other hand can encourage the creation of explicit knowledge for artefacts, skills and, to a degree heuristics but not in the case of experience and natural talent. This is not to say that the tacit and explicit words are not useful, but they are a secondary description of knowledge assets as shown in Figure 10.1. Once we have used the ASHEN model to give us a perspective on the nature of knowledge, and remember that this is not a categorisation model, and then it is legitimate to take the tacit–explicit perspective. This links to key questions about the need for, or desirability of, codification. In practice for any asset, we have two questions that need to be asked:

1. Is this knowledge, in whole or in part, capable of codification?
2. If it is capable of codification then is it desirable to do so.

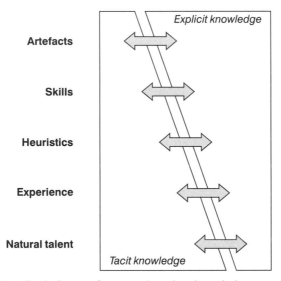

Figure 10.1   The balance of tacit and explicit knowledge

The second question is important, and the answer relates to the degree to which the knowledge is dynamic in nature and the levels of uncertainty in the surrounding environment. Generally the more dynamic and/or the more uncertain the knowledge the more likely it is that the balance will shift towards tacit at the expense of explicit; to context and narrative rather than content. The cost of codification is also a factor that links the codification decision to the time value of the knowledge. Partial codification can also be useful but is too rarely considered in many knowledge programmes where the desire for completeness tends to override common sense.

Another way of looking at the tacit–explicit balance in knowledge is to think of knowledge as being both a *flow* and a *thing*, rather like electrons are simultaneously and paradoxically waves and particles. Things are capable of codification as is, for flows we can structure and influence the channels through which the flow can take place, but the knowledge itself is too ephemeral to be codified as such, indeed (to pursue the metaphor) the attempt at codification may change the nature of the original for the worse.

Abstraction and the cost of codification

A key element in understanding the degree and nature of knowledge sharing is to understand the level of abstraction appropriate to the knowledge in question. Abstraction is key to human communication and therefore for knowledge management. By abstraction is meant the process of loss that leads to a higher level of language. This is achieved in two ways:

1. Through the use of technical language and references to books, formula and theorems that is so common among experts. This is the teachable or explicit domain of communication.
2. By reference to shared experiences, values or belief systems often only understood in full by a limited number of participants in a conversation. This is the learning, sense making or tacit domain of communication.

Even the first of this is not context-free, training programmes, different social experiences and cultural differences can all enable or handicap knowledge flow even when the language is explicit and set out in dictionaries. The general rule is that the higher the level of abstraction, the richer the communication but with a diminishing number of participants.

Figure 10.2 looks at the relationship between the level of abstraction and the cost of codification. The cost of codification might be better described as the cost of disembodiment, that is to say the process of removing knowledge from the heads of its creator/owners in such a way as to permit the use of that knowledge without the presence of the creator/owner; a process that is at the heart of much knowledge management practice. *Abstraction* and *codification* are key concepts linked to the *diffusion* of knowledge and an understanding of the relationship between the three can have a profound impact on understanding the economics of knowledge within an organisation and a market (Boisot, 1998).

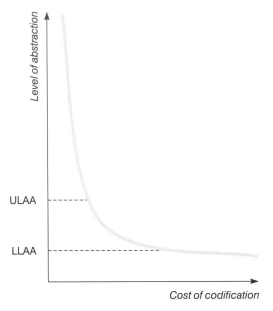

Figure 10.2 Relationship between level of abstraction and codification

The highest level of abstraction is where individuals have a conversation with themselves. Language, experience, values and beliefs are nearly always identical and as such rapid and effective communication of complex ideas is easily possible. There is some cost in note-taking or other forms of codification, but no one really expects other people to read their notes. At the other extreme where the requirement is to communicate with everyone the cost of codification is infinite as it requires not only a common language and education, but also common experiences and value systems at a level probably even denied to twins.

In between these two points we have a zone of acceptable abstraction within which any form of communication can take place. Understanding is not just a question of comprehension, but also of attitude. In a community of experts they may understand material below the lower level of abstraction (LLAA), but they will not pay attention to it, it is too simplistic given their level of understanding. Sometimes this is a form of entrainment by which they fail to see something because it does not fit the pattern of expected knowledge; often it is simply a question of available time. Those same experts may tolerate knowledge above their personal upper level of acceptable abstraction (ULAA) because they know how to gain access to it, or pride may just prevent their admission of ignorance! Levels of abstraction apply to all types of knowledge from the esoteric knowledge of a theoretical physicist, to the intricacies of a plumbing system. Understanding, or allowing the emergence or evolution of an understanding of those levels is key to any knowledge management activity which focuses on a community or communities; given that most does it is vital.

Diverse types of community

The zone of acceptable abstraction is one aspect of understanding the nature of possible knowledge flow within an organisation, the other is that ubiquitous word 'culture', generally the bucket class concept for anything that we don't fully understand or which is problematic. A useful distinction can be made between cultures as systems of rules and practices embodied within formal organisations and societies, and culture understood as a value or belief system (Keesing and Strathern, 1998). Rules and practices can be taught, measured to some degree and enforced; values on the other hand rely more on tacit understanding and factors such as ritual and obligation. Another way of describing this difference is to contrast teaching with learning. In teaching we teach what is known and there is no ambiguity as to who is the teacher and who is taught, we know what the right answer is. Learning, on the other hand, is a sense-making process of creating new meaning and insight in which there is considerable ambiguity between the teacher and taught, in fact frequently the expertise of the teacher prevents new learning in a radically new context.

Taking these two aspects, abstraction and culture allows us to identify four different domains in which functionally different communities exist and in consequence to model the dynamic flows of communities and knowledge that need to take place between those domains. This is an application of the generic Cynefin model to communities and is shown in Figure 10.3. Cynefin is a Welsh word whose literal translation into English as *habitat* or *place* fails to do it justice. Its meaning rests in the sense of multiple belonging which is an aspect of all social systems, the many tribal, religious, geographic and cultural histories that profoundly influence what we are, but of which we are only ever partially aware. The name reminds us that a full understanding of the past or present is never possible in human systems. The Cynefin model has applications in more or less all branches of management science, here it is being used in the context of communities and as such acquires the axis labels of culture and abstraction shown in Figure 10.3. Its use and background in knowledge management are more fully described in *Complex Acts of Knowing* (Snowden, 2002a).

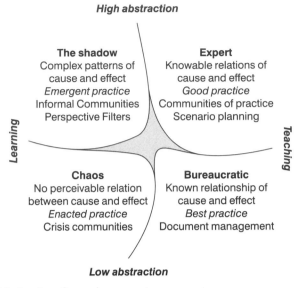

Figure 10.3 Cynefin and community

Moving anti-clockwise around the model from its southeast domain we see four types of community (Figure 10.4).

Bureaucratic These deal with relatively static knowledge, where the 'true' answer is known and people can be trained at a low level of abstraction to follow due process or reuse, generally codified, knowledge. It is the domain of expense rules, safety procedures and

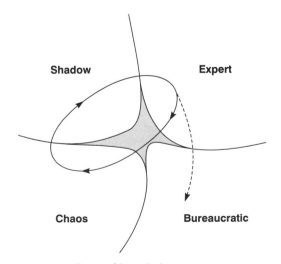

Figure 10.4 Dynamic flows of knowledge

response to known threat or opportunity. It is also the space in which reality is imposed through a corporate decision, we often forget that many organisations impose reality on their employees and that something that is true in one organisation may be false in another. Knowledge management in this domain is about standards and committees more than spontaneity.

Expert This is the dominant area in most conventional knowledge management practice and, while it is one of the most useful, it is not as universal as many commentators would claim. Expert communities share a common language, often-based on advanced training, and are able to communicate at a high level of abstraction to other experts. Such communities need to preserve the boundaries for both people and material to prevent compromise of this level of abstraction; a community of experts in which trainees take part as full members will soon result in the non-use of the system by real experts who have limited time for collaboration and have to prioritise into areas where new learning will be more readily achieved. These very boundaries are in turn a danger as the expertise becomes entrained and may not see opportunities or threats that fall outside the habituated patterns of meaning within that community. A brief study of the history of science, and the history of breakthrough innovations demonstrates that few innovations come from established experts, but from accidents and heresy!

The Shadow All organisations have an extensive informal network of communities that arise through common value systems, the experience of working together on projects, joining the organisation at the same time, common social activities; the list is endless. The membership and knowledge controlled within this space is constantly shifting and adapting and is rarely codified. One study in IBM revealed 65,000 informal communities in about 150,000 staff as against 50 formal communities of practice, and that was only a count of those who used virtual tools to share experiences so the actual ratio is probably more extreme. Similar ratios are found in most organisations down to about 500 employees although there are no hard and fast rules. The Shadow is also the domain of emergent leadership. Too many organisations try to repeat past success by selecting against competences 'measures' based on past practice rather than using the informal community to throw up natural leaders equipped to handle newly emergent situations.

Chaos The domain of chaos in which all existing patterns cease to exist is low abstraction because we have no formal language of experts, nor the experience of the shadow; the situation is completely new and therefore one in which new sense-making has to take place. In modern knowledge management this is a space in which we have to assemble knowledge assets to deal with a new situation. The language of ASHEN can help us in identifying appropriate deployment strategies for this domain; one of the neglected functions of knowledge management practice is the creation and deployment of crisis teams. The other use of chaos is the deliberate move of entrained experts into a position where their established patterns of knowledge are disrupted and challenged on a cyclical basis to prevent the otherwise inevitable ossification of entrained expertise. Positioned in advance as a part of the creation of an expert community such a programme will be welcomed and embraced, initiated as remedial action after the event it will be fiercely resisted.

The dynamic flow of knowledge

Understanding the different domains of the Cynefin model enables a more sophisticated approach to the creation and mapping of knowledge within an organisation. One shift that has already been identified is the shift of expert communities into Chaos on a controlled basis. The second move is from the shadow to expert sometimes known as *Just in Time* knowledge flow. The metaphor to JIT in manufacturing is deliberate. We used to store all of our stock on the factory floor until we realised it was too expensive, at which point we created new relationships with suppliers to bring stock in when, and if, it was needed. The same applies to knowledge management; the sheer volume of knowledge in the shadow domain exceeds our capacity for formalisation and we do not know what we need to know until we need to know it, so attempts to anticipate that need through taxonomies and the like will inevitably lead to the wrong knowledge being in the wrong place at the wrong time. Techniques for JIT-KM include expertise location as an alternative to Yellow Pages and the use of pre-existing communities to form formal communities rather than attempting to engineer the creation of an ideal. The main advantage of this latter practice is that informal communities naturally work out their own acceptable zone of abstraction and use pre-existing trust relationships. The formal creation of either of these is an expensive, time consuming and frequently unsuccessful process best avoided. Finally the amount of knowledge subject to formal codification is limited and is not a part of the main dynamic.

We can now return to an earlier reference to the separation of knowledge management into three: context, narrative and content. Content management is a necessary activity in the bureaucratic and to some extent the expert domains, where the stability of knowledge permits the investment necessary for codification. Context management applies in the main to chaos and to the shadow with some intrusion into the expert domain. Narrative straddles shadow, expert and to a degree bureaucratic. The essence is to apply the appropriate tool in the appropriate space.

The other aspect of the flow of knowledge within organisations are the various formal and informal social networks that build over time as a result of multiple interactions between people and communities. Social network theory is often associated, but should not be used with concepts of social capital that it supports, but on which it is not predicted.

Social networks

There is a broad body of theoretical and practical work on the nature of social networks in organisations, some of the best and most recent coming from Robert L. Cross (2001) of the University of Virginia, formerly a researcher with the Institute for Knowledge Management. The basis of social network analysis (SNA) is to work with a population of individuals each of whom answers a series of questions about each other individual within the network. These range from basic questions about information sourcing, through aspects of comprehension and trust. The results are plotted on a network diagram which shows the centrality or otherwise of each individual within the network in respect of each question. Measures of centrality and connectivity are also created and the resulting figures and diagrams provide a powerful diagnostic tool in respect of network-based communication with a firm. SNA also allows modelling of impact, for example removing the most networked individual and seeing the consequences of that removal for communication.

SNA between individuals is dependent on the truthfulness of the individuals' answers, and there are non-trivial problems here in that the results are visible to colleagues and superiors. The author of this chapter prefers to use SNA between significant *entities* within an organisation. An entity is a significant actor; mainly communities but this can also include powerful individuals or roles (the two are not necessarily the same). The same process is applied as for individuals but where the entity is a community either a proxy, or a poll or a workshop is used to elicit the answers. An additional process is the use of the Cynefin model to provide a perspective on the space that will stimulate the identity of informal as well as formal communities, crisis groups as well as committees. In addition the anecdote capture techniques earlier identified as a means of discovering KDPs can also provide substantial evidence of the existence of entities.

The resulting models permit a deeper understanding of community interaction, and can also separate, for example, the formal and informal aspects of a committee meeting or conference. The results can be used to determine a policy for community formation in which naturally occurring communities can now be used for knowledge management, rather than attempting to impose some ideal model that may, or may not be capable of operation. We also start to see differences between organisations, to take a recent example in which the core informal community in one part of the organisation was a cohort group comprising a year's intake into the organisation who had maintained contact; it was the group that most people referred to for meaning and trust, whereas the formal organisation was used for information. In a closely related section of the same organisation a social club provided the same function. More conventional approaches to building communities of practice would have first designed the ideal form and function of a knowledge community; far less effective than using established trusted relationships.

Knowing what you know

Knowledge is different from process. The way that we carry out our initial investigation and the way in which we create a knowledge programme are, in consequence, different. It is also an evolutionary process. The creation of a knowledge map will nearly always reveal knowledge vulnerable to loss, communities that are unsustainable, opportunities for quick wins; all of which means that the process of mapping is a process of discovery not prescription, the initiation of a series of journeys. Knowledge mapping is about creating a series of lenses through which the knowledge strategy of an organisation can be perceived. The main lenses are:

1. A mapping of knowledge objects in relationship to core organisational process or activity. This is achieved through the ASHEN model, and by creating a simple matrix to link process or activity with key knowledge assets.
2. A view of the communities and structures that possess or create knowledge, both formal and informal. The Cynefin

model represents different types of community and different functions and is also a dynamic sense-making model that allows an understanding of diversity of type and function in communities.

3. An understanding of the flows of knowledge and information dependency between those communities and structures. This is provided by SNA that demonstrates the relationship between existing communities and provides clues for the stimulus or creation of new communities based on natural patterns of relationship and trust.

The three considered together allow us to chart a way forward for a knowledge management initiative, or better a portfolio of initiatives.

This is a bottom-up approach to knowing what we know. Traditional approaches based on prior determination of management goals are less effective in that they are based on partial understanding of an organisation's knowledge. A conservative estimate of an individual's awareness of their own knowledge is 5 per cent, and a similar percentage can be applied to an organisation's awareness of the knowledge possessed by its members; 5 per cent of 5 per cent is a very small number! By first of all creating an awareness of an organisation's current *de facto* knowledge practices, through the three lenses of ASHEN, Cynefin and SNA an organisation's knowledge strategy can be informed by, and evolve from reality rather than attempting to achieve some idealised utopia. Utopianism has been an all too frequent companion of management initiatives from process re-engineering to much current knowledge management practice.

Finally we should return to the place we started, the contrast between efficient and effective systems. Machines are efficient; we optimise the whole by optimising the parts and then reassembling them. Human systems need to be effective, which requires a degree of sub-optimal behaviour by the identities that comprise its elements. Attempts to introduce machine-like efficiency into human interactions are doomed to failure in all but the most structured of tasks. In contrast, allowing a degree of self-organisation, utilising existing patterns of meaning and trust can produce a highly effective and above all human system; but it all starts with the map. We have to know what we know, how we know it, where it is located and how it flows. We also have to be aware that like all human knowledge the map is never complete, in some cases it will be annotated with the modern equivalent of the medieval cartographer's *here be dragons and other strange beasts*; such ambiguity is at the heart of human endeavour, exploration and ingenuity.

Acknowledgement

Some of the material used in this chapter was originally published in a series of three articles on Organic Knowledge Management in *Knowledge Management* from the ARK organisation www.ark-group.com

Note

1. Dava Sobel's best selling book *Longitude* provides a powerful example of the restrictive practices of existing experts and their ability to stifle innovation.

References

Boisot, M. (1988) *Knowledge Assets*, London: Oxford University Press.

Clark, A. (1997) *Being There: Putting Brain, Body, and the World Together Again*. MIT.

Cross, R., Parker, A., Prusak, L. and Borgatti, S. (2001) Knowing What We Know: Supporting Knowledge Creation and Sharing in Social Networks. *Organizational Dynamics*, 3(2), pp. 100–120.

Klein, G. (1994) *Sources of power: how people make decisions*. MIT.

Keesing, R. and Strathern, A. (1998) *Cultural Anthropology: A Contemporary Perspective*. Orlando: Harcourt Brace & Co (third edition, first edition published 1976).

Nonaka, I. and Takeuchi, H. (1995) *The Knowledge-creating Company*. London: Oxford University Press.

Snowden, D. (2002a) Complex acts of knowing: paradox and descriptive self-awareness. *The Journal of Knowledge Management*, 6, No. 2, (May).

Snowden, D. (2002b) Narrative patterns: the use of story in the third age of knowledge management. *The Journal of Information and Knowledge Management*, 00:1–5.

Stacey, R. (2001) *Complex Responsive Processes in Organizations: Learning and Knowledge Creation*. Routledge.

Weissman, D. (2000) *A Social Ontology*. Yale University.

11

Building your KM toolkit

For HR to play a strategic role in building a knowledge-centric culture one of the areas that it needs to invest in is acquiring and applying the right tools. The previous chapter introduced some of the tools and approaches relating to knowledge mapping. This chapter describes some of the other tools that could be incorporated into HR's KM toolkit, as well as drawing on some case study examples to further illustrate the use of Storytelling and Social Network Analysis.

The chapter is not intended to provide an exhaustive list of KM tools, but a selection of those that seem most valuable. Many of these tools are not new. What is different, however, is how they are being applied to help organisations manage their knowledge. As with managing change, it is easy to get carried away and think that we need to radically change the way we do things. Often it is a question of adapting existing practices, combined with introducing a few key changes.

As has been raised earlier, in the knowledge economy it is just as important that we reuse what we already have, provided that it is fit for purpose, rather than having to create new all the time.

The next chapter discusses the role of technology in building a knowledge-centric culture, including the different types of IT tools that can be used to help locate people with different sources of information and knowledge, as well as to facilitate collaborative working and learning.

Some basic tools

The Consultancy Cycle

Increasingly HR are having to take on the role of internal consultant, as part of their Business Partner and Change Agent role discussed earlier in Chapter 8. In order to be able to perform in this way HR needs to be familiar with the Consultancy Cycle.

Phase 1 – Gaining entry: This is where HR either decides for itself that it is going to need to get involved in a specific business situation/problem, or where they are invited in by their business colleagues (i.e. the internal client) to help identify a solution to a specific business problem. In the former scenario HR will need to capture the attention of their business colleagues, in order to get them to listen. This is where HR needs to come across as being knowledgeable (a) about issues that are getting in the way of business performance, (b) options for addressing performance issues and (c) current and future trends, drawn from the external world.

As many business leaders are more comfortable working with quantitative data than qualitative data, then it is important to draw on this type of data to build a persuasive argument.

Given the topic of knowledge management some of the quantitative data that could be drawn on here is: hard to fill vacancies, breakdown of staff turnover figures, number of suitable candidates coming forward for new positions, reduced response time for HR issues being resolved.

Phase 2 – Contracting: Having got the internal client interested in a particular issue/problem then the next step is to agree on who is going to do what and when, so in essence agree what the next steps are. This could simply be a matter of agreeing to do some more diagnostics, or take some soundings from others within the organisation.

Phase 3 – Data gathering: Depending on the outcome of Phase 2, a period of data gathering will often be needed. Some of the choices that need to be made here are (a) what type of data is needed (b) how will it be collected (c) how much data is needed and (d) who will do the data gathering. Each of these areas will need to be discussed and agreed with the internal client.

Phase 4 – Making sense of the data: This involves drawing on various analytical tools as well as different conceptual models to help make sense of the data that has been gathered. This can be a joint process with clients, depending upon their needs and expectations. Certainly the client can be used as another means of validating the data that has been gathered.

Phase 5 – Generating options, planning for change: This is where HR as the internal consultant needs to offer some creative solutions, and not just suggest standardised training and development solutions.

Here there needs to be a discussion about responsibilities for implementation, so who needs to what and when and also what resources need to be made available? Again there are some choices to be made. Will HR be fully responsible for implementation? Will the client be responsible for the implementation? Will it be a partnership approach? or Should others be brought in to manage the implementation?

It may also be necessary at this point to re-visit some of the earlier steps, prior to going into more detailed implementation planning. It certainly is important at this stage to map out key success criteria for the project.

Phase 6 – Implementation: This is fairly explanatory, in that it is the execution of the agreed plan. However, as difficulties often emerge at the implementation stage it is important to ensure that there is a continuing dialogue with clients during this phase. This is one of the value-adding aspects of the internal consultancy role. Implementation is never seamless, but it needs to be seen as rich ground for learning.

Phase 7 – Disengaging: Some of the areas that need to be considered here include planning a learning review session, agreeing a maintenance plan, ensuring some form of celebration to mark the end of the project, helping the client think about the next steps and evaluating outcomes.

The change cycle

One of the competencies required of successful change agents is demonstrating an understanding of the change cycle, in terms of the reactions and emotions experienced by individuals when undergoing change in their lives. Geraldine Brown of the Domino Consultancy has developed the classic transition curve, turning this into a model that can be used by change agents working within an organisational context, see Table 11.1.

Table 11.1: An adaptation of the classic transition model

Transition phase	Likely reactions	Ways of helping individuals move on
Reluctance	Uncertainty, antagonism towards the proposed change	● Open dialogue ● Space to think
Awareness	That change is desirable	● Drip in options and possibilities ● Share stories from outside
Interest	In the possibilities that the change might bring	● Listen ● Help in visualising the outcomes and benefits
Mental tryout	Imagining the new situation and how this might impact on self and others	● Tease out positive forces ● Help establish connections
Real-life practice	Piloting new ways of working or experimenting with new ways of being	● Provide resources to help set up pilots ● Help in spreading success stories
Implementation	Extending the pilot across a broader population	● Provide more resources ● Support with evaluation
Commitment	Enthusiasm and commitment to make the change work	● Ensure that enthusiasm is recognised and rewarded
Integration	Changes become embedded into day-to-day practice	● Help people to reflect on the change process – What helped? What hindered? What next?

Ways of thinking about tough or challenging situations

This tool, based on Edward de Bono's six thinking hats, developed by Joanna Howard (1999), can often help to unlock people when they are struggling with a tough or challenging situation. It encourages them to use left and right brain thinking as a way of clarifying their feelings about a particular situation, as well as to come up with more creative solutions.

To use this tool, take a large sheet of paper and write down at the top of the paper the situation/problem that you are facing. Review what you have written. How clear is the statement you have written?

Next, divide the rest of the paper into six boxes and label each section with a question, as illustrated below.

What are my emotions about this situation/problem?	What are the difficulties and risks I can see in this situation/problem?
What are the possibilities and constructive opportunities?	What creative alternatives can I generate to address this situation/problem?
What factual information do I have about this situation/problem?	What is my overall purpose and what needs to be done?

Then write down your thoughts against each of these questions. Now stand back and ask yourself the following questions: What is this telling me about the situation/problem I am facing and how I am responding? What might I do next about what I have discovered? When used in group contexts, this tool can help to unlock team members through providing a way of building shared understanding.

Questions to facilitate transformative learning

Questions are one of the most simple and powerful tools that we have at our disposal in our knowledge management toolkit, yet so often people use convergent (closed) questioning techniques, which do not provide such a rich source of data. An alternative approach is to practise using divergent questioning techniques. Some examples being:

Divergent questions	Examples
Questions to broaden awareness	*What are you noticing or hearing at this point in time?*
Questions to generate options	*What are five ways you could approach this problem?*
Questions to make new connections	*What patterns are you noticing here?*
	How does this relate to. . .?
Questions to encourage thinking out of the box	*If you were observing this problem from a helicopter how might you see it differently?*
	Imagine you are a gardener how might she/he approach this problem?

Tools to open up a dialogue

Self-managed learning model

This tool is often used by developers when helping individuals create a personal development plan, but the underlying questions, of which there are five, can also be used as a basis for strategic change. The model can be used with senior managers, as well individuals at other levels within the organisation, and the outputs used to identify the extent to which there is an overlap in thinking. The five key questions are:

Where have we come from as an organisation?
This question is designed to get people to reflect on the organisation's history, so there is an understanding of why things are as they are and why certain values have come to be important.

Where are we now?
This creates an opportunity to explore what is currently working well and why this is the case. It can create an opportunity to explore current capabilities and which of these will be important to develop further in the future, as well as where there are gaps.

Where do we want to get to, or be in the future?

Here individuals will need to be encouraged to visualise and articulate the future that they are trying to craft, in quite graphic terms. This articulation can come in the form of words, or in pictures – whichever works best for the audience that you are working with.

How will we get there?

Here we are dealing with some of the pragmatics of getting from A to B. Who needs to be involved? What expertise can we draw on to help us, either within the organisation, or outside? What projects might we need to set up? What things might we want to experiment with?

How will we know when we have got there?

This question is intended to get people thinking about what the end position will really look like. What will the observable differences be?

Appreciative Inquiry – the art of the impossible

A technique that seems to be gaining popularity as a tool for organisational change is Appreciative Inquiry (AI). AI has been developed by David Cooperrider and colleagues at Case Western University in New Mexico, together with the Taos Institute.

Cooperrider (1998) argues that successful change requires:

Novelty – new and innovative possibilities
Continuity – of those practices that an organisation wants to maintain as it moves through its journey of change
Transition – specific and tangible areas to change

The philosophy behind AI is that change follows from what is studied, since the inquiry process plants the seeds of change. AI is an engaging and inclusive process, its aim being to produce a dialogue among different stakeholders about what is currently working well and to establish what is happening when an organisation is working at its best.

The process of AI starts by asking people to consider a simple question, 'What works around here?', which then leads on to a future-orientated dialogue. Often the change process in an organisation starts by asking 'What are the problems here?', which leads to a problem-solving approach.

Some of the underlying principles behind AI are:

- Accentuate the positive – AI is based on the assumption that life-giving forces are present in people, organisations and relationships, but that these can get overshadowed by negative elements. In traditional approaches to change, the positive elements, i.e. what is currently working well, often gets lost among things that are not working. This can be de-moralising and also reduce energy levels.
- We are masters of our own destiny – we create our world and we therefore need to consciously set about creating the sort of world that we want. It is a hopeful and pragmatic philosophy, based on the assumption that we can choose whether to be optimistic or pessimistic.
- Discovery – seek out positive stories of what is working well and promoting these throughout the organisation.
- Inclusivity – engage the whole of the organisation, not just particular groups, thus maximising opportunities for discovery.
- Respect for history – what has contributed to the success of the organisation in the past.

The start point for any AI would be the identification of an area that the organisation wants to learn about, or become better at, in order to enhance their business. As a tool for generating an interest in and developing a more knowledge-focused culture it would seem to have many possibilities. AI could be used at the start of the change process to engage different groups in a dialogue about how to build a knowledge-centric culture.

Some of the underlying tools used as part of an AI are ones that most HR professionals will be familiar with, e.g. Focus Groups, 1:1 interviews, Story Circles. Each of these tools will need to be combined to ensure that as many people as possible within the organisation get an opportunity to voice their positive thoughts about the organisation as it is now, as well as their thoughts and dreams for the future. As well as being used to gather key information at the beginning of a culture change process, Appreciate Inquiry sessions can be used to start to drip in some of the behaviours that the organisation wishes to encourage, such as: the importance of narrative forms of communication; encouraging more 'rapport talk'; good ideas are meant to be borrowed and everyone's ideas are important, irrespective of levels of seniority.

Appreciative Inquiry seems to fit with the Balanced Approach to culture change discussed earlier, where the aim is to preserve existing cultural benefits, and build on existing strengths. As AI can be resource intensive, clearly there is a need to ensure that senior management are supportive of the need for change and are willing to invest the necessary resources. Strengthening and Balancing an organisational culture is easier than trying to change everything about the existing culture.

Although seen as being an important tool for use in change programmes, AI also has applications in Personal Development, Career Development, as well as a tool for leaders to draw on as part of their overall leadership approach.

Tools to facilitate the sharing of tacit knowledge

After-action reviews

The tool, *Retrospect*, developed at BP to help capture tacit knowledge at the end of major projects (Collinson and Parcell, 2001) includes the following steps:

- Call a meeting with key players who have been involved in the project
- Re-visit project objectives and deliverables, using the help of a skilled facilitator
- Re-visit project plan
- Discussion and dialogue
- What went well and why?
- What could have gone better?
- What are the key messages others need to know about? The learning that is captured needs to be expressed as being beneficial for the future
- Ensure participants leave the meeting feeling that they have achieved something
- Agree next steps if appropriate
- Record the meeting and make available to others

End of Project Learning Review

This example of an End of Project Learning Review, developed by the author (Evans, 2000), is offered as a starting point for conducting learning reviews within your organisation. It is designed to capture learning in three areas: learning about the task, the process, as well as learning at the individual/organisational level.

Your views about the task
What was the project designed to achieve?
What did it actually achieve?
Why did these differences occur?
What can we learn from this?

Your views about the process

What worked particularly well in terms of the way we worked together as a team on this project?

What worked less well for you in terms of the way we worked together as a team? How might we have worked SMARTer together?

How might we have made better use of different levels of expertise and skills?

What were the surprises for you on the project and why?

Your views on individual/organisational learning

What have been the key benefits for you personally of taking part in this project, for example what new insights, ideas, or skills have you acquired?

How have you applied, or are you intending to apply, these to your other roles?

Who else have you shared your insights/ideas with?

Who else do you think would benefit from the lessons learnt on this project?

What be the best way(s) of sharing and disseminating these lessons?

Storytelling

One of the tools that is gaining popularity as a way of helping to elicit tacit knowledge, as we saw in the preceding chapter, is the use of narrative techniques such as Storytelling. Storytelling is not a new tool, its roots are in ancient traditions. In tribal cultures, for example, community members gather around the campfire to tell and re-tell tales of important events. During these gatherings different individuals offer their recollections of a major event (e.g. wars, change of leadership) and the leader (often referred to as a shaman) offers a commentary of the story thus helping to bring the story's significance to light.

Stories, according to J.S. Bruner (1986), a social psychologist, are 'polysemic' i.e. they have layers of meaning and significance, which we become aware of as we grow in experience and insight. As individuals we return to stories time and time again to get fresh insights. Stories, according to Gareth Morgan (1986), are a valuable tool for reconciling paradoxes and of transforming our understanding of organisational dilemmas.

Storytelling can provide a means for organisations to collectively reflect on past experience and draw out lessons learnt, so that these can be proactively taken forward.

Storytelling is both a process as well as a product, the product being a compelling story which conveys key messages. These messages can often be about the organisational values, norms, or rules that have previously got in the way on a particular project, or of organisational change.

Geoff Mead, an Organisational Development consultant, suggests that if OD consultants and developers use story as a way of describing actual events and relationships, then it can help to unlock individuals through opening up creative possibilities, thus making people more open to change[2].

The Oxford Group, a major change consultancy, stress the importance of creating a shared 'One Story' during change programmes. This was the approach adopted for the closure of C&A, in the late 1990s. C&A had been a household high street name up until this point. Having taken the difficult decision to close their high street stores, the organisation set an objective of making it the best closure on the high street. This was the story that senior managers communicated time and time again; this strategy seems to have paid off as profits rose during the closure period.

Storytelling can be a time consuming process. It requires the support of skilled facilitators with a diverse skill-set. However, many of these skills may already exist within the organisation, but remain untapped. For example, individuals with observation and recording skills may well exist in HR teams who carry out Assessment Centres. Qualitative research skills may well exist amongst individuals who are studying or, or who have completed, a masters programme. Some individuals may even have script writing skills developed from their interests outside of work. So it seems a good time for organisations to take a look at the broad-ranging skills which individuals have, but may not yet have been captured or exploited.

Drawing out lessons learnt, whether it be successes, or failures, so that these can be communicated across the organisation is crucial in learning-centric organisations. The use of narrative techniques, such as Storytelling, is one of the tools that organisations are now more prepared to experiment with. The case study that follows, from English Nature, shows how Storytelling is a natural fit as a knowledge management tool given the existing organisational culture and skills set.

Surfacing organisational knowledge through the use of storytelling – insights from English Nature

Organisational background

English Nature is the Government agency that champions the conservation of wildlife and natural features throughout England.

It was set up in 1990 when the Nature Conservancy Council, which had been responsible for conservation in England, Scotland and Wales, was reorganised. It is governed by a Council, which is appointed by the Secretary of State for the Department of the Environment, Food and Rural Affairs (DEFRA).

English Nature employs around 800 staff. Two-thirds of these are based in local teams, of which there are twenty-two in total. These teams are effectively small conservation communities who work in partnership with local communities and other agencies on wildlife and the natural environment. Being locally-based means that each conservation team is able to develop first-hand knowledge about conservation issues and needs within their geographical area. These local conservation teams are supported by a number of support teams (e.g. Information Technology, Finance, and Uplands and Lowlands habitat specialists) based at English Nature's headquarters in Peterborough.

Knowledge management challenges

A large proportion of the people who join English Nature are passionate about wildlife and conservation. Most staff join as graduates and go on to develop a long service record within the organisation. Currently there are pockets of staff in the same age cohort (50+) who will all potentially retire around the same time.

The organisation has a history, documented in recently unearthed oral history records, of apprenticeship schemes whereby novices learnt about conservation by working alongside experienced conservation officers.

Unlike in other organisations, ICT is not one of the main tools that conservation officers working in the local teams use as part of their day-to-day work. Thus from a knowledge management perspective ICT wasn't perceived as being one of the main enablers for facilitating knowledge sharing, as is often the case in other organisations. However, the organisation does have a limited experience of using oral history techniques and isolated experiences of what they now refer to as campfire storytelling, among its local conservation teams. It was felt that this expertise, which is currently much under-utilised, has potential to be further developed.

Earlier experiences of oral history projects

The experience within the organisation in the use of oral history techniques is something that has only recently come to light within Head Office. Over the years several oral history projects have been carried out by local teams. As part of the organisation's Millennium celebrations, for example, the Grantham team carried out an oral history project that resulted in the publication of the booklet – *The Sands of Time* – which documents the history of the Natural Nature Reserve in Lincolnshire which they part-own and help to manage. Fifty-one local people were interviewed as part of this project to gain insights into the history of the area and the relationship between people and the reserve, going back over a period of forty years.

From a knowledge management perspective key insights have been gained from this oral history project, for example:

> *Over this forty-year timeframe two, very similar, engineering projects had been carried out on the reserve, each with the same aim i.e. to straighten out a meandering stretch of the river, and each of these projects had been equally unsuccessful as the tide washed their efforts away. This 'repeated mistake' only came to light as a result of this oral history project.*

An earlier oral history project involved gathering staff's thoughts about the restructuring of the Nature Conservancy Council. This piece of research focused on questions such as: How did staff feel about the re-structure? What were their favourable memories of working for the NCC? What had prompted them to follow a career in conservation? How do they see the role of English Nature? Unfortunately this very readable and culture packed information, gathered from this piece of research, was never published due to political sensitivities at the time. Thus the insights gained from this piece of work are not widely known within the organisation.

More recent experiences of applying Storytelling techniques

The interest in developing Storytelling as a Knowledge Management tool stemmed from a partnership arrangement initiated three years ago by Dave Snowden of IBM's Institute of Knowledge Management. The partnership was perceived as being a mutual learning opportunity in which IBM could learn about the management of ecosystems from English Nature (something that is perceived as providing important insights for managing a 'knowledge ecology' within an organisation) and English Nature could learn about the principles of Knowledge Management, communities of practice and how to use the Storytelling tools being developed within IBM.

The use of Storytelling as a Knowledge Management tool is being championed by Ron Donaldson, the acting Information Services manager. He has carried out a number of Storytelling projects. These fall into two main areas.

Lessons-learnt reviews

Two key lessons-learnt projects have been completed using IBM's Storytelling techniques. One is of an office relocation project within Head Office and the other is of a Public Inquiry which English Nature were involved in.

One of the main lessons learnt from the office relocation storytelling project was that despite the fact that a lot of effort had gone into planning the physical office layout changes and the logistics of the office move, the human factor had not been given sufficient attention, i.e. how staff felt about the office move and their work environment subsequent to the move. The 'campfire tale' after the office-move review revealed that staff felt that their personal needs had been ignored as a result of the office reorganisation because they had not all been co-located with existing work colleagues in the new office layout. In addition some staff were no longer co-located with the filing cabinets (which they require regular access to) and the support staff with whom they have regular contact. This compounded the feeling of communities being broken up.

The Public Inquiry storytelling project revealed some important insights into how the project team, set up to represent English Nature, had been formed (i.e. the team selection process), how the team organised themselves for the task they had to do and also how they identified the knowledge gaps within the team and how they then filled those gaps. It also drew out valuable insights into the sensitive issues faced by the team and how the team resolved these.

The material gathered from this particular Storytelling project includes many previously unrecorded tips and techniques which have provided fruitful learning material that could be used as a resource on the organisations' media and public enquiry training courses.

Identifying Communities of Practice

This Storytelling project surfaced both formal and informal communities in place within the organisation. It has also provided some useful insights into the implications and opportunities for the organisation's overall knowledge base from different community structures.

One of the informal communities identified during the project was the Staff Canteen Community within Headquarters. This central restaurant area is where much of the day-to-day business is conducted. At coffee breaks many of the conversations are knowledge-building exchanges rather than discussions about what people watched on the television the previous evening. These discussions often develop into impromptu project meetings.

However, the physical space where this informal community meets is constantly under threat as the organisation grows in size. As the organisation expands there is pressure to convert restaurant space into office space, as was the case during the most recent office re-organisation.

In addition to this informal community a number of formal learning communities grouped around particular areas of specialist scientific knowledge were identified. The way in which three of these communities of practice are structured and managed was found to be of particular interest.

The Woodlands Community

The Woodlands Community is led by a recognised woodlands expert. Within this community the knowledge flow tends to be uni-directional, i.e. knowledge flows from the community leader to specialists in the local teams. The knowledge flow/exchanges between specialists within local teams was found to be minimal.

From an organisational perspective one of the advantages of this community structure is that it is easy to identify a woodland's expert who is able to speak knowledgeably and with authority on behalf of English Nature to external bodies. However, one of the downsides of this community structure is that local woodland experts (like shoots around a mature tree) can live in the shadow of the community leader. This has implications for the organisation's overall knowledge succession planning, as well as individuals' career development.

The Botanical Community

The Botanical Community is facilitated (as opposed to led) by a community leader with a general science background, rather than someone who is a recognised specialist in botany. In this community the knowledge flow was found to be more multi-directional, between the community leader and community members. In addition there was found to be more interaction and knowledge exchanges between community members. This is something that is actively encouraged by the community leader.

Although the way in which this particular community is structured and managed enables local conservation officers to enhance their personal knowledge, it generates a problem for the organisation as a whole in that it is more difficult quickly to identify a subject expert to represent the organisation to external bodies when needed.

The Freshwater Community

The leader of the Freshwater Community is different in that this was an external appointment. The knowledge flow within this community group is again more multi-directional, with knowledge flowing both ways between the community leader and experts within the local teams.

Appointing someone from outside the organisation into this role has had some unanticipated benefits. In particular it has opened up a new knowledge source through the previous contacts that the community leader already had with external organisations. This surfaces the importance of recognising already mature relationships during recruitment.

As the acting Information Services manager pointed out it is difficult to make an overall judgement as to which of these community structures is more effective from an overall knowledge management perspective. Each structure has advantages and disadvantages for the organisation as a whole, and for individuals.

The organisation needs to have experts who can be readily identified to speak knowledgeably on different aspects of conservation to external bodies in order to maintain its reputation and authority. The way in which the Woodlands Community and the Freshwater Community groups are structured makes this easier from an organisational perspective. However, the way in which the Botanical Community group is managed has the potential for a number of subject experts to be developed in parallel and perhaps a greater than average level of common knowledge.

Through this particular Storytelling project the organisation now has practical examples of the outcomes of different leadership approaches that could be used as learning materials in both internal and external leadership development programmes.

Organisational learning from the Storytelling projects

The Storytelling project that led to the discovery of how different communities of practice are structured and managed has surfaced some important questions for the organisation, these include:

- Where should the responsibilities for knowledge succession planning sit? What should the role of the centre be? What role should local teams play? What role should recognised experts play in identifying and developing their successor?
- What is the best way to develop local conservation officers so that they develop the relevant knowledge and skills needed to be capable of leading a Community of Practice in the future?
- Should local teams be expected actively to exchange knowledge with other local teams as well as with headquarters? How should this best be facilitated given that ICT isn't one of the essential tools that conservation officers within local teams use as part of their day-to-day work?
- How can technical specialists be helped to see the value of their 'know how' for the organisation as a whole?

Broader learning from the English Nature case study

- The way in which organisations are structured has implications for how knowledge is developed and retained. While decentralised structures can enable in-depth knowledge to be more easily developed, there is a danger that unless carefully managed this knowledge remains localised rather than flowing freely across the organisation.
- Knowledge management interventions need to be chosen carefully so that they are appropriate for the size of the organisation and also reflect an organisation's history and existing areas of expertise.
- The need to develop and retain specialist, as well as more generic, knowledge needs to be reflected in an organisation's overall knowledge retention plans.
- Knowledge management interventions need to begin with some form of stocktaking. What knowledge already exists within the organisation? Where is it located? Where are the gaps? How can these gaps best be addressed – is it through development, 'buying in' experts on a short or long-term basis, or through outsourcing?
- Any re-structuring/re-organisation plans need to take into account the potential impact on an organisation's knowledge assets, both short-term and longer-term.

- Leaders have an important role to play in helping technical specialists see the value of their specialist knowledge within a broader context.
- Organisations that recruit employees in cohorts from a particular source i.e. the graduate population, need to plan for the time when this cohort moves on, in order to retain their corporate memory.

Tools for identifying key knowledge resources and players

Social Network Analysis

One of the biggest difficulties organisations face today, particularly those that have a flexible, mobile and global workforce, is knowing who knows who and who knows what. Although there are formal systems for communicating and channelling information within organisations, a lot of the information that people use in their day-to-day work comes from their informal networks.

Networking has been identified as a crucial skill in knowledge-based businesses as it is the means by which individuals acquire and develop business-critical knowledge. Shapiro and Varian point out that 'Whether real or virtual, networks have a fundamental economic characteristic: the value of connecting to a network depends on the number of other people connected to it ... other things being equal, it is better to be connected to a bigger network than a smaller one. It is this "bigger is better" aspect of networks that gives rise to the positive feedback so commonly observed in today's economy' (Shapiro and Varian, 1999:174).

However, given the changing landscape of careers, networking is also important because of the way in which it contributes to the development of social capital. Through networking individuals build appropriate support structures, that are seen as being important for ensuring continuing psychological health, particularly when experiencing career transitions (Minor, Slade and Myers, 1991).

So how can organisations uncover the informal networks that exist within their organisation, as well as the different roles that people play within these networks?

A tool that seems to be gaining in popularity within the business world is Social Network Analysis. However, this is not a new tool. It evolved from the work of a group of social anthropologists, Barnes, Mitchell and Bott, in the 1950s and 1960s[3]. In its original form, Social Network Analysis was used to gather and analyse information about people's social support networks in a systematic way. From Burns *et al.*'s pioneering work four key categories of social support were identified:

- Informational support – the provision of information
- Instrumental support – support that is of a more practical nature
- Companionship – i.e. friendship
- Emotional support – this is support that is linked to areas of a more intimate nature such as self-confidence and self-esteem

The way in which individuals mobilise support can be broken down into two categories. The first is 'solicited requests', this is where an individual actively seeks help from others. The second is 'unsolicited requests' where support is volunteered without an individual having directly to ask for it. The size, density and level of interconnectedness of an individual's support network all have a bearing on the type, and speed, at which support can be mobilised.

Mobilising social support does have a number of associated costs. One cost is that of having an unbalanced exchange process, i.e. an unequal exchange of resources between individuals. Women in particular can suffer from 'network overburden' as they are often more responsive to requests for help, than men. In certain contexts, women may have limited access to supportive helpers e.g. when working in male-dominated organisations. Other costs associated with mobilising social support include: not wanting to create a negative impression by admitting that you have a problem which you cannot solve yourself; the issue of ensuring confidentiality, as well as not wanting to become dependent on others for support.

How are organisations using Social Network Analysis to help them manage their knowledge?

One way is in identifying the informal networks that exist within the organisation, how information flows through these networks, and the different roles that people play in this process. Used appropriately, Social Network Analysis can help identify:

Knowledge connectors – individuals who are good at linking different people within networks. The people who can be heard saying 'I don't know the answer to that myself, but I know a man/ woman who will'. These individuals have a good insight into who knows what and who knows who, and thus are able quickly to direct others to the information, or person, that colleagues are looking for. PAs and administrative staff are often very good at playing the role of knowledge connectors, as their work brings them into contact with lots of different people, for different reasons.

Knowledge brokers – these individuals help keep different sub-groups within the network together, by communicating what is happening within these different sub-groups.

Boundary spanners – these individuals form links with other networks, either within the organisation, or outside. They tend to have a broad overview of different functional areas and what they are doing. Boundary spanners can often be formal connectors between departments, because of the insights that they have into what other departments are doing.

Knowledge specialists – these individuals are the ones that others consult when they need some expert advice. These may not be the same people whom the formal system recognises as being a particular subject expert. This could be because the individuals themselves prefer to play a peripheral role, rather than be in the spotlight. They may be the ones who write the leading-edge articles, but not the ones who volunteer to give presentations at conferences, either internal or external.

What is important from an organisation's perspective is to recognize that these different roles exist and that they are each valuable in their own way. Armed with this information, organisations can then make more informed decisions about their reward and recognition, retention planning, succession planning, career management systems. In addition, line managers can take these informal roles into account when agreeing key task and deliverables with team members.

Other areas in which organisations can benefit from using Social Network Analysis are the recruitment and exit interview process, career management programmes, management development programmes, to highlight where individuals need to build more, or develop closer, working relationships.

In my own practitioner work, helping individuals who are in some form of career transition, I use Social Network Analysis as a way of helping these individuals review their personal networks. We look at the people in their existing network and the different types of support that each contact provides. This helps individuals become more aware of the gaps between support needed and received. We also look at the level of inter-connectivity between contacts in their network. This is important for information flow. Connectivity can also affect the extent to which individuals have to ask for direct help, as opposed to help being offered. Reviewing one's social network when in some form of transition is important as it is likely that individuals will need to invest in building new relationships, as well as possibly letting go of some existing relationships.

Figure 11.1 provides an example of the social network of an individual making the transition from a traditional career to an independent career, drawn from my own research (Evans, 2001).

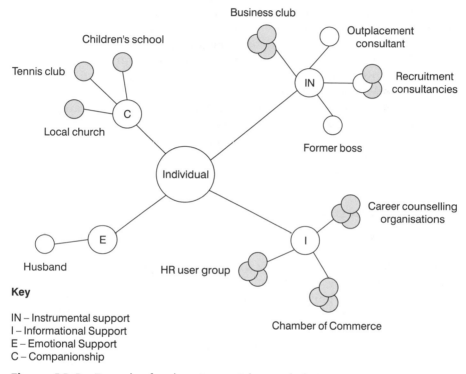

Figure 11.1 Example of a changing social network during a career transition

This particular individual was interesting in that in the immediate period prior to pursuing an independent career she had been on sabbatical, and had not worked for a period of around eighteen months. Part of her networking strategy during her career transition involved renewing old contacts (indicated by the unshaded nodes in Figure 11.1), as well as building new contacts (indicated by the shaded nodes in Figure 11.1). Her objective in renewing old contacts was twofold. First, to update her network contacts on her future plans. Second, to enlist their support in helping her make connections with organisations that might have a need for her expertise.

As Figure 11.1 shows the type of support she received from the different contacts in her network varied (indicated by the capital letters in each of the network nodes). As she was no longer in traditional employment most of her *Companionship* needs were satisfied through the contacts in her community networks: the local tennis club, local church and her children's school.

Most of her *Informational Support* needs were met through more formal bodies, such as an HR User Group that she belonged to, as well as her local Chamber of Commerce. *Instrumental Support* (i.e. practical support) was provided through her contacts in recruitment consultancies, business clubs, as well as an existing contact in an outplacement consultancy. Looking at her social network we can see that there was no interconnectivity between the different groups, so the information flow was uni-directional and tightly bounded.

Of course what we must remember is that social networks are not static entities, they are subject to change. People come and go. Relationships form and end. As a key resource in today's knowledge rich world networks need active management, both personally and for the organisation as a whole.

Rethinking evaluation

Evaluation, as discussed in Chapter 1, is one of the critical components of an effective knowledge management approach. However evaluation, particularly evaluating training and development programmes, is often considered as the Achilles heel of HR's work. Evaluation is often an afterthought, rather than something that is designed into training and development interventions from the outset.

With the increasing emphasis on learning in today's knowledge economy I think that there is a need to reframe our view of evaluation. Below I have reproduced an earlier article of mine in which I argue for the evaluation process to be seen as a valuable source of learning in its own right, rather than as a proving process, or as a way of catching people out.

Evaluating learning – Achilles heel or valuable source of learning?*

To stay successful in today's ever-changing business world organisations are investing millions on training and development

---

* This article first appeared in CCH Personnel Management Newsletter, July 2001, published by Croner.CCH and available as part of a subscription to Croner.CCH British Personnel Management Service.

interventions. Statistics from the DfEE indicate that in 2001 organisations spent £23.5 billion on training (this figure includes both off-the-job training and on-the-job training)[4]. But how do organisations know whether they are investing wisely? How do they know whether they are focusing on the right learning needs? and How do they know whether what has been learnt is being applied, developed and shared as part of the daily routines of working life? These are the types of questions that should be addressed as part of any evaluation process.

Evaluating training and development programmes has always been seen as the Achilles heel of HR's work. Yet with HR now taking on a more strategic role there has never been a better time for HR to grasp evaluation by the throat, using it as a tool to help demonstrate added value to the business. For this change to happen HR will need to work at changing some of the deep-rooted assumptions held about the purpose and anticipated outcomes from evaluation projects.

This article argues that instead of seeing evaluation as a proving process there are benefits to be gained from seeing evaluation as a learning process in its own right. It sets out where the learning points in the evaluation process are and what needs to happen to maximise these learning opportunities.

Intellectually, evaluation makes sense, so why the reluctance?

Evaluation, like post-implementation reviews, is one of those tasks that people rarely get over-enthused about. Management developers know that to be a good all-round learner individuals need to allocate time for giving and receiving feedback and for personal reflection – all part of the evaluation process. As Wilhelms (1971) points out, human beings, like all organisms, depend on feedback for their survival. We ponder over how a situation has worked out up to a particular point, what problems we are likely to face going forward and from there work out what is our next move. The feedback gained from learning programmes is vital for planning the next developmental steps, both for individuals, developers, and senior management. If feedback is so important to our ongoing development, and through evaluation we get valuable feedback, why are people so reluctant to invest in this process? There are a number of possible explanations. One is that different stakeholders hold different views on the purpose and expected outcomes from the evaluation process. In some organisations evaluation is perceived as a proving exercise, or a way of identifying failures. In these situations the evaluation process is conducted on the lines of an inspection or audit. Wilhelms points out that '*Most evaluators rush in too soon and concentrate too much on the catching of failures.*' If individuals feel that the evaluators are trying to catch them out, it is no wonder that they are unwilling to engage with the evaluation process, or indeed see the value or relevance to them.

An alternative perspective on evaluation is that of evaluation being about improving and developing. Adopting this perspective can help to free people up in terms of what they are willing to contribute to the process.

Another explanation is that having completed a learning project most developers want to move on to their next project. Indeed participants themselves are often so keen to get back to work that they do not want to spend time completing evaluation sheets. '*I need time to think before completing this*' or '*I have to dash off to ... I'll complete it later and post it to you*' are some of the responses that developers receive when evaluation sheets are handed out at the end of a programme. Sometimes these make it back, but often they gather dust in delegates' in-trays.

One final explanation is that while some individuals are good at reflection others require the stimulus of other people to help them with this process. It never ceases to amaze me when conducting evaluations how much individuals value the opportunity to talk to someone else about what they have learnt on a development programme and what development steps they have taken since. Sadly not all individuals have an opportunity for this type of one-to-one learning conversation once a development event is over – a missed opportunity then from an evaluation perspective.

Evaluation – a politically sensitive task

Conducting evaluations requires a politically sensitive approach. Each evaluation needs to take into account the different interests and expectations of the multiple stakeholders with an interest in the learning programme being evaluated; these stakeholders and their interests are likely to include:

- The Finance Director whose primary interest will be Return on Investment.
- The Commissioning Manager whose primary interest will be identifying the extent to which the learning programme is helping to address a specific business issue in his or her area.
- The developers who will be interested in whether or not the delivered solution meets the customer's expectations, and whether or not they receive favourable feedback on their personal impact as trainers. The developers are also likely to want to focus on their own learning, for example what new

techniques, skills or knowledge have they acquired as a result of designing and implementing a particular learning programme.

- The head of HR who will be interested in whether or not the customer is likely to want to purchase the HR team's services again in the future.
- The individual learners who will no doubt have a myriad of personal objectives that they hoped to gain from the learning programme, some of which they will share willingly with others and some of which they keep to themselves.

Evaluators need to be aware of the many factors that can affect the way in which different stakeholders engage with the evaluation process. These factors include:

- Assumptions held by stakeholders about the purpose of the evaluation – is it for proving or improving purposes?
- General attitudes towards evaluation – is it seen as a necessary evil, or a means of learning?
- Previous involvement with evaluation projects – was it an enjoyable and engaging experience, or stressful?
- Nature of the learning intervention to be evaluated – is it a self-contained area, or is it more broad-ranging?
- Clarity and openness about the overall process, including the dissemination of findings.
- Level of attachment to the learning intervention – a high level of attachment by stakeholders can mean that individuals are less able to be objective with their input.
- Criteria for participation in the evaluation – is it voluntary or imposed?

The experienced evaluator will be attuned to these different factors and by investing time in getting to know the different stakeholders personally will identify the extent to which these factors apply on any given evaluation.

It is never too early to start

Many writers agree that the evaluation process needs to start much earlier in the development cycle than is often the case. The best time to start thinking about evaluation is as soon as the business problem is being teased out. However, evaluations frequently get tagged on as an afterthought, rather than being planned in at the outset of the overall learning project. It is hardly surprising then when having spent thousands of pounds on developing a learning programme developers ask for more money to evaluate it, their request is met with little enthusiasm. It is far better that any additional resources needed to conduct the evaluation are identified at the overall planning stage.

If evaluation is to be seen as a learning tool in its own right then it is particularly important that the evaluation scope and approach is discussed at the outset of the project. Wherever possible, evaluators should try to encourage a partnership approach whereby different stakeholders work together to ensure that the evaluation scope and approach meets their collective needs. Again this helps to maximise the opportunities for learning among the different stakeholders.

Learning points in the evaluation process

Identification of learning needs

Sometimes it is all too easy for developers to offer a standard solution to a presented business problem, particularly where the developer thinks that cost is likely to be the main decision criterion.

By investing a little extra time at this stage the developer can ensure that they have a clear picture of what the real problem is, rather than take at face value the initial reported business problem. Often this requires spending some time learning about what is currently working well with a business area, rather than focus on the reported what is not working well. For example the reported '*I need to send all of my team on a creativity course so that they become more creative*' after some further diagnostics, may transpire to be a case of the team are very creative but are not allowed the space to demonstrate this, or the reward system doesn't reinforce creativity. In either of these cases the solution would be quite different to running a creativity course.

Focusing on evaluation at the needs identification stage can thus help ensure that the right intervention gets planned at the outset. For those in the organisation interested in Return on Investment this means minimising the chances of unnecessary expenditure. Sadly this type of information often doesn't get reported.

Engaging different stakeholders in a discussion about evaluation at the outset can help them broaden their perspective on the overall measures that need to be used to assess the programme's success. One leading practitioner in the field of e-learning, for example, encourages her clients to consider measures such as 'time to competency' or 'time to market', rather than applying more traditional Return on Investment criteria[5].

Programme design

One of the other opportunity points for learning in the evaluation process comes at the programme design stage. A key decision for the lead developer at this point is who to involve in the project. The bigger the project the greater the opportunity for involving more people and hence more learning. However, teams are often put together based upon individuals' prior experience of working on similar learning programmes..

However, if at the design stage we put our diversity and/or knowledge management hats on this could bring a different result, creating an opportunity for injecting new energy and/or approaches into the design.

I have a well-respected colleague who, although she doesn't do much actual delivery these days, is regularly invited to design meetings. Her ability to challenge some of the underpinning assumptions upon which learning programmes are developed, as well as her ability to encourage others to come up with creative design solutions, is invaluable. Her involvement, albeit for a limited time, increases the learning opportunities for other team members.

Where a knowledge management perspective is adopted at the programme design stage this could help focus on the lessons learnt from other relevant learning programmes, for example, what were the key successes, sticking points and turning points? This approach has two benefits, one being an improved product, and another being the enhanced knowledge of the developers in the design team. One generic evaluation criterion that could be adopted is ensuring that the way of working adopted by the design team maximises the opportunities for the transfer of knowledge.

Delivery

At the delivery stage, the evaluation process should focus on the individual learner according to Wilhelms so that the individual moves towards a *'valid and healthy view of him/herself'*. The evaluation processes used during the actual learning programme needs to focus on helping individuals be clear about their strengths, so that they can build upon their self-concept. This does not mean avoiding areas of weakness. However, the feedback obtained needs to be balanced, so that individuals develop the insights and energy needed to take their learning forward. This is particularly important given that individuals who have had positive learning experiences feel more positive about themselves and their achievements, and hence are more likely to seek out further learning opportunities and challenges in the future. In organisations that are striving to become a learning organisation, or where there is a goal to encourage life-long learning, willingness to participate in additional learning programmes ought to be one of the broader criteria taken into account in the evaluation process. Happiness sheets will not capture this sort of data as the questions asked are too context specific.

Beyond implementation

When the euphoria of a learning event is over, it is often only then that individuals really start to take stock of what they have actually learnt, how they will put their learning into practice, as well as identify current gaps in their knowledge. Yet many evaluations rarely get beyond the first level in the Kirkpatrick evaluation model, i.e. the reaction level.

I was reminded of this recently when as a novice sailor I attended a three-day yacht sailing course and then immediately went off flotilla sailing with my family. While the yacht course gave me a good theoretical base for sailing it wasn't until we were out on our own boat that I really started to apply what I had learnt on the course. I quickly learnt that the instructor had lots of tacit knowledge that she hadn't been able to pass on to me given the type of training course that I had participated in. Had I had the opportunity to give feedback to the instructor after the flotilla holiday, it would have been of more value than that given immediately after completing the course.

So what can we learn from this particular experience? As learners we need time, beyond the learning event itself, to assimilate and put into practice what we have learnt. It makes sense then for the evaluation process to extend beyond the delivery stage. But we already send out evaluation sheets three months after a training course I hear you say, and the response rate is always very low. If this is the case, perhaps it is time to adopt a different approach.

We need to consider which stakeholders are likely to benefit most from the evaluation process at this point? Very often it is the individual learners as ongoing feedback, following a learning programme, is crucial to the learning process. One approach that could be incorporated into the evaluation process is to utilise a tool that enables individual learners to gain regular ongoing feedback on the development areas that they have chosen to work on. A new tool that I have recently come across that makes this a simpler process for both individuals and HR is Pulse Feedback[6].

This tool enables individual learners to receive regular feedback, in an electronic format, on the progress that others see them making against their defined development areas. Although centrally administered, the individual learner is in control of the feedback that is most relevant to them.

In viewing evaluation as a learning process in its own right, it can be a valuable tool in HR's toolkit. From a knowledge management perspective developing the skills in learning how to learn, as well as facilitating the transfer of knowledge, is as important as what is actually learnt. Any evaluation process needs to acknowledge and capture this difference.

Pause for thought

- How might you start to draw on some of the tools outlined in this chapter to help develop your organisation's knowledge management capabilities?
- How might you integrate these into central learning resources?
- What other tools are colleagues using to help them manage their knowledge?
- How extensively do you use evaluation as a valuable source of learning?

Notes

1. Some additional references on Appreciative Inquiry, other than the Cooperrider one in the main references, include: S. Hammond (1998) *The Thin Book of Appreciative Inquiry* (2nd edn). Thin Book Publishing, Plano Texas and C. Elliott (1999), *Locating the Energy for Change: An Introduction to Appreciative Inquiry.* The International Institute for Sustainable Development, Winnipeg, Canada.
2. Geoff Mead. A Winter's Tale: myth, story and organisations. *Self & Society*, Volume 24, No. 6, January 1997.
3. For an introductory book on the use of Social Network Analysis see J. Scott. (1991), *Social Network Analysis.* Sage Publications.
4. Learning and Training at Work 2000. In *Labour Market Quarterly.* DfEE Skills and Enterprise Network Publication. May 2001.
5. D. Raths, Measure of Success. *www.onlinelearningmag.com*
6. For further details about Pulse Feedback™ see *www.psymmetry.com*

12

Using technology wisely

Having made the point at the outset of this book that although technology is an important enabler for managing knowledge, it is not the total solution, it may seem a little strange to find a chapter dedicated to the use of technology. My reason for wanting to include this chapter was that I felt that if HR are to be more influential in the knowledge management arena they may need to enhance their own knowledge about where technology can help an organisation move forward on its knowledge management journey.

This chapter does not provide an in-depth discussion of specific technologies, instead it covers an overview of different categories of technologies, specifically those that are available to help locate and connect people with specific 'know of' and 'know how', as well as to facilitate collaborative working. It is hoped that this will generate some common language to have a meaningful dialogue with IS and IT colleagues.

Rob van der Spek and Jan Kingma (1999) point out that an organisation's strategy for managing knowledge should address two areas. First, the exploitation and application of existing knowledge and second, the creation of new knowledge, including building the capabilities to create new knowledge faster than in the past. They argue that delivering an effective knowledge management strategy requires:

● Processes and tools to help to connect knowledgeable people, working in different geographical locations and time zones.

- Processes and tools to ensure corporate-wide access to information about best practice, experience and ideas.
- The provision of learning tools for individuals and teams to help them adopt a learning perspective on their work.

One of the dangers in today's technological world is automatically to look for a technological solution for organisational problems, whereas in practice this is not always feasible, cost-effective, or indeed necessary. Linda Emmett, Information Manager, CIPD Professional Knowledge, shared some thoughts with me about the appropriate use of technology for managing knowledge.

One of the first areas to consider, Linda suggests, is exploring whether an IT solution is needed, not what is needed. This involves asking questions like:

- What do you really want KM to achieve?
- What do you think KM would look like in the organisation – what does your end vision look like? Is it about streamlining to improve workflow? Or do you want to automate a manual process? Would IT provide that framework as the enabler/ facilitator?
- What would be a good 'organisational fit'? What do the different users – the knowledge creators, knowledge translators and knowledge users – need? Remember that there is a difference between what users say they need, what they want, and what they actually use! There may be a need to observe the different users in action to find out what they actually do and then derive needs from these direct observations.
- What kind of Board support is available, both financially and culturally?

The next area to consider, if it is identified that there is a need for an IT solution, is to consider whether any existing systems can be adapted, or whether there is a need to buy a packaged solution, or build a bespoke system. Some considerations here include:

- What sort of usability/functionality does the organisation want? Accepting that this will depend on what you want the technology to do, the main consideration is to keep things simple and not to get lost in terminology and jargon.
- One option would be to follow generic marketing principles to segment the organisation into different user sectors, so that you can match solutions to needs, recognising that one size does not usually fit all, particularly where different parts of the organisation have different skill levels.

● Another consideration is that of what has been the organisation's experience of introducing new technology? Has it had positive or negative experiences? Does it have 'baggage' that needs to be addressed? How will this be addressed?

Other general areas to consider include:

Accessibility

Is there a common IT platform across departments/locations?
Are there existing standards for data entry/input?
How will content be added/updated and removed? How easy is it for content to be added? Who has responsibility? Who will ensure that out-of-date data is removed?
What sort of archiving mechanisms is needed?

Employee skills and development

Is there a common level of skill and usage?
What are the skills/competencies of employees – is there a need for training and developing?

Technical issues

Can the existing network cope? Is there enough memory for storage and archiving?
What about response times, especially when remote working?
Maintenance and security – who and how?

Cultural issues

What use is made of networks/shared drives/collaborative emails? Are these part of the 'How we do things around here'?
Is there a need for interaction – real-time updating?
Is our organisational culture ready for the systems that we want to introduce?

Privacy/security

Will everyone require the same access, or are different levels of access required? What about temporary workers, those on short-term contracts, and strategic partners; what restrictions, if any, will they have?
Updating for all? What is the trade-off between the need for gatekeepers versus accessibility?
How will access to sensitive information be managed?

What has all of this got to do with HR?

In the introduction to this book I made the point that one of the ways in which HR, in their strategic partner role, can add value in the knowledge management arena is to challenge other people's thinking about what does, and does not, need changing within the organisation. Although HR may not necessarily be as closely involved with the detailed design of any technological solution for managing knowledge, they could add value by at least finding out whether the questions outlined above have been asked. HR could get away with asking what might seem the naive questions – Could we do KM without technology? – something that the technologists may never consider, because they are often motivated by designing and building systems, irrespective of the real need.

There is growing consensus that when developing knowledge management solutions a multi-disciplinary team approach should be adopted drawing on resources such as: Information Services, IT, HR, Marketing, Chief Knowledge Officer and/or Knowledge Management team, Communications Department, as well as representatives from different user groups.

One model of working identified as background research for this book involved:

- The Head of IT putting forward an outline suggestion for ways of enhancing IT systems from a knowledge management perspective.
- This is followed by the organisation setting up a series of focus groups as a way of building an understanding of what is required versus what is possible.
- The output from the focus groups are then incorporated into a formal proposal, which is then fed back to senior managers and focus group members for approval, before any development work commences.

Practitioner tips

From my background research, which includes discussions with different HR, IT and IM professionals, I have identified the following practitioner tips which could be applied if the organisation is considering introducing a technological solution for managing knowledge.

Tip 1: Understand the value of the information that you have

One of the issues that many individuals complain of today is information overload. However, Shapiro and Varian (1999) suggest that this isn't because the quantity of information has changed significantly, but that technology has made it more accessible; as a result this has affected the value that people ascribe to information.

New technologies have also made it possible to manipulate information in ways that were not feasible in the past; again this has added to the value of information. However, the value that people place on information is not static. Equally, different people can ascribe a different value to the same piece of information.

Having access to information in business is one thing, but what is also important is whether or not people then act on that information (thus bringing more value). A story to illustrate this point follows:

An HR manager in a pharmaceutical company that I met while writing this book talked about how she happened to stumble across a news item about how a rival pharmaceutical company was planning to open an office about twenty miles away from her company's offices. She immediately alerted her senior management team about this piece of information, pointing out some of the implications for the organisation.

Together the HR manager and the senior management team worked out a plan for minimising any potential fallout from this change. They looked at who their most vulnerable employees were, i.e. the ones whom they did not want to lose, but who might be attracted to the other company. A decision was taken to bring forward a salary review. They also looked at the development plans for those employees whom they wanted to retain, looking at what could be done to enhance their development opportunities. The physical work environment was reviewed too, recognising that the building that their competitors were moving into would be more modern, and hence possibly have better facilities.

Despite the initial concerns, the organisation did not lose any of the key people that they wanted to retain. The HR manager couldn't be certain that this was entirely linked to the speed at which the management team had responded to this potential threat, but felt it must have been a contributing factor.

This story illustrates how information and knowledge are not the same thing. We can each have the same piece of information in front of us, but how we interpret, or apply that information, is different depending upon our prior experience, i.e. our pre-existing knowledge.

Tip 2: Get a better handle on managing information

Making the information that people need to do their jobs more accessible is often a key goal for organisations when they start off on their KM journey.

Some of the sources of information that people need to do their jobs effectively include:

- Contact details for all employees – name, telephone, e-mail addresses
- Departmental information – What departments exist and what do they do?
- My PC is broken, who do I contact to get it fixed?
- Products and services – What do we offer now? What new products and services are in the pipeline?
- Customer information – Who are our customers? What do we know about them? Do they have any outstanding problems? What business issues are they struggling with?
- Supplier information – Who are our major suppliers? Who are the key contacts? Where are they located?
- Organisational procedures – How do I complete an expense claim form?
- Who is the expert on XYZ?
- Is there a template for writing a client a proposal?
- What customer reports have been written on XYZ?
- What are the latest Project Management guidelines?
- How do I prepare for a performance review?

However, one of the biggest challenges for organisations is ensuring ease of access to the vast range of information that people need to do their jobs effectively, as well as ensuring that this information is kept up-to-date. In the past, much of the information that people needed to do their jobs was held in procedures manuals. Often these manuals gathered dust on employees' shelves, largely because they quickly became out-of-date. However, through the use of web-based technologies many organisations have been able to find a way of centralising key information. Intranet systems are quickly becoming the central repository for organisational procedures.

But managing information is a skill in its own right. Information management professionals need to understand and effectively manage information from its conception, including its role in the organisation's ability to meet its strategic goals. Today's information management professionals need to demonstrate an understanding of how and why data is created, who should have access to it, how long data should be kept and hence when it is safe for it to be destroyed. They also need to be able to demonstrate an understanding of where technologies can help in managing an organisation's information sources.

Tip 3: Keep it simple

Work with real needs, rather than what someone/some department thinks is needed. This will require building an understanding of the issues that get in the way of people doing their jobs effectively.

Tip 4: Treat managing knowledge as a task that has a deliverable and therefore requires an allocation of time

Often a key reason why people do not share their knowledge is not because they don't want to, but because they do not have the time to do so, as they are too busy doing other things, some of which may be more valuable, or perceived to be more valuable. If it is so important for people to acquire, build and share knowledge then it is important that they are allowed to plan for this in the same way as they plan their other work activities.

In Chapter 7, I described how working, learning and knowledge-building was very much integrated into the lives of independent consultants. They plan for and manage this aspect of their lives. For these individuals there is a more direct relationship between knowledge and income, i.e. if they don't keep their knowledge up-to-day their in-demand factor goes down, which in turn can affect their income. However, in organisations this relationship is not so clear. Individuals may be set targets, but how those targets are met, or whether they actively contribute from a knowledge perspective, may not be taken into account in the reward system.

Tip 5: Provide basic tools and train people in how to use them

In many organisations some of the basic knowledge management tools already exist, e.g. e-mail, Internet access, word processing facilities, video conferencing facilities, as well as conference call facilities. Before introducing more tools, a start point could be to look at how these facilities are currently being used. Does everyone have access to these facilities? How frequently do they use them? Are they over-utilised, or under-utilised? Do some teams/departments use these tools more frequently than others? If, so what is the outcome?

KPMG, for example, has invested significantly in the technologies needed to facilitate knowledge sharing and to encourage collaborative working among its own staff, and with clients. The corporate intranet is one of the key tools used by staff as part of their day-to-day work. As this was felt to be such an important vehicle for knowledge sharing a separate training programme was developed to help staff get the most out of the intranet as a tool for use in their day-to-day work.

As different people use technology in different ways, depending on the nature of their jobs, this needs to be taken into consideration in the training provision. Rather than go into too much depth initially, provide people with the basics to get them started, followed by opportunities to go into more depth at a later stage, as and when individuals are ready to use additional facilities. One area to consider would be to set up a network of experts who would be willing to offer one-to-one advice/coaching to others in the organisation, at the time when they need to know more.

Tip 6: Examine the feasibility of adapting existing systems to provide just-in-time knowledge

Davenport and Glaser (2002) suggest that instead of developing separate knowledge management systems, an alternative strategy would be to build the specialist knowledge that people need to do their jobs into existing IT systems. This is an approach adopted by Partners Healthcare, a Boston-based group of hospitals. The challenge facing this particular hospital group was one of doctors finding it difficult to keep their clinical knowledge up-to-date. Something that is not untypical among highly skilled professionals, such as doctors. However, instead of developing a separate knowledge management system the organisation decided to link large amounts of constantly changing clinical information to the existing IT systems that their doctors use during their day-to-day work. The organisation started by linking critical knowledge to their order-entry system; a system that Partners' doctors regularly use to order tests, drugs and treatments.

By linking the existing order-entry system with a clinical database (knowledge-management system) doctors are offered 'real-time' up-to-date information about new drugs, or whether a particular drug is compatible with those that a particular patient is already taking. Instead of having to search out critical information, as in the past, the information that they need to do their job is automatically presented to them. But what is also different about the system that Partners' have introduced is that it still enables doctors to apply their professional judgment to the decision-making process. In other words the system was designed so that doctors are presented with suggestions, not commands. This was also a critical element in getting buy-in to invest in developing such knowledge management systems.

Tip 7: Make sure that any new KM systems addresses a real need

One of the traps that many organisations have fallen into is introducing a KM system because the technology is there, or because other businesses have them and therefore feel that their organisation should have one too, rather than because it addresses a real business need. It has been a case of technology in search of a business solution, as opposed to the other way round.

When introducing KM into the organisation, the KM team needs to spend time gaining an understanding of the difficulties that individuals currently experience gaining access to information, locating who is who, and also who knows what. From here a decision can then be taken as to how best to address these difficulties. Is an IT systems solution needed, or a human systems solution needed, or a combination of the two?

When Compaq were introducing a portal for its global sales force the first stage of the project involved building an in-depth understanding of how the organisation's global sales force actually worked[1]. Many of the sales people were home-based, therefore having access to key information from different locations was something that was a key requirement. The portal development team spent five months gaining this insight through a combination of e-mail surveys, focus group discussions and one-to-one discussions with sales people. It was the one-to-one sessions with sales people that provided some of the most valuable insights for the portal development team.

Tip 8: Pilot new systems with a small, but representative group, of users before rolling out to the wider user population

This was one of the key lessons learnt by QinetiQ during the early stage of its knowledge management journey (see the QinetiQ case study that follows later in this chapter). If well managed the pilot phase can be used to generate wider interest in knowledge management. As with other types of change programmes running a pilot enables users to make a mental shift and to start to see new possibilities.

Tip 9: Learn from other people's mistakes

This was a strategy introduced in Chapter 6 that discussed ways of enhancing learning in the knowledge economy. Ways of gaining access to this type of information include: informal networking at conferences; organisational case studies; research reports produced by academic institutions, or specialist technology research institutions, such as Gartner, or Butler Cox, or carrying out a study tour and/or benchmarking activity.

Tip 10: Ensure that new KM systems interface with existing systems

This was one of the criteria specified by QinetiQ when selecting software to help tap into the organisation's intellectual assets, in this way avoiding wasteful duplication of data, as well as making it easier from the user's perspective.

The rest of this chapter discusses the different types of technologies that are available to help locate and connect people, as well as to facilitate collaborative working. This is not meant to be an in-depth discussion. The aim is to provide an overview of what technologies are available and how they are being used, so that as practitioners you will be able to engage in a dialogue with your IT colleagues.

Technology to connect a mobile and global workforce

Tools here include:

Video conferencing facilities – though not a new technology, its usage seems to have greater appeal when the organisation is looking to reduce its travel expenditure.

Messaging and conference call facilities – when these facilities are combined with Instant Messaging facilities this can enable individuals to have a second dialogue going with selected members of those participating in the conference call.

E-mail – used appropriately e-mail is a great tool for communicating across different locations and time zones. However, many people today complain of e-mail overload, so much so that some organisations are starting to monitor usage more closely. E-mail-free Fridays (or an equivalent) seem to be creeping in alongside dressing down on Fridays. Individuals need to be provided with training and/or guidelines for using e-mail as a communications tool, alongside the training available for other forms of communication.

Team rooms or chat rooms – these are virtual spaces that can be used for exchanging knowledge among virtual project teams.

Information portal – this is an intranet site that can be used to hold information that mobile workers may need to access remotely. This can be anything from internal marketing information, business news, product updates, even information on how to get the best usage out of different technologies. It is also possible for individuals to create their own personal web-page, containing any information about themselves that they want to share with colleagues. The free-format nature of these web-pages means that the information held is likely to be very different to that held in a CV database.

Web camera technology – one small technology-based company that I discovered as part of the background research for this book had introduced web cameras in its staff restaurant. The thinking behind this was to try to eliminate queuing at peak times in the restaurant. However, the organisation quickly discovered additional benefits of using this technology. First, it helped to create a greater sense of community between employees working in different locations. As a small number of the organisation's employees work in America, being able to see pictures of their colleagues in the restaurant in the UK site helps them feel part of a wider community. Staff in the UK quickly started to use the web camera technology to time their visits to the restaurant to catch up with colleagues whom they particularly wanted, or needed, to talk to. Of course there is a danger that if this technology becomes over-used, as with mobile phones, staff and managers alike might find that there is no way of escaping work.

Technologies to locate and connect people

'I am writing a paper on "xyz" who might be able to help me?', or 'I have got to give a presentation to a client on "xyz", has anyone else given a similar presentation?'. These are fairly typical problems that people within organisations have to resolve. In small to medium sized organisations, say around two hundred to three hundred people, it is likely that individuals will know a large percentage of their colleagues personally. If not, it is likely that they will only have to make one or two calls in order to make contact with the person who can be of most help. But where organisations consist of larger numbers of people, and these people are located in different locations, then locating and connecting to the right person can be more problematic.

Directory systems are one of the more common knowledge management systems. Often referred to as 'Yellow Pages', basic directory systems can provide a central point for listing who is who within an organisation, together with some basic contact details (e-mail address, telephone number, mobile number, work-place location).

However, directories can be used in more extensive ways than this, depending on the needs of the organisation. Most of the big consultancies use directories as a way of making it easier to locate, connect and tap into the explicit and tacit knowledge of their consultants. KPMG's Kclient, for example, helps individuals locate particular knowledge experts, as well as facilitating knowledge sharing among different professional teams. Ericsson's Stargate system is a centralised resource designed to enhance global collaboration. The system enables individuals to locate information about customers, identify someone in the organisation with a specific skill, or area of specialist knowledge, create a new community of practice, as well as providing easier access to published documents.

Before implementing directory systems, some cultural questions need to be considered. To what extent do people currently share their 'know how' freely with others? What are some of the existing political behaviours that get in the way of knowledge exchanges? How will people be encouraged/enticed to use the system? Who will be responsible for keeping the information in the directory system up-to-date? Will the directory be available to all staff, or just certain groups?

As usage of 'Yellow Pages' type systems in most organisations is voluntary, some of the ways in which people can be encouraged to use the system is by enabling them to personalise their own directory entry, either by including their hobbies and interests outside of work, or including a photograph of themselves, or latest holiday pictures. Adding photographs, and other personal details, is seen as a way of helping to establish trust among users; an essential ingredient for knowledge exchanges. Giving people a free hand to personalise their directory entry may provide the initial stimulus to encourage people to start to use the system. But getting them to keep their details up-to-date, may need more innovative incentives. While knowledge is normally freely, or relatively freely, available within organisations, HP have adopted a slightly different approach. Users of HP's internal search engine pay a monthly charge that goes some way to enabling providers to recover the costs incurred in delivering knowledge services to their customers[2]. What would happen if a similar approach were adopted for rewarding individual knowledge contributors and sharers? Might this lead to a change in behaviours?

As well as helping individuals quickly to locate the right expert to help them with a specific problem, directory systems can also be used as a management tool, for example, to locate individuals with a particular area of expertise to work on a client project. One HR Director pointed out to me that while informal networking is an important way of matching individuals to projects, in a project-working environment, their 'Yellow Pages' system is an important tool for matching people and projects.

Using technology to identify, connect and leverage organisational 'Know how' within QinetiQ

Organisational background

QinetiQ is currently a wholly government-owned UK plc, competing to deliver innovative technology-based solutions to customers and their communities worldwide. QinetiQ, formed in July 2001, comprises the greater part of DERA, the British Government's 'Defence Evaluation and Research Agency', with Dstl remaining part of the MOD and continuing to handle the most sensitive areas of defence research.

In its new form, QinetiQ aims to leverage the breadth of its knowledge base, which consists of 9,000 staff working in 42 different locations in the UK, to help its customers maximise advantage from technology. This includes making optimal use of existing systems and developing, building and implementing new solutions.

The organisation's strategic aim is to position QinetiQ for a Public Offering within the next two to four years, but it is currently looking for a strategic investor. As a public–private partnership, QinetiQ will have greater freedom and access to capital, allowing it to exploit its technologies and capabilities in wider markets. It has the potential to become a globally recognised brand, and the world's leading technology-based solutions provider.

The organisation's knowledge management journey

The organisation's knowledge management journey started in about 1996, before QinetiQ was formed. Many of the scientists, engineers and technologists that work within QinetiQ have grown up in an environment that closely mirrors that of an academic research environment. Thus to a certain extent many of the disciplines required for effective knowledge management are ones that individuals are familiar with, as these have been developed as part of their scientific practice. None the less the organisation has adopted a more strategic approach to knowledge management over the past six years. There have been several stages to the organisation's knowledge management strategy. The key stages, requirements and deliverables are summarised in Table 12.1.

Despite acknowledging the role of technology in facilitating knowledge building and sharing the organisation recognised early on, in its knowledge management journey, that IT solutions alone would not be sufficient to bring about the changes that it wanted to achieve. Thus in addition to investing in different technological solutions, other organisational changes were introduced to help develop the cultural aspects needed to support the organisation's knowledge management goals. One of these changes related to encouraging and supporting more collaborative team working, particularly among virtual teams.

Another change involved changes to the physical work environment to support more open communications and collaborative working. This transformation had started prior to the organisation becoming privatised. At the Farnborough offices, for example, the coffee lounge area in the staff restaurant was redesigned to create an environment that was more conducive to holding informal meetings with colleagues. Since becoming QinetiQ, the number of these informal meeting spaces has been increased. In addition the organisation is making it easier for people to make more use of outside meeting areas. Parts of walls have literally been taken out and replaced with doors, making access to the outer courtyards easier. Staff now also have the ability to connect into the organisation's networks from home, so that they are better able to balance work and home needs. These changes act as a powerful symbol of the culture that the organisation wants to encourage, i.e. a culture where people are trusted to do their job and deliver what they have committed to deliver, rather than being judged by the actual hours spent at work.

One of the biggest challenges for QinetiQ was that despite having an accreditation system for identifying and categorising the knowledge of its scientific community, through the 'QinetiQ Fellow' system, the breadth of knowledge held by 'QinetiQ Fellows' was often only available to a tightly knit group of colleagues. Given the organisation's aim of maximising advantages from technology for its customers, it is important that it knows what expertise exists within the organisation and is able quickly to bring together experts from different disciplines to create new business opportunities.

Although the K-NET system, introduced in 1998, provided a central repository for scientists and technologists to store some basic details about themselves, e.g. name, contact numbers, qualifications, and membership of professional bodies, in practice this did not bring the expected business benefits. There were a

Table 12.1: Stages in QinetiQ's strategic approach to knowledge management

Date	Key priority area	Key requirements	Key deliverables
1996	Stage 1: Focus on codified knowledge	• Provide easy access to explicit knowledge • Create an environment where it is easy to share knowledge • Locate where the tacit knowledge is	• Intranet established, containing information about who is doing what and when, citation index • Appointment of Chief Information Officer, reporting directly to the Board
	Stage 2: Focus on tacit knowledge	• Identify what tacit knowledge is available	• Introduction of K-NET, designed to hold details about individuals and 'know how'
1998	Focus on the organisational culture	• Clarify the business benefits of knowledge management • Identify KM priorities for different DERA sectors • Develop just-in-time knowledge delivery	• Knowledge management steering group established • Appointment of Manager to manage the cultural aspects of KM • Identification of 56 key KM initiatives, linked to 4 main categories • K-NET web enabled to allow direct input by staff
1999			• FISP(PeopleSoft) introduced to provide a central repository for organisational information, such as personnel data, finance, contracts etc
2001/2002 (Now QinetiQ)		• System to make it easier to tap into the organisation's intellectual capital	• New technology – 'Knowledge Store' – introduced

number of reasons for this. First, the WIFM factor had not been fully addressed. While it was the scientists and technologists who were expected to input information into K-NET, the main users of K-NET came from a small sub-section of the organisation, i.e. the Resource Managers (responsible for matching people to projects) and the Bid Managers (responsible for winning new business). There was a disconnect between the WIFM factor for contributors (individual scientists) and users (the management population). Second, the use of the K-NET system had not been embedded in a business process and therefore did not form an integral part of people's day job.

Despite these difficulties, the organisation learnt some valuable lessons from the introduction and usage of K-NET, which it was able to take on board when designing the Knowledge Store. These lessons included:

- It is better to adopt a phased implementation approach, rather than go for a big bang approach.
- It is important to ensure up front that any existing systems that the new system needs to interface with, or co-exist with, are fully operational.
- Agreeing on some common design principles. For example acknowledging that there will be different users with different needs, ensuring that there will only be one master information source to avoid wasteful duplication and where information is already known about an individual, but available in another source, don't ask users to input this information again.

The development of the Knowledge Store

The Knowledge Store, which was developed by iFramework Limited, a Knowledge Management Software provider, supports three different working requirements: an expertise database (i.e. who is who, and who is working on what projects – this is what other organisations often refer to as a Yellow Pages); capabilities information (i.e. what people know, documented in reports, or working papers) and a resource to support collaborative team working.

The Knowledge Store integrates a range of standard Microsoft products. iFramework were chosen as the software supplier because their software was capable of interfacing with the organisation's existing systems, such as PeopleSoft and Siebel. This means that certain categories of existing Human Resource data can be accessed via the Knowledge Store without the need for duplicating this type of information.

The Knowledge Store has been designed from a specification produced by QinetiQ's Information Systems department, based upon requirements gathered as part of the organisation's knowledge management strategy. The development involved a multidisciplinary team approach with representatives from the scientific user population, the business development areas, the Knowledge Management and Technology Intelligence Information Services team and the Human Factors department (this department has knowledge about the people aspect of implementing technology systems).

The system design reflected the fact that there are different consumers and contributors of the information and knowledge held within the Knowledge Store. While primarily seen as a tool to help connect and encourage collaborative working among the organisation's scientists and technologists, Business Group Managers are able to utilise the system to locate particular areas of expertise when putting client proposals together and for finding information about an individual's knowledge contribution, prior to carrying out a performance review.

The Knowledge Store provides an open publishing environment in which scientists at different levels within the organisation can make their 'know how', in the form of written reports and working papers, available to colleagues. The author (i.e. individual scientist) is responsible for managing and publishing his/her own content and for deciding who else it would be valuable to share their knowledge with. Scientists can choose to share their formative ideas with a smaller community, or to make reports and working papers available to the rest of their team, or make these available to all users of the Knowledge Store.

In addition to being used as a publishing repository the Knowledge Store can be used to search for information about people, projects, departments, company presentations, or external market research data. Searches can either start from requesting information relating to a pre-defined set of science and technology keywords (of which there are around 15,000). From here an inquirer can then search for further details about the author of a particular paper, such as the types of projects that the author has worked on, or the author's contact details.

The cultural shift needed to gain full advantage of the Knowledge Store

The success of the Knowledge Store is dependent upon the continued usage of the system by the initial user base, together with a critical mass forming through the addition of more and more users, together with material that users want to use. Gaining this critical mass requires individuals within the scientific community being self-motivating and self-regulating.

Usage of the Knowledge Store is entirely voluntary; there are no separate rewards or sanctions to encourage scientists to use it. The organisation works on the assumption that peer recognition is a key reward factor in itself, therefore opportunities to become known as an expert, and to form new networks, is seen as being a key motivator.

Because usage of the Knowledge Store is entirely voluntary, the Knowledge Store project development team wanted to ensure that the system was particularly user friendly, thus making it easy for users to locate the right people, as well as making it easy for scientists to publish their 'know how'. This was an important lesson learnt by those leading the organisation's knowledge management programme in the early stage (i.e. prior to the organisation being formed out of DERA). One of the tactics employed in the early stage of the organisation's knowledge management journey was 'leaving users hungry for more' by tempting them with a taster of what is possible and then working with them to shape systems in a way which more closely matches their needs. This was the approach adopted when developing the software to support virtual team working.

One of the other design features to encourage scientists to use the Knowledge Store was to ensure that it is user-friendly. Scientists have a free-hand here, but are encouraged to use the system as a vehicle for self-promotion, and as a vehicle for letting their colleagues know about their interests and activities outside of work too, thus adding to a wider sense of community.

The Knowledge Management and Technology Intelligence Information Services team are now working on collecting and disseminating usability stories, as a way of encouraging other scientists to start to propagate the system. The Technical Managers forum will also be used as a forum to promote and encourage usage of the Knowledge Store.

One of the expected pay-backs for those who regularly contribute to the Knowledge Store, either by ensuring that their CV details are kept up-to-date, or through publishing papers that are accessible to the wider community, is that they will enhance their knowledge reputation, track-record and deployment (i.e. an individual's in-demand factor on projects). In an environment where individuals are expected to manage their own career, and have to meet utilisation targets, then clearly there are direct benefits of contributing to the Knowledge Store and indeed other knowledge management initiatives and forums.

From a broader business perspective, however, QinetiQ wants to see their investment in the Knowledge Store bringing commercial benefits. With the nature of the business changing, the company wants to be able to draw on the different scientific and technological disciplines to generate new commercial services. One of the current challenges for the Knowledge Management and Technology Intelligence Information Services team is to demonstrate how the business benefits are being realised.

The way forward for the Knowledge Store

The Knowledge Store has now been successfully piloted with a group of seventy users. It has been propagated with the contact details for 9,000 QinetiQ employees and 25,000 projects, as well as over 600 documents. Now that initial usability problems have been ironed out, there are plans to roll the system out to other groups within QinetiQ, in a phased approach.

Other potential areas for development include:

- Building in a business taxonomy to compliment the scientific taxonomy
- Providing management information from the data contained within the Knowledge Store. This could help support that the business benefits are being realised.
- Having developed in-house expertise for delivering knowledge management solutions this expertise could be packaged as an offering to QinetiQ's clients.

'Yellow Pages' then, or more sophisticated directory systems, provide a vehicle for individuals working in a market economy to really sell themselves, through the quality of the information that they provide in their personal entries. Individuals therefore need to develop the discipline of ensuring that their personal pages are regularly updated, in this way maintaining their 'in demand' factor.

One final thought, while the initial stimulus for introducing directory systems is to make it easier for individuals and teams to locate and connect 'know how' within an organisation, these systems can be used as effective management tools too. From HR's perspective one of the basic questions to be asked is what information can directory type systems provide that will help HR become more effective. For example:

Will it enable you to identify who is talking to who, and who the 'Knowledge connectors', 'Knowledge brokers' and 'Boundary spanners' are, and whether enough is being done to recognize and support their contributions?

Will it enable you to identify what new ideas are emerging from the interactions with knowledge workers?

Will it enable you to identify what development needs are emerging?

Will it help you identify some of your most vulnerable assets, i.e. the ones you would least like to lose?

Will it enable you to identify how much time people are spending on knowledge sharing activities?

Summary

Too often organisations can get drawn into introducing a techno-logical solution for managing their knowledge before having fully considered what it is that they are trying to manage or assessing the organisation's readiness for new systems. HR, as we have seen in this chapter, has an important role to play in asking some basic questions about how best to address the information needs of employees, in order for them to perform at their optimum. This chapter also sets out some practitioner tips, drawn from the wisdom of different knowledge management practitioners, to help with the decision-making process when selecting technological solutions for managing the organisation's knowledge.

The chapter has discussed some of the different types of technologies available to help locate and connect people with specific expertise, as well as technologies to facilitate collabora-tive working. It has also raised some questions about how these new technologies could be used as a tool to help HR become more effective too, thus reflecting the different users and usage of knowledge management technologies.

Notes

1. Portal Pitfalls, *Knowledge Management Magazine*, October 2000. See *www.destinationKM.com*.
2. Skyrme, D. J. (2001), *Capitalising on Knowledge. From e-business to k-business*. Butterworth-Heinemann.

13

Summary and conclusions

Leveraging the intellectual assets of the organisation continues to be a key strategic concern for many business leaders and should be one of the top priorities for HR.

New markets, new ways of doing business, together with new organisational structures to support these broader changes, all call for a greater focus on managing knowledge. The survey findings reported in Chapter 1 on how seriously organisations are taking knowledge management, indicate that this is moving higher up the strategic agenda for business, and now for the HR community too. However, this has not been the case to date for HR. Indeed, HR have come under criticism for not being more proactive in the knowledge management arena. This is despite the fact that managing 'know how', which if we unpack this is about managing and getting the best out of knowledgeable people, maps directly onto HR's core competence.

The need to get a better handle on managing knowledge has more of a direct impact on some types of businesses than others. In high-tech businesses, as well as in consultancies, it is easier to see the link between managing knowledge and business results. After all what these types of organisations are selling is their 'know how' – no 'know how', no sale, or certainly no repeat sale.

However, managing knowledge is now moving higher up the strategic agenda in other business sectors. Public sector organisations, for example, are under pressure to become more performance orientated, which includes adopting a more customer-focused approach. This requires a different mindset, skills-set and way of working. Collaborative working and partnership working are now more prevalent within the public sector, bringing implications and opportunities from a knowledge management perspective. While partnership working can open up access to 'know how' and help minimise the risk factor of new ventures, to work effectively partnership working requires building relationships of trust. This is something that takes time to nurture and requires different behaviours.

There is another reason why knowledge management has moved up the strategic agenda – the war for talent. More and more organisations are finding it difficult to recruit and retain talented people, i.e. people with the skills, knowledge and attitude to create value for the organisation. Even though we are supposedly in some form of economic recession, some organisations are still claiming that they cannot recruit the talent that they are looking for. Given that knowledge is now considered the key business asset this does not bode well for business, the economy, or society more generally.

Perhaps what is more worrying is that certain knowledge resources are not being replenished. In the educational system, for example, there seems to be a fall in the demand for certain subjects, particularly maths and science. While this may not be impacting on businesses today, unless this situation is rectified, it may well have implications for the future as advances in science and technology lead to new business opportunities. The question is, though, to what extent should organisations be concerned about these broader trends? How should these be addressed in their knowledge management strategy?

Recruiting, developing and retaining employees has always been part of HR's agenda, however, the implications of getting this wrong are now even greater. Without the right 'know how', organisations cannot compete in today's increasingly competitive global marketplace, where customers are more and more discerning. Speed to market is now all-important, given that customers today are not prepared to wait – if one business cannot quickly supply what the customer wants, there are others all too eager to come forward.

In the downsizing era of the late 1990s and early 1990s many businesses came unstuck because of the approach adopted for streamlining the organisation. The practice of encouraging (some would argue forcing) individuals in their early fifties to take early retirement has back-fired for some organisations. What was overlooked was the longer-term implications of losing this valuable 'know how'. In the Financial Services sector, for example, much of this lost 'grey matter' has now been re-introduced – mature customers want to build relationships with mature employees, with similar life experiences and values.

Other broader trends that are having an impact on recruitment and retention is the changing landscape of careers: boundaryless organisational structures are giving rise to boundaryless career models, which have different success criteria to that associated with traditional career models. Equally the quest to achieve a better work–life balance is leading some individuals, like the independent HR professionals referred to in Chapter 7, to work with organisations on a different contractual basis.

The prediction for the future of work, and the future workplace, is that organisations will become smaller, employing fewer people on traditional contracts. If this is the case, organisations will need to deliver their services through more contractual and partnership working. This will bring different opportunities and challenges from a knowledge management perspective, particularly given that trust is an essential ingredient for knowledge building and sharing. Developing relationships of trust in these networked organisations requires a different model of working and leadership style.

So what can HR do to help their organisation develop and retain its knowledge assets?

First it should start by helping the organisation achieve greater clarity about what a knowledge-centric culture looks like. In other words what are the essential characteristics. This book has outlined a number of core elements that exist in knowledge-centric cultures. These include: having clearly defined values and knowledge behaviours; permeable structures; fluid roles and responsibilities; energising workspaces; flexible ways of working, as well as facilitative leadership.

Second, focus on what really needs to change, in other words identify the key levers for change and channel resources into these areas. It isn't possible to change everything at once, nor indeed is this desirable. Where it isn't possible to make significant changes, consider re-branding existing practices. This will at least help reinforce the change message. Some examples drawn from my own research include:

From	To ...
Newsletters	'In the know'
Internal communications	Knowledge communicators
Librarians	Information Managers
IT	Information Resources
Internal job vacancies database	'Oceans of Opportunity'
Training	'Knowledge-pool'
Help Desk	Knowledge Hub

Of course re-branding, in itself, will not lead to change, however as part of a co-ordinated change approach it can help the organisation move forward.

Third, HR needs to re-visit its own roles and responsibilities relating to building a knowledge-centric culture. Some of the roles discussed earlier include: helping develop a common understanding of what managing knowledge means; addressing the blocks to knowledge sharing; helping teams experiment with new ways of working that can lead to enhanced knowledge creation and sharing; co-ordinating plans for the free movement of people, and hence knowledge, across the organisation, as well as developing the right form of leadership, i.e. leaders who see their role as being coaches and nurturers of talent, not necessarily the knowledge experts themselves.

Where HR has adopted the Business Partner model of working they are in a good position to spot any overlaps and gaps in an organisation's knowledge base, as well as act as 'knowledge connectors'. There is a strong argument for HR to be involved in all key business developments, even in situations where they may not initially appear to add value. This way of working will enable HR to remain in touch with business and organisational realities, as well as gathering information that can be used to develop leading-edge HR practices.

Fourth, help the organisation re-visit its assumptions about learning and how to facilitate learning in knowledge businesses. The old model of learning, where learning is seen as an activity that takes place away from the workplace, is gradually being superseded with other models of learning, particularly those based on social learning theory. The increased use of learning in Communities of Practice is an example of social learning theory in action in the workplace. Learning in communities has the added advantage that it leads to the development of intellectual and social capital. Social capital is the '. . . oil that lubricates the process of learning through interaction' (Kilpatrick, Bell and Falk, 1998). But for the organisation to take full advantage of the learning that occurs in communities they need to reconsider what counts as productive work. In the knowledge economy work and learn are less easy to compartmentalise.

Fifth, HR needs to re-visit its core practices to ensure that these are aligned with the organisation's knowledge management approach. This means revisiting practices relating to: recruitment and selection; induction; performance management; training and development; career management; resource management, as well as reward and recognition packages.

Sixth, HR needs to re-visit its own competencies to ensure that these are sufficiently developed to equip them for their new roles and responsibilities in the knowledge era.

Finally, HR needs to develop an interest, understanding and expertise in applying a broad range of tools (some technological) to help them deliver the organisation's strategic knowledge management goals. As with their business colleagues, this will no doubt require HR to invest in its own development. The time has come for HR to demonstrate its true leadership capabilities and to role model the behaviours needed to survive in the knowledge economy.

References

Abrahamson, E. (2000), Change Without Pain. *Harvard Business Review*, July-August 2000.

Ahmed, P.K., Kok, L.K. and Loh, A.Y.E. (2002), *Learning Through Knowledge Management*. Butterworth-Heinemann.

Allen, J. (1992), Post-industrialism and post-Fordism. In S. Hall (ed.), *Modernity and Its Futures*. Open University.

Alred, G., Garvey, B. and Smith, R. (1998), Pas de deux – learning in conversation. *Career Development International*, Vol. 3, No. 7, 1998. MCB University Press.

Apgar, M. IV (1998), The Alternative Workplace – Changing Where and How People Work. *Harvard Business Review*, May-June.

Bahrami, H. (1996), The Emerging Flexible Organization: Perspectives from Silicon Valley. In P.S. Myers (ed.), *Knowledge Management and Organizational Design*. Butterworth-Heinemann.

Bailey, C. and Clarke, M. (1999), Going for Gold. *Human Resources*, March 1999.

Baker, W. (1996), Building Intelligence Networks. In P.S. Myers (ed.), *Knowledge Management and Organizational Design*. Butterworth-Heinemann.

Bank, J. (1999), Dividends of Diversity. *Management Focus*. Issue 12, Summer 1999 (Cranfield School of Management).

Barley, S.R. (1989), 'Careers, Identities and Institutions: The Legacy of the Chicago School of Sociology. In M.B. Arthur, D.T. Hall and B.S. Lawrence (eds) *Handbook of Career Theory*. Cambridge University Press.

Baruch, Y. and Nicholson, N. (1997), Home, Sweet Work: Requirements for Effective Home Working. *Journal of General Management*, Vol. 23, No. 2., Winter 1997.

Becker, B.E., Huselid, M.A. and Ulrich, D. (2001), *The HR Scorecard. Linking People, Strategy and Performance*. Harvard Business School Press.

Bird, A. (1994), Careers as repositories of knowledge: a new perspective on boundaryless careers. *Journal of Organizational Behaviour*, Vol. 15, 325–344.

Bruner, J.S. (1986), *Actual Minds. Possible Worlds*. Harvard University Press.

Castells, M. (1989), *The Informational City*. Basil Blackwell.

Cockman, P., Evans B. and Reynolds, P. (1992), *Client-centred Consulting*. McGraw-Hill.

Collinson, C. and Parcell, G. (2001), Learning after doing. *Knowledge Management*, Vol. 5, Issue 2, 2001.

Coolahan, J. (1998), The Learning Age: Towards a Europe of Knowledge. UK Presidency of the European Lifelong Learning Conference. DfEE 1998.

Cooperrider, D.L. and Whitney, D. (1998), The AI Summit: Overview and Application. *Employee Relations Today*, Summer 1998.

Cross, K.P. (1981), *Adults as Learners*. Jossey-Bass.

Daudelin, M.W. (2000), Learning from Experience Through Reflection. In R. Cross and S. Israelit (eds), *Strategic Learning in a Knowledge Economy. Individual, Collective and Organizational Learning Process*. Butterworth-Heinemann.

Davenport, T.H. and Prusak, L. (1998), *Working Knowledge – How Organisations Manage What They Know*. Harvard Business School Press.

Davenport, T.H. and Glaser, J. (2002), Just-in-Time Delivery Comes to Knowledge Management. *Harvard Business Review*. July 2002.

Drucker, P.F. (1993), cited in *RSA Inquiry*. Tomorrow's Company: The Role of Business in a Changing World. Interim Report, Feb. 1994.

Edwards, R. (1993), The inevitable future? Post-Fordism in work and learning. In Edwards, R., Sieminski, S. and Zeldin, D. (eds), *Adult Learners, Education and Training*. Routledge

Evans C. (2000), *Developing a Knowledge Creating Culture*. Roffey Park Institute.

Evans, D. (2000), Changing organisational forms and technology. *Journal of Professional HRM*, Issue No. 20, July 2000. CRONER@CCH

Evans. C. (2001), The Changing Nature of Employment. How Self-Employed HR Professionals Manage Their Lives, Learning and Knowledge. Unpublished PhD Thesis. Open University.

Evans, C. (2002a), *Developing and Retaining Organisational Knowledge*. Roffey Park Institute.

Evans, C. (2002b), Volunteering – social conscience or sound business sense? *Personnel Management Newsletter*, Issue No 101 17 July 2002, CRONER@CCH.

Filipczak, B. (1994), It's just a job: generation X at work. *Training*, April 1994, V31, No. 4, pp 21–28.

Fuller, A. and Unwin, L. (1998), Reconceptualising Apprenticeship: exploring the relationship between work and learning. *Journal of Vocational Education and Training*, Vol. 50, No. 2, 1988, pp 153–171.

Giannos, V. (2002), Managing Organisational Knowledge in the UK: A Report on HRM Contribution and Implications of Knowledge Management. MA Dissertation. University of Grenwich.

Ghoshal, S. and Bartlett, C.A. (998), *The Individualized Corporation*. William Heinemann.

Glynn, C. (2000), *Work–Life Balance, Careers and the Psychological Contract*. Roffey Park Institute.

Gryskiewicz, S. (1999), *Positive Turbulence: Developing Climates for Creativity, Innovation and Renewal*. Jossey-Bass.

Gubman, E.L. (1998), *The Talent Solution: Aligning Strategy and People to Achieve Extraordinary Results*. McGraw-Hill.

Guest, D.E. (1998), Human Resource Management, Trade Unions and Industrial Relations. In C. Mabey, G. Salaman and J. Storey (eds), *Strategic Human Resource Management*. Sage Publications.

Hall, D.T. (1991), Research Needed to Advance the Field of Careers. In R.F. Morrison and J. Adams (eds), *Contemporary Career Development Issues*. Lawrence Erlbaum Associates.

Handy, C. (1996), *Beyond Certainty*. Arrow Business Books.

Herriot, P. and Pemberton, C. (1995), *Competitive Advantage Through Diversity. Organizational Learning Through Difference*. SAGE Publications.

Herriot, P., Hirsh, W. and Reilly, P. (1998), *Trust and Transition. Managing Today's Employment Relationship*. John Wiley & Sons.

Hilltrop, Jean-Marie (1998), Preparing People for the Future: The Next Agenda for HRM. *European Management Journal*, Vol. 16, No.1, February 1998.

Hirsh, W., Jackson, C. and Kidd, J.M. (2001), *Straight Talking: Effective Career Discussions at Work*. NICEC.

Holbeche, L. (1999), *Aligning Human Resources Strategy and Business Strategy*. Butterworth-Heinemann.

Holbeche, L. (2000), *The Future of Careers*. Roffey Park Institute.

Horibe, F. (1999), *Managing Knowledge Workers. New Skills and Attitudes to Unlock Intellectual Capital in Your Organization*. John Wiley & Sons.

Howard, J. (1999), *Managing More with Less.* Butterworth-Heinemann

Jain, R.K. and Traindis, H.C. (1997), *Management of Research and Development Organizations.* John Wiley & Sons, Inc.

Kavanagh, J. (2002), Bulletin Interview. *The Computer Bulletin* January 2002. The British Computer Society.

Kilpatrick, S., Bell, R. and Falk, I. (1998), The role of Group Learning in Building Social Capital. *Journal of Vocational Education and Training*, Vol. 50, No. 4. 1998.

Knight, T. (2001), A strategic approach to KM. *Knowledge Management.* Dec. 2001/Jan. 2002.

Knight, T. and Howes, T. (2002), *Knowledge Management: A Blueprint for Delivery.* Butterworth-Heinemann.

Kotter, J.P. (1995), *Leading Change.* Harvard Business School Press.

Kotter, J.P. and Cohen, D.S. (2002), *The Heart of Change.* Harvard Business School Press.

Leadbeater, C. (1999), *Living on Thin Air.* Viking.

Leonard-Barton, D. (1994), The factory as a learning laboratory. In C. Mabey and P. Isles (eds), *Managing Learning.* The Open University.

Minor, F.J., Allen Slade, L. and Myers, R.A. (1991), Career Transitions in Changing Times. In R.F. Morrison and J. Adams (eds), *Contemporary Career Development Issues.* Lawrence Erlbaum Associates.

Mirvis, P.H. and Hall, D.T. (1994), Psychological Success and the Boundaryless Career. *Journal of Organizational Behaviour*, Vol. 15, pp. 365–380.

Morgan, G. (1986), *Images of Organization.* Sage Publications Inc.

Myers, P. (1995), *Knowledge Management and Organizational Design.* Butterworth-Heinemann.

Nonaka, I. (1998), The Knowledge-creating Company. In *Harvard Business Review on Knowledge Management.* Harvard Business School Press.

Overell, S. (1999), Head for Heights. *Personnel Today.* 27 May 1999.

Pink, D.H. (2001), *Free Agent Nation. How America's New Independent Workers are Transforming the Way We Live.* Warner Books, Inc.

Probst, G., Raub, S. and Romhardt, K. (2000), *Managing Knowledge – Building Blocks for Success.* John Wiley and Sons.

Rajan, A. with Penny van Eupen. Tomorrow's People. CREATE 1997.

Reich, R.B. (1998), The Company of the Future. Fast Company. November 1998.

Roberts-Witt, S.L. (2001), Re-inventing HR. When the human resources department adopt KM, business benefits. *Knowledge Management Magazine*, September 2001

Roffey Park Institute. *The Management Agenda – 2002*.

Scase, R. (2002), *Living in the Corporate Zoo. Life and work in 2010*. Capstone Publishing Limited.

Schein, E. (1996), Career Anchors Revisited: Implications for Career Development in the 21st Century. *Http//:www.sol-ne.org/res/wp/hall.html*.

Seely-Brown, J. (1998), Research that Reinvents the Corporation. In *Harvard Business Review on Knowledge Management*. Harvard Business School Press.

Semple E. (1999), Knowledge Management in a Digital World. Liberating Knowledge. *CBI Business Guide*.

Senge, P. (2002), The leaders new work building learning organisations. In H. Mintzberg (ed.), *The Strategy Process*. Prentice Hall.

Shapiro, C. and Varian, H.L. (1999), *Information Rules, A Strategic Guide to the Network Economy*. Harvard Business School Press.

Skyrme, D.J. (2001), *Capitalizing on Knowledge, from e-business to k-business*. Butterworth-Heinemann.

Stacey, R. (1993), *Strategic Management and Organisational Dynamic*. Pitman Publishing.

Stonehouse, G.H., Pemberton, J.D. and Barber, C.E. (2001), The Role of Knowledge Facilitators and Inhibitors. *Long Range Planning*, April 2001, Vol. 34, No. 2. Strategic Planning Society.

Thompson, J.L. (1993), *Strategic Management Awareness and Change*. Chapman & Hall (1993).

Ulrich, D. (1998), A New Mandate for Human Resources. *Harvard Business Review*, January-February 1998.

Ulrich, D. (2000), Human Resources in the New Millenium: Intangibles, deliverables and capabilities. Human Resources World Conference, Paris, May 2000.

van der Spek, R. and Kingma, J. (1999), Achieving successful knowledge management initiatives, in Liberating Knowledge. *CBI Business Guide*.

Volberda, H.W., Baden-Fuller, C. and van den Bosch, Frans, A.J. (2001), Mastering Strategic Renewal. *Long Range Planning*, April 2001, Vol. 34, No. 2. Strategic Planning Society.

Wenger, E. (1998), *Communities of Practice. Learning, Meaning, and Identity*. Cambridge University Press.

Wenger, E. and Synder, W.M. (2000), Communities of Practice: The Organizational Frontier. *Harvard Business Review*, January-February.

Whatmore, J. (1999), *Releasing Creativity – How Leaders Develop Creative Potential in their Teams*. Kogan Page.

Wilensky, H.L. (1960), Careers, Life-styles and Social Integration. In B. G. Glaser (ed.) (1968), *Organisational Careers. A Sourcebook for Theory*. Aldine Publishing Company.

Wilhelms, F.T. (1971), Evaluation as feedback. In R.Hooper (ed.), *The Curriculum: Context, Design and Development*. OU Press.

Index